HAN~~DBOOK~~S
OF ~~T~~HE
BRITISH ISLES

First published in 1994 by Philip's
an imprint of Reed Consumer Books Limited
Michelin House, 81 Fulham Road, London SW3 6RB
and Auckland, Melbourne, Singapore and Toronto

All rights reserved. Apart from any fair dealing for the purpose
of private study, research, criticism or review, as permitted
under the Copyright Designs and Patents Act, 1988, no part of
this publication may be reproduced, stored in a retrieval
system, or transmitted in any form or by any means,
electronic, electrical, chemical, mechanical, optical,
photocopying, recording, or otherwise, without prior written
permission. All enquiries should be addressed to the
Publisher.

To the best of the Publisher's knowledge, the information in
this atlas was correct at the time of going to press.
No responsibility can be accepted for any errors or their
consequences.

The representation in this atlas of any road, drive or track is
no evidence of the existence of a right of way.

Cartography by Philip's
Copyright © 1994 Reed International Books Limited

Printed in Spain

CONTENTS

IV Route planner

VI Key map

VIII Road signs

XVI Motorway service areas

1 Key to map symbols *10 miles to 1 inch*

2 Great Britain *10 miles to 1 inch 1: 625 000*

73 Key to map symbols *20 miles to 1 inch*

74 Orkney, Shetland and Channel Isles
20 miles to 1 inch 1: 1 250 000

76 Ireland *20 miles to 1 inch 1: 1 250 000*

84 Index of place names

121 Key to map symbols *5 miles to 1 inch*

122 Approach mapping *5 miles to 1 inch 1: 300 000*
London, Birmingham, Leeds and Bradford,
Manchester, Edinburgh, Glasgow

132 First aid

Route planner

Key map

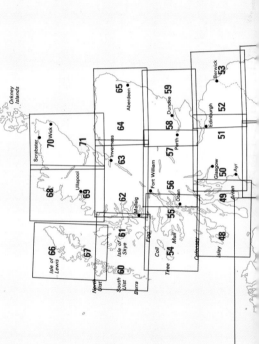

ORKNEY & SHETLAND **74**

Orkney
Islands

• Scrabster
70 • Wick

71

68

Ullapool •
69

65
• Aberdeen

64

• Inverness
63

59
Dundee •
58
57 • Perth

53
Berwick •

52

Edinburgh •
51

62
• Fort William
Mallaig •

56
55 • Oban

Glasgow •
50 • Ayr
49

Isle of **66**
Lewis
67
Isle of
Skye **61** **60**

North
Uist
South
Uist
Barra

Eigg
Coll
Tree
Mull **54**
Colonsay
Islay **48**
Arran

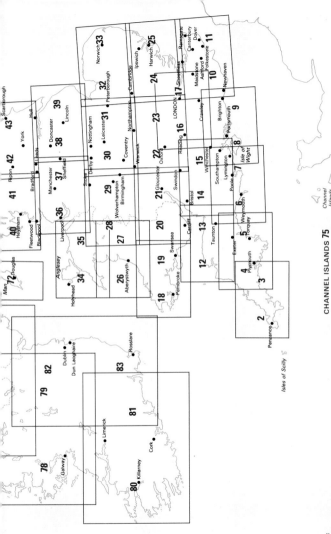

CHANNEL ISLANDS 75

Channel Islands

Isles of Scilly

Road signs

'The Highway Code', prepared by the Department of Transport and the Central Office of Information for HMSO, contains important advice for all road users. It is designed to prevent accidents by ensuring that we all adopt the same rules when using the road. The rules are not just for motorists; they apply also to pedestrians, cyclists and horse riders, and is essential reading for everyone.

Road traffic law has developed over the years into a comprehensive set of rules. Observance is best achieved by making certain that the rules are seen to be both necessary and fair and that they are as straightforward as possible. 'The

Light signals (controlling traffic)

TRAFFIC LIGHT SIGNALS

RED means 'Stop'. Wait behind the stop line on the carriageway.

RED AND AMBER also means 'Stop'. Do not pass through or start until GREEN shows.

GREEN means you may go on if the way is clear. Take special care if you intend to turn left or right and give way to pedestrians who are crossing.

AMBER means 'Stop' at the stop line. You may go on only if the AMBER appears after you have crossed the stop line or are so close to it that to pull up might cause an accident.

A GREEN ARROW may be provided in addition to the full green signal if movement in a certain direction is allowed before or after the full green phase. If the way is clear you may go but only in the direction shown by the arrow. You may do this whatever other lights may be showing.

FLASHING RED LIGHTS

Alternately flashing red lights mean YOU MUST STOP

At level crossings, lifting bridges, airfields, fire stations etc

ighway Code' helps to ensure that the rules are more easily nderstood. Most people follow the rules, but for those who do ot, road traffic law lays down both general bad driving offences nd more specific ones aimed at particular types of behaviour. he Road Traffic Act 1991 redefined the major bad driving ffences and increased the penalties available to deal with them.

It is important to follow the rules for your own safety and the afety of others. All road users share a personal responsibility o reduce the terrible toll of death and injury on the roads. If we ll obey the rules, many more precious lives will be saved.

The road signs illustrated in this atlas, reproduced from he Highway Code', provide vital information for all road users. owever, for more detailed advice it is recommended that the eader refers directly to a copy of 'The Highway Code', which an be obtained from any branch of HMSO.

MOTORWAY SIGNALS

Do not proceed further in this lane.

Change lane.

Reduced visibility ahead.

Lane ahead closed.

Temporary maximum speed limit and information message.

Leave motorway at next exit.

Temporary maximum speed limit.

End of restriction.

LANE CONTROL SIGNALS

Green arrow – lane available to traffic facing the sign. Red crosses – lane closed to traffic facing the sign. White diagonal arrow – change lanes in direction shown.

Traffic signs

Mostly circular and those with red circles are mostly prohibitive

Entry to 20 mph zone

End of 20 mph zone

School crossing patrol

Maximum speed

National speed limit applies

Stop and give way

Give way to traffic on major road

No vehicles

No entry for vehicular traffic

No right turn

No left turn

No U-turns

No overtaking

Give priority to vehicles from opposite direction

No motor vehicles

No motor vehicles except solo motorcycles, scooters or mopeds

Manually operated temporary 'STOP' sign

No vehicles with over 12 seats except regular scheduled, school and work buses

No cycling

No pedestrians

No goods vehicles over maximum gross weight shown (in tonnes)

No vehicle or combination of vehicles over length shown

No vehicles over height shown

No vehicles over width shown

WEAK BRIDGE

No vehicles over maximum gross weight shown (in tonnes)

Axle weight limit in tonnes

No stopping (Clearway)

Permit P holders only

Parking restricted to use by people named on sign

No stopping during times shown except for as long as necessary to set down or pick up passengers

Plates below some signs qualify their message

End

End of restriction

Except for loading

Exception for loading/unloading goods

Except for buses

Exception for regular scheduled, school and work buses

Except for access

Exception for access to premises and land adjacent to the road where there is no alternative route

Signs with blue circles but no red border mostly give positive instruction.

One-way traffic (note: compare circular 'Ahead only' sign)

Ahead only

Turn left ahead (right if symbol reversed)

Turn left (right if symbol reversed)

Keep left (right if symbol reversed)

Route to be used by pedal cycles only

Segregated pedal cycle and pedestrian route

Minimum speed

End of minimum speed

Mini-roundabout (roundabout circulation – give way to vehicles from the immediate right)

Vehicles may pass either side to reach same destination

Buses and cycles only

Trams only

Pedestrian crossing point over tramway

With-flow bus and cycle lane

Contra-flow bus lane

With-flow pedal cycle lane

WARNING SIGNS   Mostly triangular

Distance to 'STOP' line ahead

Crossroads

Junction on bend ahead

T-junction

Staggered junction

Distance to 'Give Way' line ahead

Sharp deviation of route to left (or right if chevrons reversed)

Double bend first to left (symbol may be reversed)

Bend to right (or left if symbol reversed)

Roundabout

Uneven road

Plate below some signs

Dual carriageway
ends

Road narrows on right
(left if symbol reversed)

Road narrows
on both sides

Two-way traffic
crosses one-way road

Two-way traffic
straight ahead

Traffic signals

Failure of traffic light signals

Slippery road

Steep hill downwards

Steep hill upwards

Gradients may be shown as a ratio
i.e. 20% = 1:5

Children going to
or from school

School crossing
patrol ahead
(Some signs have
amber lights
which flash when
children are
crossing)

Elderly people (or
blind or disabled as
shown) crossing
road

Pedestrians
in road ahead

Cycle route ahead

Pedestrian crossing

Road works

Hump bridge

Worded warning
sign

Loose chippings

Risk of
grounding

Light signals
ahead at level
crossing, airfield
or bridge

Level crossing
with barrier or gate
ahead

Level crossing
without barrier or
gate ahead

Level crossing
without
barrier

Trams
crossing
ahead

Cattle

Wild animals

Wild horses
or ponies

Accompanied
horses or
ponies

Quayside or
river bank

Opening or swing bridge ahead

Low-flying aircraft or sudden aircraft noise

Falling or fallen rocks

Available width of headroom indicated

Overhead electric cable; plate indicates maximum height of vehicles which can pass safely

Distance to tunnel

Distance over which road humps extend

Other danger; plate indicates nature of danger

School bus (Displayed in front or rear window of bus or coach)

DIRECTION SIGNS

Mostly rectangular

Signs on motorways – blue backgrounds

At a junction leading directly into a motorway

On approaches to junctions (junction number on black backgrounds)

Route confirmatory sign after junction

Downward pointing arrows mean 'Get in lane'

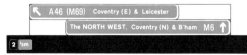
The panel with the sloping arrow indicates the destinations which can be reached by leaving the motorway at the next junction

Signs on primary routes – green backgrounds

On approaches to junctions

On approaches to junctions (The blue panel indicates that the motorway commences from the junction ahead. The motorway shown in brackets can also be reached by proceeding in that direction)

At the junction

Route confirmatory sign after junction

Airport

Ring road

Signs on non-primary routes – black borders

On approaches to junctions

On approaches to junctions (A symbol may sometimes be shown to indicate a warning of a hazard or prohibition on a road leading from a junction)

At the junction

Direction to toilets with access for the disabled

Other direction signs

Picnic site

Advisory route for lorries

Ancient monument in the care of English Heritage

Tourist attraction

Route for pedestrians

Direction to camping and caravan site

Holiday route

Diversion route

Symbols showing
emergency diversion route
for motorway traffic

Recommended route for pedal
cycles to place shown

INFORMATION SIGNS

All rectangular

Start of motorway and point
from which motorway
regulations apply

One-way street

Priority over vehicles
from opposite direction

No through road

Hospital ahead

End of motorway

Parking place
for towed
caravans

Advanced warning of
restriction or
prohibition ahead

Motorway service area sign
incorporating the operator's
name (the current price of
petrol may be shown)

Tourist information
point

Recommended route
for pedal cycles

Appropriate traffic lanes at
junction ahead

'Countdown' markers at exit from motorway
(each bar represents 100 yards to the exit).
Green-backed markers may be used on primary
routes and white-backed markers with red bars on
the approaches to concealed level crossings

Entrance to controlled
parking zone

End of
controlled
parking zone

Temporary lane closure
(the number and position of arrows
and red bars may be varied
according to lanes open and closed)

Bus lane on road at
junction ahead

xv

Motorway service areas

⊨ Overnight accommodation available **●** Hot meals or snacks available at night **⤙** Repair facilities **C** Facilities for young children **⊼** Picnic area **▣** Tourist Information Centre

M1

	Between Access Numbers
Scratchwood ⊨ ● ⤙ C	2 – 4
Toddington ⊨ ● ⤙ ⊼ C	11 – 12
Newport Pagnall ⊨ ● ⤙ C	14 – 15
Rothersthorpe Turn off at ● ⤙ C ⊼	Exit 15A
Watford Gap ● ⤙ C ⊼ ▣	16 – 17
Leicester Forest East ● ⤙ C	21 – 22
Trowell ⤙ C ⊼ ▣	25 – 26
Woodall ● ⤙ C ▣	30 – 31
Woolley Edge ⊨ ● ⤙ C ⊼	38 – 39

M2

Medway ⊨ ● ⤙ C ⊼ ▣	4 – 5

M3

Fleet ⊨ ● ⤙ C ⊼	4A – 5

M4

Heston ⊨ ● ⤙ C ⊼	2 – 3
Chieveley Turn off at exit 13 ● ⤙ C ⊼	
Membury ⤙ C ⊼	14 – 15
Leigh Delamere ⊨ ● ⤙ C ⊼	17 – 18
Severn View Turn off at ⊨ ● ⤙ C ⊼ exit 21	
Magor Turn off at exit 23 ⊨ ● ⤙ C ⊼ ▣	
Cardiff West Turn off at ⊨ ● ⤙ C ⊼ exit 33	
Sarn Park Turn off at exit 36 ⊨ ● ⤙ ▣	
Swansea Turn off at exit 47 ⊨ ● ⤙ ▣	
Pont Abraham ● C ⊼ ▣	49

M5

	Between Access Numbers
Frankley ⊨ ● ⤙ C ⊼	3 – 4
Strensham ● ⤙ C ⊼	7 – 8
Michaelwood ● C ⊼	13 – 14
Gordano Turn off at exit 19 ⊨ ● ⤙ C ⊼ (▣ Summer only)	
Sedgemoor ⊨ ● ⤙ C ⊼	21 – 22
Taunton Deane ⊨ ● ⤙ C ⊼	25 – 26
Exeter Turn off at exit 30 ⊨ ● ⤙ C ⊼ ▣	

M6

Corley ● ⤙ C	3 – 4
Hilton Park ⊨ ● ⤙ C ⊼ ▣	10A – 11
Keele ⊨ ● ⤙	15 – 16
Sandbach ● ⤙ C ▣	16 – 17
Knutsford ⊨ ● ⤙ C	18 – 19
Charnock Richard ⊨ ● ⤙ C ▣	27 – 28
Forton ⊨ ● ⤙ C ⊼ ▣	32 – 33
Burton (N'bnd only) ⊨ ● ⤙ C ⊼	35 – 36
Killington (S'bnd only) ● ⤙ C ⊼ ▣	36 – 37
Tebay ⊨ ● ⤙ C ⊼ Caravan site	38 – 39
Southwaite ⊨ ● ⤙ C ▣	41 – 42

M8

Harthill ● C	4 – 5

M9

Stirling Turn off at exit 9 ⊨ ● ⤙ C ⊼ ▣	

M23

Pease Pottage ● C	11

M25

	Between Access Numbers
Clacket Lane ● ⤙ C ⊼ ▣	5 – 6
South Mimms Turn off at ⊨ ● C ⊼ ▣ exit 23	
Thurrock ⊨ ● ⤙ C ⊼ ▣	30 – 31

M27

Rownhams ⊨ ● ⤙ C ⊼ ▣	3 – 4

M40

Cherwell Valley ⊨ ● ⤙ C ⊼	10
Warwick ⊨ ● C ⊼	12 – 13

M42

Tamworth Turn off at exit 10 ⊨ ● ⤙ C ⊼	

M61

Rivington ● ⤙ C ⊼	6 – 8

M62

Burtonwood ⊨ ● ⤙ C	7 – 9
Birch ⊨ ● ⤙ C ⊼	18 – 19
Hartshead Moor ⊨ ● ⤙ C ⊼	25 – 26
Ferrybridge Turn off at ⊨ ● ⤙ C exit 33	

M74

	Dumfries & Galloway
Gretna Green ⊨ ● ⤙ C ▣	
Bothwell (S'bnd only) ● C ⊼	4-5
Hamilton (N'bnd only) ⊨ ● ⤙ C	5-6
Abington ⊨ ● C ⊼ (▣ Summer only)	13

M90

Kinross ⊨ ● C ⊼ (▣ Summer only)	6

A1(M)

	Notts
Blyth ⊨ ● ⤙ C	
Washington Tyne & Wear ⊨ ● ⤙ C	

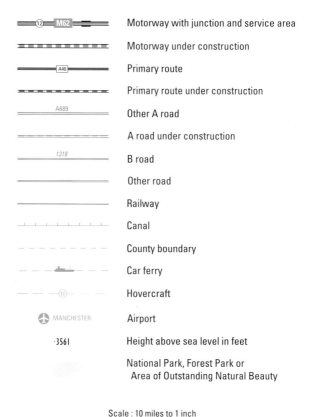

	Motorway with junction and service area
	Motorway under construction
	Primary route
	Primary route under construction
A689	Other A road
	A road under construction
1318	B road
	Other road
	Railway
	Canal
	County boundary
	Car ferry
	Hovercraft
MANCHESTER	Airport
·3561	Height above sea level in feet
	National Park, Forest Park or Area of Outstanding Natural Beauty

Scale : 10 miles to 1 inch

R

Pads

Trevose Hd

St. M

Watergate B.
St. M
ST. MAWGA
Towan Hd.

Newquay

Crantock Pe

Penhale Pt. New

Ligger B. Cubert Summ

Perranporth
A307

Perranzabuloe
A30
St. Agnes Hd. 328
St. Agnes A30 A3

Mount Hawke Tr
3277 328
Porthtowan
Portreath Illogan A390 Chacewater Ple
3300 St. Day Pl
Godrevy I. 330 **Redruth** Gwennap A39
St. Ives **Camborne** Devora Do
B. Lanner A393 Cdrn

S

Troon 329 Four Lanes Ponsanooth S
St. Ives A3074 3280 Stithians Mylor
Zennor Lelant Hayle Praze Brid
Gurnard's Hd. 3306 -an-Beeble A394 Pen **Falmouth**
331 **826** Ludgvan A30 St. Erth 3280 Fa
Pendeen 3318 3302 Mawna
Madron Marazion Constantine Smith
C. Cornwall Goldsithney 329 Gweek
St. Just A307 **Penzance** Germoe **Helston** Helford
3285 Perranuthnoe A394 3304 St. Keverne
Whitesand Bay Newlyn Breage 329
Sennen 3288 Mousehole Porthleven A3083 Cove
Land's End 3315 St. Buryan *Mount's Bay* Black
Porthcurno **Mullion**
Gwennap Hd. St. Levan 3296
Ruan Minor
Cadgwith
Lizard Landewednack

T *Wolf Rock* Lizard Pt.

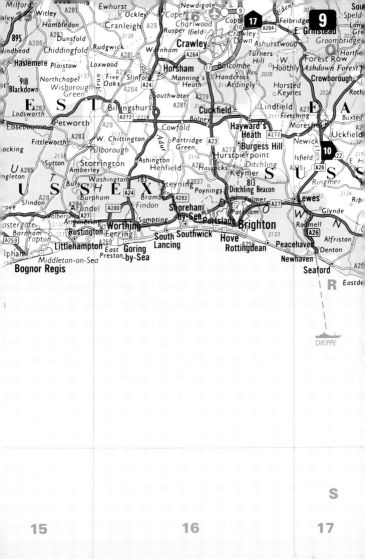

ch

Swale

Whitstable   **Herne Bay**   Westgate **Margate** Cliftonville
The   2205   -on-Sea   North Foreland
salter   Herne   A299   Birchington   A28   St. Peters
eney   A298   St. Nicholas   A299   I. of Thanet   **Broadstairs**
A299   Sturry   A29 Upstreet   at Wade   Monkton   A255   2892
Blean   Hersden   Sarre   Minster   **Ramsgate**
Str.   A2   Preston   Stour   A256   Pegwell Bay
Canterbury   Littlebourne   Ash   A257   **Sandwich**   Goodwin
Wingham   Woodnesborough   Sands
m   Chartham   Staple   Worth
Shalmsford   Adisham   2046   Eastry   A258   DUNKIRK
Street   2068 Aylesham   Nonington   Betteshanger
Petham   Barham   Northbourne   **Deal**
Wye T   Womenswold   Tilmanstone   **Walmer**   The
Kythorne   A256   Downs   Q
ngton   Shepherdswell   Ringwould
rd   Elham   Lydden   A2   Whitfield   Kingsdown
Lyminge   Temple Ewell   A258   St. Margaret's
Brabourne   A260 Alkham   at Cliffe
Lees   W. Hougham   South Foreland
2068   A20   **Dover**
20   Saltwood   11   12   13   Capel le Ferne   Withdrawn from service
2067   OSTEND
Lympne   **Folkestone**
rmarsh   A259   **Hythe**   Sandgate   CALAIS
ey   **Dymchurch**
h   St. Mary's Bay   CHANNEL TUNNEL

w Romney

Dungeness   BOULOGNE

R

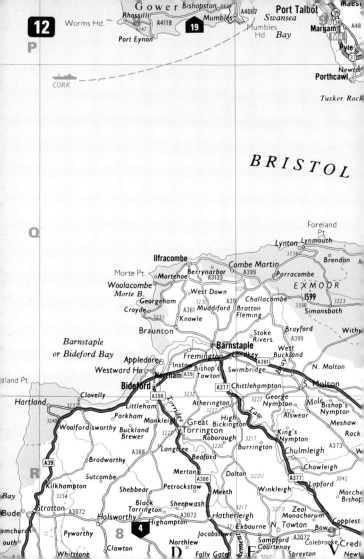

LAMORGAN
A4061 Treforest A470 A468 Caerphilly 20 Newport 13 Severn Beach
Llanharan A473 A473 Nantgarw Taffs-Well 28 Redwick Almo
A4119 Llantrisant Pentyrch A469 29 Marshfield A40
Bryncethin Pont-y-clun 33 Radyr Whitchurch St Mellons Seve Avonmouth 18
encoed A4222 34 A4232 Llandaf Rumney A4139 P
Bridgend A473 Fagans Portishead A369 Portbury 19 Easton-in- BRIS
A48 Llandaff CARDIFF Portbury Gordano
Ewenny SOUTH A48 Dinas CARDIFF Clevedon A370 Nailsea Long
C. Brides Cowbridge Powys A4160 Weston-in- Gordano Ashton
Major A4266 A4222 Wenvoe Penarth Gordano A370 Backwell
ick Llantwit A4055 GLAMORGAN Clevedon 20 Yatton Wrafford
Major St Hilary A48 A370 Yatton Congresbury A38 Che
St Athan CARDIFF 420 Wrington
E. Aberthaw Rhoose Barry Sand B. Congresbury Churchill Blagdon
Flat Holm Kewstoke 21 Banwell A368 Shipham
Steep Holme Weston- Winscombe Me Compto
ANNEL super-Mare Uphill Bleadon Loxton Axbridge Marti
A N N E L Loxton A371 Cheddar
Bridgwater Lympsham A38
B a y Brent Knoll Draycot A371 3135 Westbur
Weston Huntspill Wedmore 3139 Men
elworthy Minehead Burnham Brent Wookey Hole
-on-Sea 22 Mark Wookey
Dunster Watchet Highbridge 3141 Theale Coxley
con Old Kilve Stogursey Woolavington Westhay Meare A:
Carhampton Cleeve 3191 Holford Combwich Cossington A39 Glastonbury
Timberscombe A39 Washford Nether Cannington Moorlinch Ashcott
Wheddon Brendon Brett Stowey Wembdon A39 Walton Street
Cross Hills Stogumber A358 A361 Westonzoyland Cary E
1391 Bradford Bishop's Nth. 24 Middlezoy A372 Keinton
Brompton St. Lawrence Lydeard Petherton A361 High Ham Mandevil
Regis Res. 3224 Kingston Lyng Othery Pitney Somer
Wiveliscombe Halse Vale of Taunton Deane Langport Kingsdo
Morebath A3190 Norton N. Curry Curry Long Sutton
A396 Fitzwarren Rivel Ilchester
Bampton Milverton Bradford Hatch Martock A303
kford on-Tone TAUNTON Beauchamp Ilton Petherton sub Hamdor
Holcombe Wellington Trull A38 Corfe A358 Montac
Tiverton Rogus 26 M5 3176 Broadway Seavington E. Co
A396 Sampford Blackdown Hills Combe Ilminster Chinnock
Halberton Peverell Culmstock 1035 St. Nicholas A3037 Merriott A30 Crewkerne Haselbury
Cullompton Uffculme A303 Chard Winsham Misterton Plucknett
Bickleigh Willand Dunkeswell Yarcombe Chardstock A358 S. Chard Broadwindsor S. Perrotts
horverton Kentisbeare A373 Broadhembury Stockland Mosterton Beamin
ke Canon Plymtree Wilmington A35 Hawk Marshwood A306
5 bury Honiton 6
O M5 Broad Whimple Kilmington Axminster SOUTH A35
Clyst Ottery A375 Musbury 3164

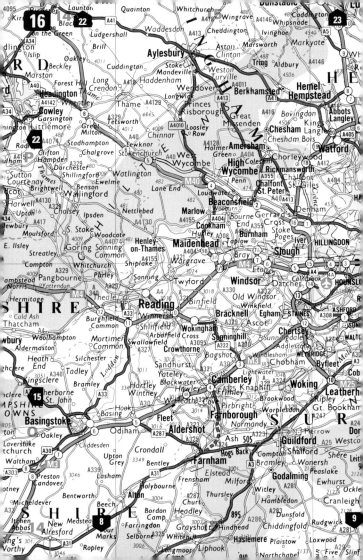

6

7

O

Cemaes Hd.

Aberporth

4548

4544

Cardigan

St. Dogmaels

4331

B

Llechryd

ROSSLARE

Strumble Hd.

Fishguard Bay

Dinas
Hd.

Moylgrove

A487

Cilgerran

Teifi

4332

A40

Dinas

Nevern

4582

Ne

Goodwick

A487

Newport

Eglwyswrw

Boncath

St. Nicholas

Fishguard

4329

Crymmych
Arms

A478

D

Trevine

Mathry

A
4219

4313

Mynydd Prescelly
1760

Llanfyrn

St. David's
Hd.

Llanrhian

4337

Puncheston

Greenway

Whitesand B.

A487

Letterston

Little
Newcastle

Maenclochog

T

4583

A40

4329

St. Davids

4330

Wolf's Castle

4313

A478

Solva

Llandissilio

Llanb

Ramsey I.

Roch

4330

Spittal

Clarbeston
Road

Taf

N

Camrose

Wiston

Llawhaden

Whitland

St. Bride's B.

A487

Nolton

Haverfordwest

A40

Narberth

Llanddowr

4341

A478

4328

Little Haven

Johnston

Llangwm

Martletwy

Templeton

L

P

A4076

4327

Rosemarket

A4115

A477

Pendine

Skomer I.

Marloes

Herbrandston

A4707

A4075

Begelly

Amroth

St. Ishmael's

Neyland

Lawrenny

4586

Kilgetty

Skokholm I.

Dale

Milford Haven

Coshsheston

Saundersfoot

St. Ann's Hd.

Angle

4325

Pembroke
Dock

Lamphey

A477

Sageston

A478

Tenby

4320

Pembroke

St. Florence

A4139

Castlemartin

A4139

4318

Penally

ROSSLARE

Linney Hd.

4319

Bosherston

4584

Manorbier

A4139

Caldy I.

C

St. Govan's
Hd.

Q

6

7

Llanon
Aberaeron
Cilcennin
4577
4343
New Quay
Llangeitho
4342
Tregaron
Llanarth
Mydroilyn
A486
A482
Llanfihangel-Ystrad
Llanddewi-Brefi
A487
4242
Llangybi
A485
Beulah
Talgarreg
A338
Cribyn
4343
Garth
Cwrt-newydd
Llanwnen
Lampeter
Llanwrtyd
Wells
A486
A475
Llanybydder
A482
Mynydd Eppynt
1560
Llandysul
A485
Pumpsaint
Cilycwm
A483
Llanfihangel-
ar-arth
Rhydcymerau
Pencader
Llansawel
F   E   D
Brechfa
Talley
Llansadwrn
Llandovery
A40
Llanpumsaint
Llanfynydd
Llanwrda
Myddfai
A40
Sennybri
A4069
Llangadog
Trecastle
Def
Usk
Res.
Cray
A4
Llandeilo
2632
Fforest
20
A40
A483
Fawr
Carmarthen
Abergwili
Llanarthney
A4069
Mynydd
Llandybie
A48
Pen-   Groes
Glanamman
Brynamman
Cwmllynfell
Clears
Llangendeirne
Drefach
Cross Hands
A4068
Ystradgynlais
Coelbren
Ystra
Llanstephan
Tumble
Ammanford
Cae-Gurwen
Seven
Sisters
Onllwyn
Ferryside
Pontyberem
Tycroes
Ystalyfera
Glen
Neath
Pont Henry
A4067
A4109
Llansaint
Llannon
Hendy
Crynant
Blaengwrach
Hirw
Kidwelly
Pont Yates
Five Roads
Pontardawe
1969.
Trimsaran
A475
Llangennech
Pontardulais
Alltwen
WEST
Glyncorrwg
Treherbe
Pembrey
A484
Llwyn-hendy
Llangyfelach
Clydach
GLAMORGAN
Treor
Burry
Port
Llanelli
Loughor
Gorseinon
Skewen
Tonna
Cymmer
Burry
River
Penclawdd
Gowerton
Neath
Briton
Ferry
Cwmavon
Ystrad R
Llanmadoc
Dunvant
Killay
Bryn
Pontycymmer
MID
Burry Holms
Llanrhidian
Bishopston
Swansea
Port Talbot
Maesteg
GL
Worms Hd.
Gower
Rhossili
A4118
Mumbles
Swansea
Margam
A48
Tondu
Port Eynon
Mumbles
Hd.
Bay
M4
Pyle
Newton
Bri
ORK
Porthcawl
Ogmore-
by-Sea.

Tusker Rock

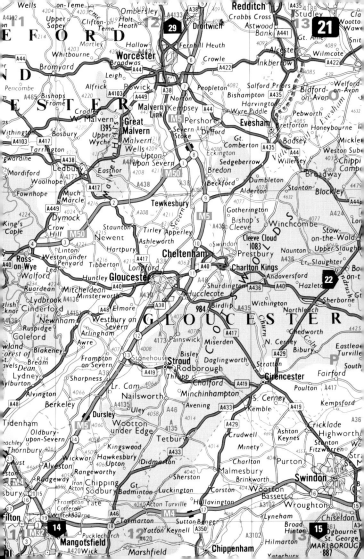

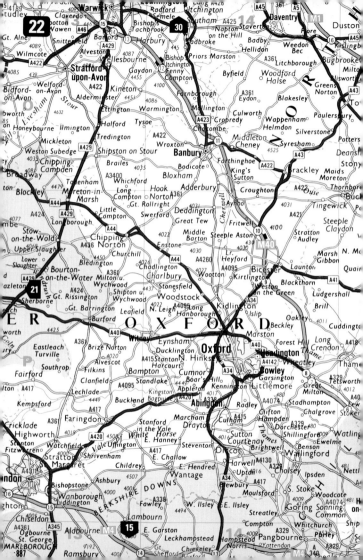

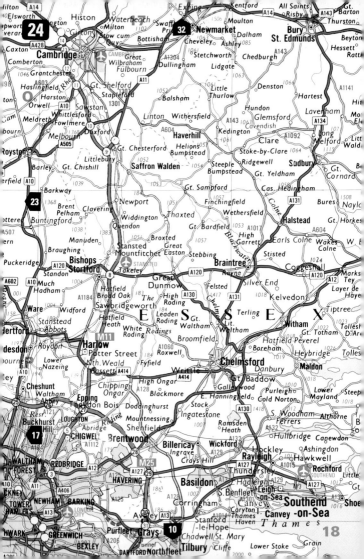

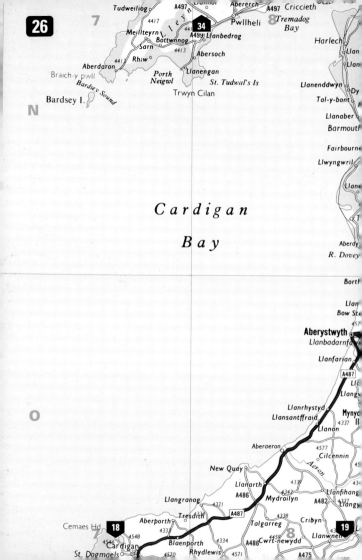

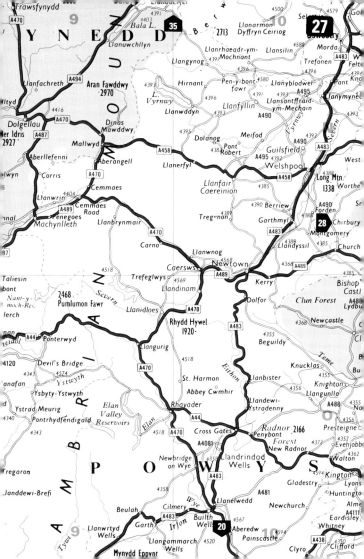

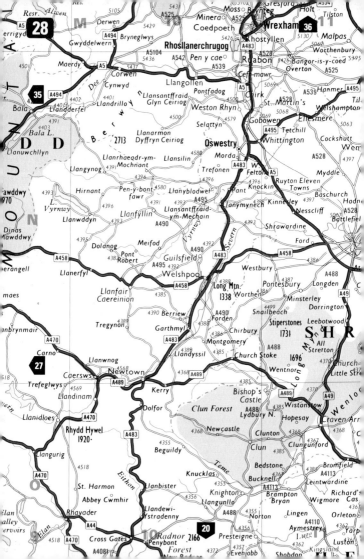

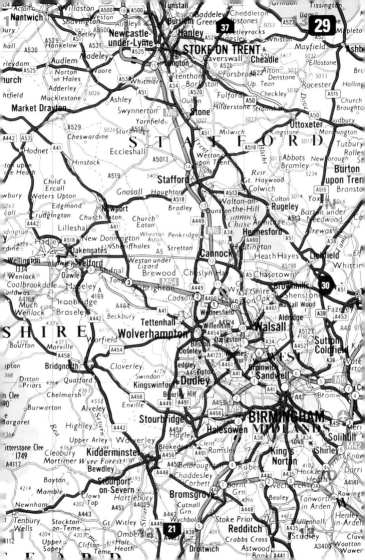

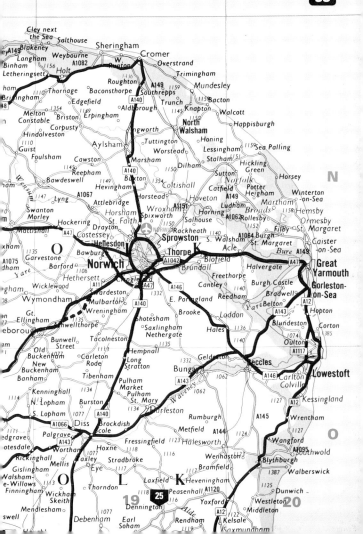

7

8

The Skerries
Carmel Hd.

Bull
Bay
Cemaes Bay
Pt. Lynas
Amlwch
Penysarn
Moelfre

Holyhead
Bay
Llanfechell
Llanfaethlu
A5025
Alaw Res.
Rhosybol

DUBLIN
DUN LAOGHAIRE

Llanddeusant
Llanerchymedd
Benllech
Red Wharf Bay

Llanfachraeth
5112
5110
A5025
Llanddona
Llc

Holyhead
A5
Bodedern
5109
Pentraeth
Beaum

4545
Valley
A n g l e s e y
5109
A5
Llangefni
5108
Beaun

Holy I.
Gwalchmai
5109
A5
Menai Bridge
Bangor

Rhoscolyn
5420

Cymyran Bay
Rhosneigr
Llanfaelog
Gaerwen
A5
Llanfairpwll
Ala

Aberffraw
A4080
4422
4410
411
Bryn
Siencyn
Dinorwi

Newborough
4417
Dwyran
4366
Deiniol

Caernarfon
Llanrug
A4086

Menai St.
Bontnewydd
A487
Llanberis

C a e r n a r f o n
Llandwrog
A499
Waenfawr
Gl
Pass of
Llanberi

B a y
A4085
Snowdo
3561
Carmel
4418
Nantlle
Rhyd-dd

Pen y Groes
Tal y sarn

Llanllyfni

Clynnogfawr
Moel Hebog
2566
Bed
A

Trevor
A499
Garn-
Dolbenmaen

Llanaelhaearn
4417
A487
A498
Garreg

Morfa Nefyn
Four
Crosses
Llanystumdwy
Tremadog
Borth-y-
Gest
Porth

Nefyn
4354
A487

Edern
A497
Llannor
Abererch
A497
Criccieth

Tudweiliog
Pwllheli
Tremadog
Bay

Meillteyrn
A499
4415
Llanbedrog
Harlech

Bottwnnog
4413
Abersoch

Sarn
Rhiw
Llanf

Aberdaron
441
Llanengan
Llanf

Braich-y-pwll
Porth
Neigwl
St. Tudwal's Is
Llanenddwyn
Dy

Bardsey Sound
Trwyn Cilan
Tal-y-bont

Bardsey I.
Llanaber
Barmouth

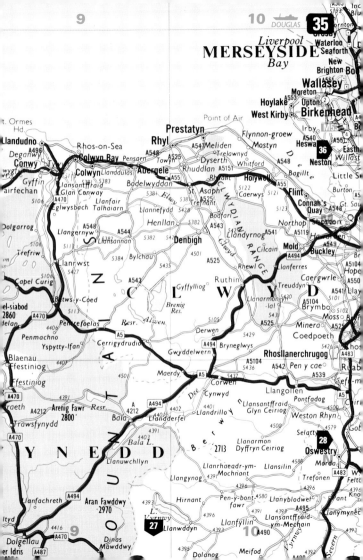

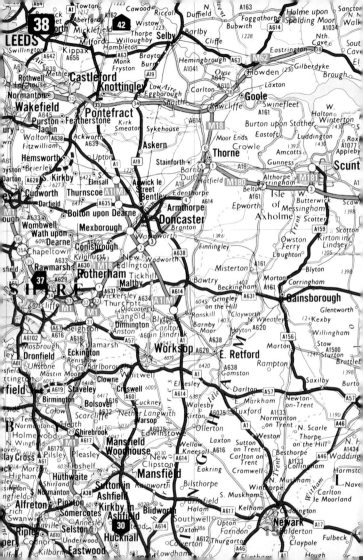

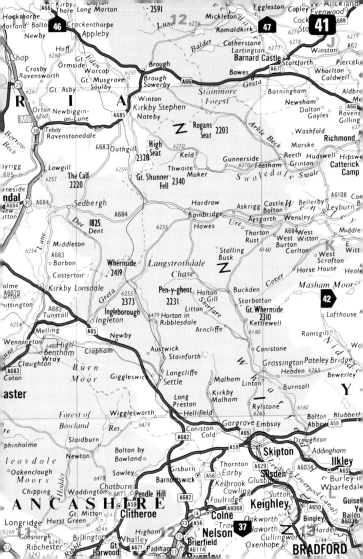

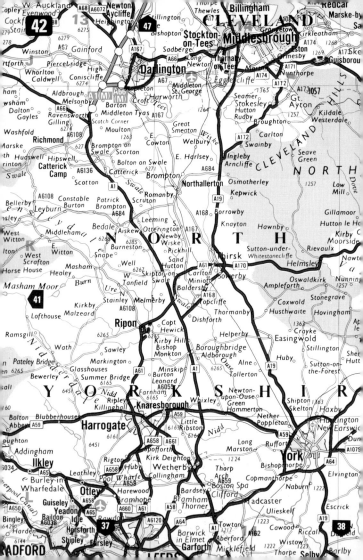

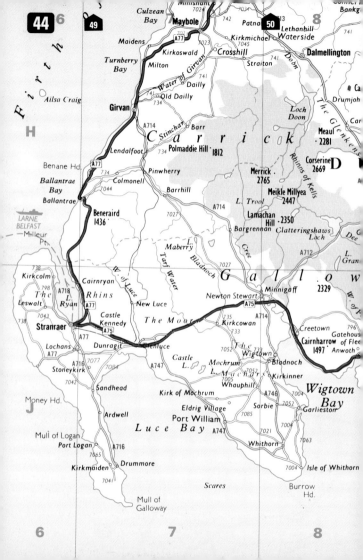

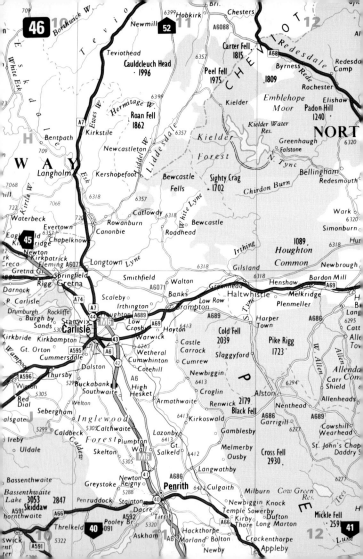

F

Z

I

G

H

3   4   5

Colonsay

8086

Kiloran

OBAN
(Summer
only)

Scalasaig

L. Staosnaig

8085

Oronsay

Passage of Oronsay

Corpach B.

Beinn
1527

Shian
B.

A846

J u r a

Rubha a' Mhail

L. Tarbert

Jura Forest

Paps of
Jura   · 2571

Sound of Islay

Sound of Oronsay
(Summer
only)

Nave I.
Ardnave Pt.

Bunnahabhainn

Ruadh-phort Mor

An Clachan

Port Askaig

L. Gruinart

8018

L. Gorm

8017

Ballygrant

A846

Lagg

A846   Keils
Craighouse

Coul Pt.

Kilchoman

Bridgend

McArthur's Hd.

Machir Bay

Bruichladdich

Kilchiaran

Port
Charlotte

L. Indaal

I   s   l   a   y

Beinn Bheigeir
1609

Lossit Pt.

A847

Laggan

Laggan
Pt.

A846

ISLAY

8016

Claggain
B.

Ardmore Pt.

Gigha

Rubha na Faing
Portnahaven

Rhinns
Pt.

Laggan
Bay

Risabus

Lower
Killeyan

The Oa

Mull of Oa

Laphroaig

A846

Port
Ellen

Ardbeg
Lagavulin

Ca

Rubha nan
Leacan

Glenegedale

Mach

Earadale Pt.

3   4   5

Mull of Kintyre

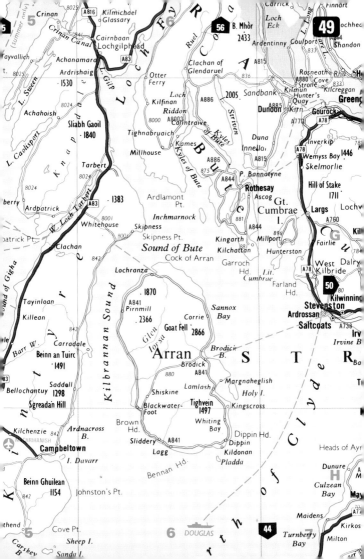

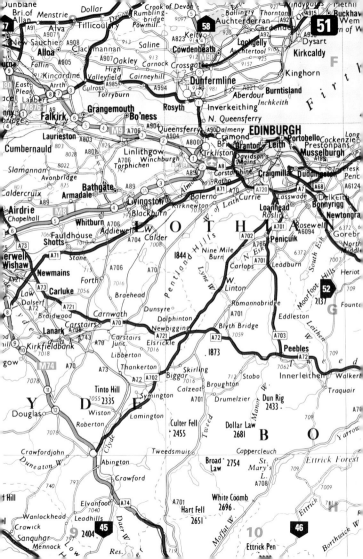

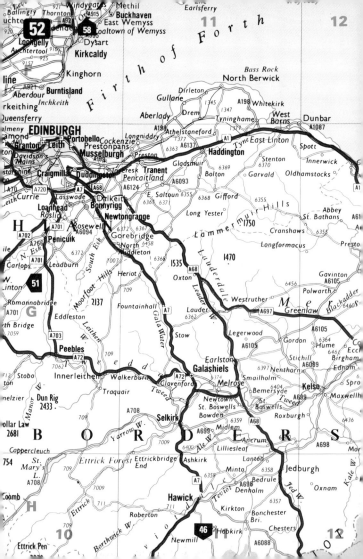

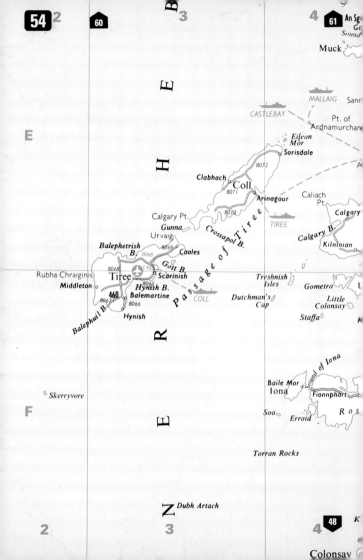

3
4 An Sg
Go
Soun

Muck

E

H

E

MALLAIG   Sanr

CASTLEBAY

Pt. of
Ardnamurchan

*Eilean
Mòr*
Sorisdale

Clabhach   **Coll**
8071   8072

Calgary Pt.

8070

Gunna

Urvaig

Balephetrish

B.   8069   Caoles

Rubha Chraiginis   **Tiree**
Middleton

460   *Hynish B.*
Balemartine

Balephuil B.

Hynish

Arinagour

TIREE

Caliach
Pt.   *Calgary*

Calgary B.

Kilninian

Crossapol B.

Gott B.

Scorinish

*Treshnish
Isles*   *Gometra*

*Dutchman's
Cap*   *Little
Colonsay*

COLL   *Staffa*

Passage of Tiree

Rubha Chraiginis

Skerryvore

Baile Mòr
Iona

Soa   *Erraid*

Fionnphort

Ros

Torran Rocks

Dubh Artach

2   3   4

Colonsay (

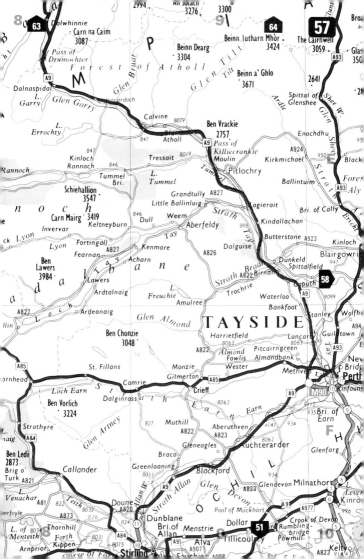

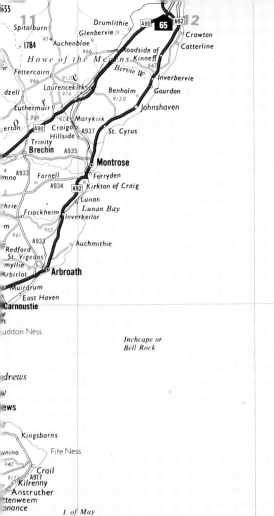

555

Spitalburn

Drumlithie

Glenbervie

A90 65 A92 12

Crawton

Auchenblae

Catterline

1784

974

966

Roadside of Kinneff

Howe of the Mearns

967

Fettercairn

9120

Bervie W.

Inverbervie

966

Laurencekirk

Benholm

Gourdon

dzell

974

9120

Luthermuir

Johnshaven

erton

996

974

Marykirk

A90

Craigo

Hillside

A937

St. Cyrus

Trinity

Brechin

A935

Montrose

E

4

A933

Farnell

Ferryden

mno

A934

A92

Kirkton of Craig

hrie

Lunan

Friockheim

Lunan Bay

Inverkeilor

m

961

965

A933

Redford

Auchmithie

St. Vigeans

myllie

Arbirlot

Arbroath

Muirdrum

East Haven

Carnoustie

h

uddon Ness

Inchcape or
Bell Rock

drews

v

ews

F

Kingsbarns

nino

Fife Ness

940

Crail

917

A917

Kilrenny

Anstruther

ttenweem

onance

I. of May

2

r t 1h

12

53

13

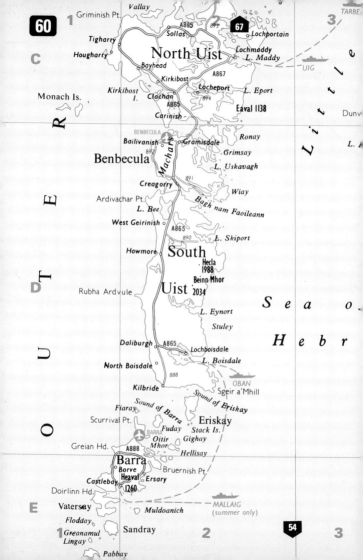

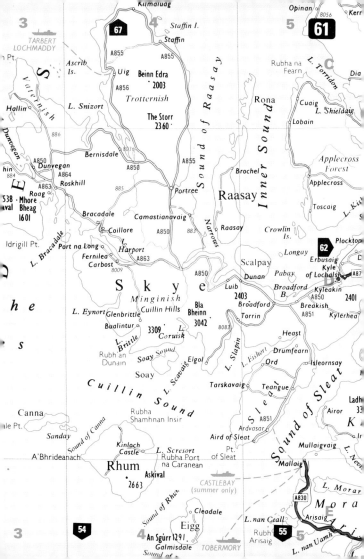

This is a map of the Isle of Skye and surrounding areas.

Grid/navigation markers: 3, 4, 5, 67, 61, 62, 54, 55

Places and features:

Kilmaluag, Staffin I., Staffin, Opinan, Kerr, 8056

TARBERT LOCHMADDY, Pt., Ascrib Is., A855, A855, Rubha na Fearn, L. Torridon, C, Dia

S, Vaternish, Uig, A856, Beinn Edra 2003, Trotternish, L. Snizort, 886, Cuaig, L. Shieldaig, Lobain, Rona

Hallin, The Storr 2360, Sound of Raasay, Inner Sound, Applecross Forest

hin, 884, Dunvegan, A850, A864, Roskhill, Bernisdale, A850, A856, Portree, Brochel, Raasay, Applecross, Toscaig, L. Kis

E, Roag, A863, Mhore Bheag, 1601, 538, val, Bracadale, 885, Camastianavaig, Narrows, Raasay, Crowlin Is., Longay, Plockton

Idrigill Pt., L. Bracadale, Coillore, A850, 883, Scalpay, 62, Erbusaig, Kyle of Lochalsh, A87

D, Port na Long, L. Harport, A863, 8009, Fernilea, Carbost, Dunan, Pabay, Broadford B., Kyleakin, 2401

S   k   y   e, Minginish, Luib, 2403, Broadford, A850, A851, Breakish, Kylerhea

he, L. Eynort, Glenbrittle, Cuillin Hills, Bla Bheinn 3042, Broadford, Torrin, A851, Heast

s, Bualintur, 3309, L. Coruisk, 8083, L. Slapin, Drumfearn, Ord, Isleornsay

Rubh' an Dunain, L. Brittle, Soay Sound, Elgol, L. Eishort, Sleat, Ladh, 33

Soay, Cuillin Sound, Tarskavaig, Teangue, Airor, K, Ir

Canna, Rubha Shamhnan Insir, Sound of Canna, Ardvasar, Mullaigvaig, L. Nev

le Pt., Sanday, A'Bhrideanach, Kinloch Castle, L. Scresort, Rubha Port na Caranean, Aird of Sleat, Pt. of Sleat, Mallaig, Sound of Sleat, L. Morar

Rhum, Askival, 2663, CASTLEBAY (summer only), A830, Mora, L. Morar, Ari

Cleadale, Eigg, L. nan Ceall, Arisaig, E

3, 54, 4, An Sgurr 1291, Galmisdale, 55, 5, Rubh' Arisaig, L. nan Uamh, TOBERMORY, Sound of

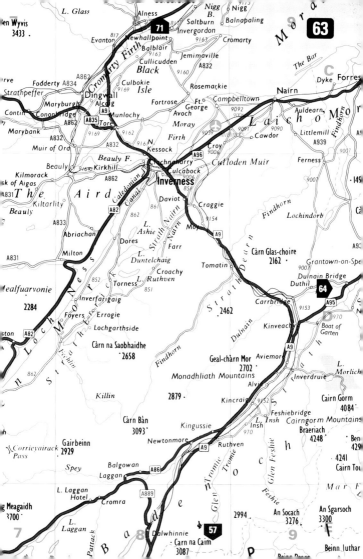

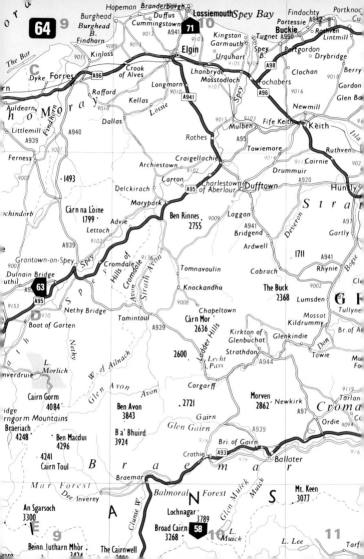

A

B

4

3

2

S

E

D

I

R

B

Lews

WESTERN

Butt of Lewis
P. of Ness
801/4
Lionel
N E S S
801/5 Skigersta
Cross
Cellar Hd.

Tolsta Hd.

Tiumpan Hd.
Portnaguiran
Shulishader
Eye Peninsula
Bayble
Knock
Chicken Hd.

Aird Dell
South Dell
A857
Five Penny
Borve

Muirneag
808
North Tolsta

895
Broad
Bay
Garrabost
Melbost
STORNOWAY
Sandwick

North Tolsta
Coll
Back
Gress

A857

Lower Shader
Barvas
Aird Barvas
Brue
Bragar
A858
Carloway
Ben Barvas
918

Newmarket
Laxdale
Stornoway
A859
Leurbost
897
Grimshader

North
Shawbost
South Shawbost

Breasclete
Callanish
A858
Achmore

E. Loch Roag
Gt.
Bernera
Breaclete

8059

W. Loch
Roag

8011
L o c h s

Gallan Hd.

Uig
Camus Uig
Miavaig
L. Suainaval
Isliving

U i g

Aird

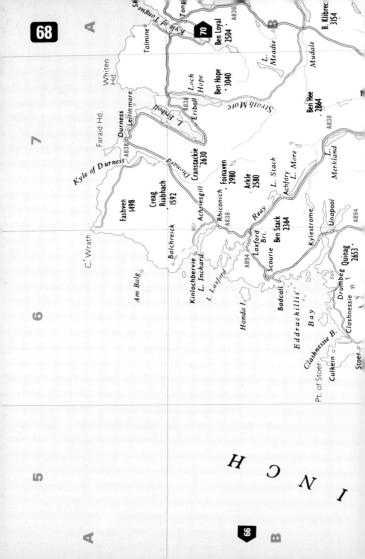

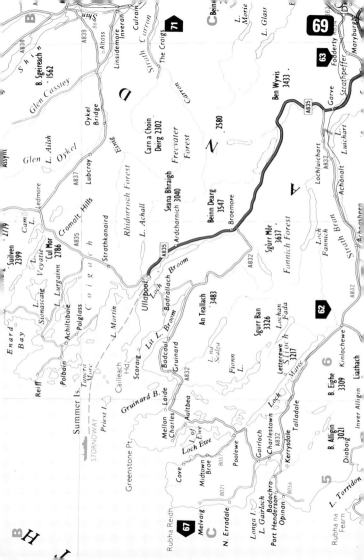

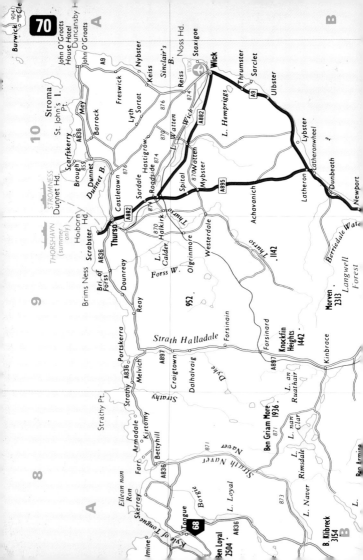

ARDROSSAN

Point of Ayre

10 Bride
19
Jurby Hd. Jurby
Ballasalla 17
The Cronk Churchtown
Ballaugh 3 Sulby Glen
Auldyn
Kirk Michael Snaefell **Barrule** Maughold
2034 **1860**
Agneash Glen Mona
Laxey

Peel

Patrick St. Laxey B.
Glenmaye John's 18 Baldrine
Crosby Clay Hd.
Dalby
Foxdale Onchan
S. Barrule St. Union
Niarbyl **1585** Mark's Mills **Douglas**
Bay 3 5 Douglas Hd.
Bradda Hd. Colby
Port Erin RONALD Ballasalla FLEETWOOD
Cregneish Port 5 Derbyhaven (summer only)
St. Mary Castletown HEYSHAM
Calf of Langness
Man Spanish Dreswick Pt.
Hd.

ISLE OF MAN

Glen Helen

K

L

BELFAST
(summer only)

DUBLIN
(summer only)

LIVERPOOL
(Summer only)

Ramsey
Ramsey
Bay

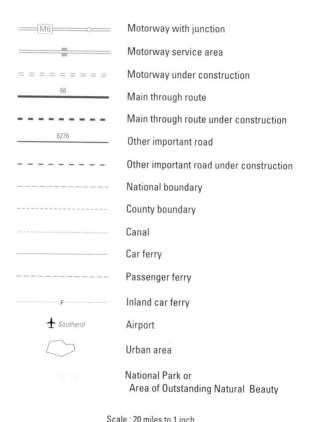

Motorway with junction

Motorway service area

Motorway under construction

Main through route

Main through route under construction

Other important road

Other important road under construction

National boundary

County boundary

Canal

Car ferry

Passenger ferry

Inland car ferry

Airport

Urban area

National Park or
Area of Outstanding Natural Beauty

Scale : 20 miles to 1 inch

| 0 | 10 | 20 | 30 | 40 | 50 | Miles |
| 0 | 20 | 40 | 60 | 80 | Kilometres |

Shetland Islands

20 miles to 1 inch

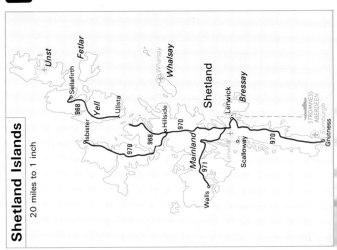

Orkney Islands

20 miles to 1 inch

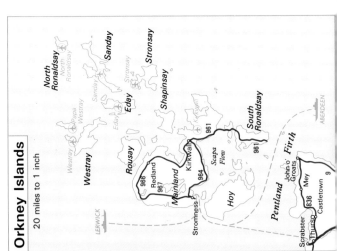

Channel Islands

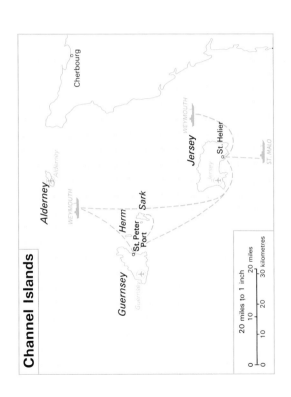

Cherbourg

Alderney

Alderney

WEYMOUTH

Jersey

o St. Helier

Jersey

WEYMOUTH

ST. MALO

Guernsey

Guernsey

Herm

Sark

St. Peter Port

20 miles to 1 inch

0	10	20 miles
0	10	20	30 kilometres

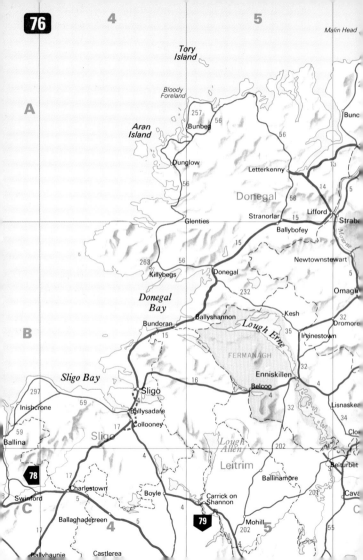

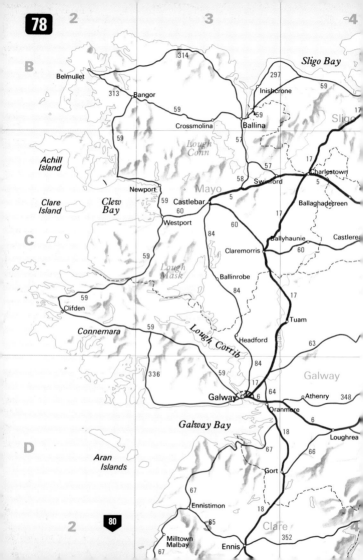

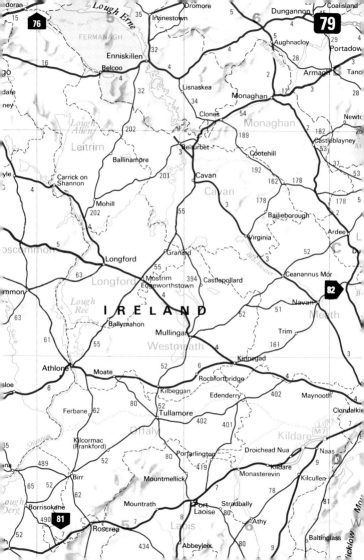

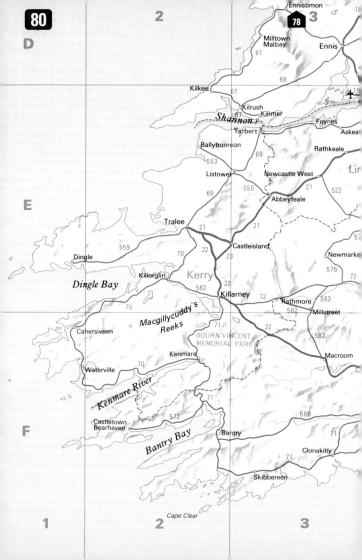

2

3

D

Ennistimon

Milltown
Malbay
67

Ennis

68

Kilkee
67

Shannon
19

Kilrush
Kilimer

Shannon

Foynes

Askea

Tarbert

Ballybunnion

Rathkeale

69

553

Lir

Listowel

Newcastle West

69

555

21

522

Abbeyfeale

E

Tralee
21

21

559

22

Castleisland

Dingle

70

28

Newmarke

Killorglin

Kerry

576

72

562

22

Killarney

70

Macgillycuddy's
Reeks

72

Rathmore

582

583

Millstreet

Dingle Bay

71

BOURN VINCENT
MEMORIAL PARK

22

582

Cahersiveen

Kenmare

Macroom

Waterville
70

71

Kenmare River

586

572

Castletown
Bearhaven

F

Bantry

71

Bantry Bay

71

Clonakilty

Skibbereen

Cape Clear

1

2

3

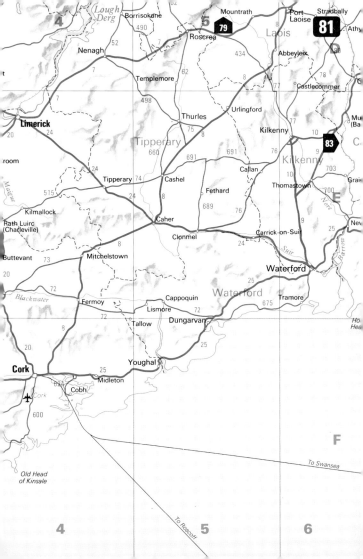

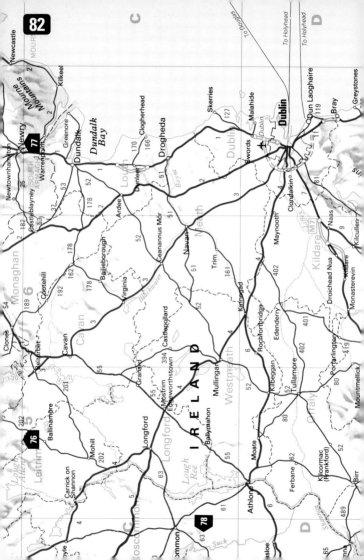

ABBREVIATIONS

Beds	*Bedford*	Hants	*Hampshire*	Northum	*Northumberland*
Berks	*Berkshire*	Heref/Worcs	*Hereford and*	Notts	*Nottingham*
Bri.	*Bridge*		*Worcester*	N Yorks	*North Yorkshire*
Bucks	*Buckinghamshire*	Herts	*Hertford*	Oxon	*Oxford*
Cambs	*Cambridge*	H'land	*Highland*	S'clyde	*Strathclyde*
Chan Is.	*Channel Islands*	Hth.	*Heath*	S Glam	*South Glamorgan*
Ches	*Cheshire*	Humber	*Humberside*	Shetl'd	*Shetland*
Clevl'd	*Cleveland*	I of Man	*Isle of Man*	Shrops	*Shropshire*
Cornw'l	*Cornwall*	I of Scilly	*Isles of Scilly*	Som'set	*Somerset*
Cumb	*Cumbria*	I of Wight	*Isle of Wight*	Staffs	*Stafford*
Dumf/Gal	*Dumfries and*	Lancs	*Lancashire*	S Yorks	*South Yorkshire*
	Galloway	Leics	*Leicester*	Tyne/Wear	*Tyne and Wear*
E Sussex	*East Sussex*	Lincs	*Lincoln*	W Glam	*West Glamorgan*
Glos	*Gloucester*	Lit.	*Little*	Wilts	*Wiltshire*
Gramp	*Grampian*	Lo.	*Lodge*	W Isles	*Western Isles*
Grn.	*Green*	Lr.	*Lower*	W Midlands	*West Midlands*
Gt.	*Great*	Mersey	*Merseyside*	W Sussex	*West Sussex*
Gtr Man	*Greater Manchester*	Mid Glam	*Mid Glamorgan*	W Yorks	*West Yorkshire*
Gwyn	*Gwynedd*	Northants	*Northampton*		

A

Abbey Cwmhir *Powys*	27 O10	Abersychan *Gwent*	20 P10	Adwick le Street *S Yorks*	38 L14
Abbey Dore *Heref/Worcs*	20 P11	Abertillery *Gwent*	20 P10	Ae Village *Dumf/Gal*	45 H9
Abbey St. Bathans *Borders*	52 G12	Abertridwr *Mid Glam*	20 P10	Afton Bridgend *S'clyde*	50 H8
Abbey Town *Cumb*	45 J10	Aberuthven *Tayside*	57 F9	Agneash *I of Man*	72 K8
Abbots Bromley *Staffs*	29 N13	Aberystwyth *Dyfed*	26 O8	Ainsdale *Mersey*	36 L10
Abbots Langley *Herts*	16 P16	Abingdon *Oxon*	22 P14	Ainsworth *Gtr Man*	36 L12
Abbotsbury *Dorset*	6 R11	Abington *S'clyde*	51 H9	Aird of Sleat *H'land*	61 D5
Abbotskerswell *Devon*	5 R9	Aboyne *Gramp*	64 D11	Airdrie *S'clyde*	51 G9
Aber *Gwyn*	34 M8	Abriachan *H'land*	63 D8	Airor *H'land*	61 D5
Aberaeron *Dyfed*	19 O8	Abridge *Essex*	17 P17	Airth *Central*	51 F9
Aberaman *Mid Glam*	20 P10	Aby *Lincs*	39 M17	Aiskew *N Yorks*	42 K13
Aberangell *Powys*	27 N9	Accrington *Lancs*	36 L12	Akeld *Northum*	53 G12
Abercarn *Gwent*	20 P10	Achahoish *S'clyde*	49 G5	Albrighton *Shrops*	29 N12
Aberchirder *Gramp*	65 C11	Achanalt *H'land*	62 C7	Alcaig *H'land*	63 C8
Abercynon *Mid Glam*	20 P10	Achanamara *S'clyde*	49 F5	Alcester *Warwick*	21 O13
Aberdare *Mid Glam*	20 P10	Acharacle *H'land*	55 E5	Alconbury *Cambs*	31 O16
Aberdaron *Gwyn*	34 N7	Acharn *Tayside*	57 E8	Aldborough *Norfolk*	33 N19
Aberdeen *Gramp*	65 D12	Achavanich *H'land*	70 B10	Aldborough *N Yorks*	42 K14
Aberdour *Fife*	51 F10	Achfary *H'land*	68 B7	Aldbourne *Wilts*	15 Q13
Aberdyfi *Gwyn*	26 N8	Achiltibuie *H'land*	69 B6	Aldbrough *N Yorks*	42 K13
Aberedw *Powys*	20 O10	Achleck *S'clyde*	54 E4	Aldbrough *Humber*	43 L16
Abererch *Gwyn*	34 N8	Achmore *W Isles*	66 B3	Aldbury *Herts*	16 P15
Aberfeldy *Tayside*	57 E9	Achnacroish *S'clyde*	55 E6	Aldeburgh *Suffolk*	25 O20
Aberffraw *Gwyn*	34 M8	Achnasheen *H'land*	62 C6	Alderbury *Wilts*	15 Q13
Aberford *W Yorks*	38 L14	Achnashellach *H'land*	62 D6	Alderholt *Dorset*	7 R13
Aberfoyle *Central*	57 F8	Achranich *H'land*	55 E5	Alderley Edge *Ches*	37 M12
Abergavenny *Gwent*	20 P10	Achriesgill *H'land*	68 B7	Aldermaston *Berks*	15 Q14
Abergele *Clwyd*	35 M9	Acklam *N Yorks*	43 K15	Alderminster *Warwick*	22 O13
Abergwili *Dyfed*	19 P8	Ackworth *W Yorks*	38 L14	Aldershot *Hants*	16 Q15
Abergynolwyn *Gwyn*	27 N9	Acle *Norfolk*	33 N20	Alderton *Glos*	21 P13
Aberlady *Lothian*	52 F11	Acomb *Northum*	47 H12	Alderton *Suffolk*	25 O19
Aberlemno *Tayside*	58 E11	Acton *Ches*	36 M11	Aldford *Ches*	36 M11
Aberllefenni *Gwyn*	27 N9	Acton Burnell *Shrops*	28 N11	Aldingham *Cumb*	40 K10
Aberllynfi *Powys*	20 O10	Acton Turville *Avon*	21 P12	Aldridge *W Midlands*	29 N13
Abernethy *Tayside*	58 F10	Adderbury *Oxon*	22 O14	Aldwincle *Northants*	31 O15
Abernyte *Tayside*	58 F10	Adderley *Shrops*	29 N11	Alexandria *S'clyde*	50 G7
Aberporth *Dyfed*	18 O7	Addiewell *Lothian*	51 G9	Alford *Lincs*	39 M17
Abersoch *Gwyn*	34 N8	Addingham *W Yorks*	41 L13	Alford *Gramp*	65 D11
		Addlestone *Surrey*	16 Q15	Alfreton *Derby*	38 M14
		Adisham *Kent*	11 Q19	Alfrick *Heref/Worcs*	21 O12
		Adlington *Lancs*	36 L11	Alfriston *E Sussex*	10 R17
		Advie *H'land*	64 D10	Alkham *Kent*	11 Q19

All Saints *Humber*	39	L16
All Stretton *Shrops*	28	N11
Allendale Town *Northum*	46	J12
Allenheads *Northum*	46	J12
Allerston *N Yorks*	43	K15
Allestree *Derby*	37	M13
Alloa *Central*	51	F9
Allonby *Cumb*	45	J10
Alloway *S'clyde*	50	H7
Alltwen *W Glam*	19	P9
Almeley *Heref/Worcs*	20	O11
Almondbank *Tayside*	58	F9
Almondsbury *Avon*	14	P11
Alne *N Yorks*	42	K14
Alness *H'land*	71	C8
Alnmouth *Northum*	53	H13
Alnwick *Northum*	53	H13
Alphington *Devon*	5	R9
Alpraham *Ches*	36	M11
Alresford *Essex*	25	P18
Alrewas *Staffs*	30	N13
Alsager *Ches*	37	M12
Alswear *Devon*	12	R9
Altass *H'land*	69	C7
Althorne *Essex*	24	P18
Althorpe *Humber*	38	L15
Alton *Hants*	16	Q15
Alton *Staffs*	29	N13
Alton Barnes *Wilts*	15	Q13
Altrincham *Gtr Man*	37	M12
Alva *Central*	51	F9
Alvechurch *Heref/Worcs*	29	O13
Alveley *Shrops*	29	O12
Alvescot *Oxon*	22	P13
Alveston *Avon*	21	P11
Alveston *Warwick*	22	O13
Alvie *H'land*	63	D9
Alvington *Glos*	21	P11
Alwinton *Northum*	47	H12
Alyth *Tayside*	58	E10
Amberley *W Sussex*	9	R15
Amble *Northum*	47	H13
Ambleside *Cumb*	40	K11
Amcotts *Humber*	38	L15
Amersham *Bucks*	16	P15
Amesbury *Wilts*	15	Q13
Amlwch *Gwyn*	34	M8
Ammanford *Dyfed*	19	P9
Amotherby *N Yorks*	43	K15
Ampfield *Hants*	15	Q14
Ampleforth *N Yorks*	42	K14
Ampthill *Beds*	23	O15
Amroth *Dyfed*	18	P7
Amulree *Tayside*	57	E9
Ancaster *Lincs*	31	N15
Ancroft *Northum*	53	G12
Ancrum *Borders*	52	G11
Andover *Hants*	15	Q14
Andoversford *Glos*	21	P13
Angle *Dyfed*	18	P6
Angmering *W Sussex*	9	R16
Anlaby *Humber*	39	L16
Annan *Dumf/Gal*	45	J10
Annat *H'land*	62	C5
Annesley *Notts*	38	M14
Annfield Plain *Durham*	47	J13
Ansley *Warwick*	30	N13
Anstey *Leics*	30	N14
Anston *S Yorks*	38	M14
Anstruther *Fife*	59	F11
Anwick *Lincs*	31	M16
Anwoth *Dumf/Gal*	44	J8
Apperley *Glos*	21	P12
Appleby *Humber*	38	L15
Appleby *Cumb*	41	J12
Applecross *H'land*	61	D5
Appledore *Kent*	11	Q18
Appledore *Devon*	12	Q8
Appleton *Oxon*	22	P14
Appleton *Ches*	36	M11
Appleton-le-Street *N Yorks*	43	K15
Arbirlot *Tayside*	59	E11
Arborfield Cross *Berks*	16	Q15
Arbroath *Tayside*	59	E11
Archiestown *Gramp*	64	D10
Ardbeg *S'clyde*	48	G4
Ardcharnich *H'land*	69	C6
Ardelve *H'land*	62	D5
Ardentinny *Central*	57	F8
Ardfern *S'clyde*	55	F5
Ardhasig *W Isles*	67	C3
Ardingly *W Sussex*	9	Q16
Ardmolich *H'land*	55	E5
Ardpatrick *S'clyde*	49	G5
Ardrishaig *S'clyde*	49	F6
Ardrossan *S'clyde*	50	G7
Ardtalnaig *Tayside*	57	E8
Ardvasar *H'land*	62	D5
Ardvourlie Castle *W Isles*	67	C3
Ardwell *Dumf/Gal*	44	J7
Ardwell *Gramp*	64	D10
Aribruach *W Isles*	67	B3
Arinagour *S'clyde*	54	E3
Arisaig *H'land*	61	E5
Arlecdon *Cumb*	40	J10
Arleigh *Essex*	25	P18
Arlesey *Beds*	23	O16
Arley *Warwick*	30	N13
Arlingham *Glos*	21	P12
Armadale *Lothian*	51	G9
Armadale *H'land*	70	A8
Armathwaite *Cumb*	46	J11
Armitage *Staffs*	29	N13
Armthorpe *S Yorks*	38	L14
Arncliffe *N Yorks*	41	K12
Arncroach *Fife*	58	F11
Arnisdale *H'land*	62	D5
Arnold *Notts*	30	N14
Arnprior *Central*	50	F8
Arnside *Cumb*	40	K11
Arrington *Cambs*	23	O16
Arrochar *S'clyde*	56	F7
Arundel *W Sussex*	9	R15
Ascog *S'clyde*	49	G6
Ascot *Berks*	16	Q15
Asfordby *Leics*	30	N15
Ash *Kent*	11	Q19
Ash *Surrey*	16	Q15
Ashbourne *Derby*	30	M13
Ashburton *Devon*	5	R9
Ashbury *Oxon*	15	P13
Ashby de la Zouch *Leics*	30	N14
Ashcott *Som'set*	14	Q11
Ashford *Kent*	10	Q18
Ashford *Surrey*	16	Q16
Ashford *Derby*	37	M13
Ashford Carbonel *Shrops*	28	O11
Ashill *Norfolk*	32	N18
Ashingdon *Essex*	24	P18
Ashington *Northum*	47	H13
Ashington *W Sussex*	9	R16
Ashkirk *Borders*	46	H11
Ashleworth *Glos*	21	P12
Ashley *Cambs*	24	O17
Ashley *Staffs*	29	N12
Ashley *Ches*	37	M12
Ashover *Derby*	37	M14
Ashstead *Surrey*	16	Q16
Ashton *Gtr Man*	37	M12
Ashton in Makerfield *Gtr Man*	36	M11
Ashton Keynes *Wilts*	21	P13
Ashton-under-Lyne *Gtr Man*	37	L12
Ashurstwood *W Sussex*	9	Q17
Ashwater *Devon*	4	R8
Ashwell *Herts*	23	O16
Ashwell *Leics*	31	N15
Ashwellthorpe *Norfolk*	33	N19
Ashwick *Som'set*	14	Q11
Askam-in-Furness *Cumb*	40	K10
Askern *S Yorks*	38	L14
Askham *Cumb*	40	J11
Askrigg *N Yorks*	41	K12
Aslackby *Lincs*	31	N16
Aspatria *Cumb*	45	J10
Aspley Guise *Beds*	23	O15
Astbury *Ches*	37	M12
Aston *Herts*	23	P16
Aston Clinton *Bucks*	16	P15
Astwood Bank *Heref/Worcs*	21	O13
Atcham *Shrops*	28	N11
Athelstaneford *Lothian*	52	G11
Atherington *Devon*	12	R8
Atherstone *Warwick*	30	N13
Atherton *Gtr Man*	36	L12
Attleborough *Norfolk*	33	N19
Attlebridge *Norfolk*	33	N19
Atwick *Humber*	43	L16
Atworth *Wilts*	14	Q12
Auchenblae *Gramp*	59	E12
Auchencairn *Dumf/Gal*	45	J9
Auchencrow *Borders*	53	G12
Auchertyre *H'land*	62	D5
Auchinleck *S'clyde*	50	H8
Auchleven *Gramp*	65	D11
Auchmithie *Tayside*	59	E11
Auchnagatt *Gramp*	65	D12
Auchterarder *Tayside*	57	F9
Auchterderran *Fife*	58	F10
Auchtermuchty *Fife*	58	F10
Auchtertool *Fife*	51	F10
Audlem *Ches*	29	N11
Audley *Staffs*	37	M12
Aughton *Lancs*	36	L11
Auldearn *H'land*	63	C9
Aultbea *H'land*	69	C5
Aust *Avon*	21	P11
Austwick *N Yorks*	41	K12
Avebury *Wilts*	15	Q13
Aveley *Essex*	17	P17
Avening *Glos*	21	P12
Averton Gifford *Devon*	4	S9
Aviemore *H'land*	63	D9
Avoch *H'land*	63	C8
Avonbridge *Central*	51	G9
Avonmouth *Avon*	14	Q11
Awre *Glos*	21	P12
Axbridge *Som'set*	14	Q11
Axminster *Devon*	6	R11
Axmouth *Devon*	5	R10
Aycliffe *Durham*	42	J13
Aylburton *Glos*	21	P11
Aylesbeare *Devon*	5	R10
Aylesbury *Bucks*	16	P15
Aylesford *Kent*	10	Q17
Aylesham *Kent*	11	Q19

Aylsham *Norfolk* 33 N19
Aymestrey *Heref/Worcs* 28 O11
Aynho *Northants* 22 P14
Ayr *S'clyde* 50 H7
Aysgarth *N Yorks* 41 K12
Ayton *N Yorks* 43 K16
Ayton *Borders* 53 G12

B

Babbacombe *Devon* 5 S9
Back *W Isles* 66 B4
Backwell *Avon* 14 Q11
Backworth *Tyne/Wear* 47 H13
Baconsthorpe *Norfolk* 33 N19
Bacton *Norfolk* 33 N19
Bacup *Lancs* 37 L12
Badachro *H'land* 69 C5
Badby *Northants* 22 O14
Badcall *H'land* 68 B6
Badcaul *H'land* 69 C6
Baddeley Green *Staffs* 37 M12
Baddesley Ensor *Warwick* 30 N13
Badenscoth *Gramp* 65 D12
Badrallach *H'land* 69 C6
Bagillt *Clwyd* 35 M10
Bagshot *Surrey* 16 Q15
Bagworth *Leics* 30 N14
Baildon *W Yorks* 42 L13
Baile Mor *S'clyde* 54 F4
Bailivanish *W Isles* 60 D2
Baillieston *S'clyde* 51 G9
Bainbridge *N Yorks* 41 K12
Bainton *Humber* 43 L15
Bakewell *Derby* 37 M13
Bala *Gwyn* 35 N9
Balallan *W Isles* 66 B3
Balbeggie *Tayside* 58 F10
Balblair *H'land* 63 C8
Balchreik *H'land* 68 B6
Balcombe *W Sussex* 9 Q16
Baldersby *N Yorks* 42 K14
Balderton *Notts* 38 M15
Baldock *Herts* 23 P16
Baldrine *I of Man* 72 K8
Balemartine *S'clyde* 54 F3
Balerno *Lothian* 51 G10
Balfron *Central* 50 F8
Balgowan *H'land* 63 D8
Balgray *Tayside* 58 E11
Balintore *H'land* 71 C9
Ballantrae *S'clyde* 44 H7
Ballasalla *I of Man* 72 K7
Ballasalla *I of Man* 72 K7
Ballater *Gramp* 64 D10
Ballaugh *I of Man* 72 K7
Ballchraggan *H'land* 71 C8
Ballingry *Fife* 58 F10
Ballintuim *Tayside* 58 E10
Balloch *S'clyde* 50 F7
Ballygrant *S'clyde* 48 G4
Balmacara *H'land* 62 D5
Balmaclellan *Dumf/Gal* 45 H8
Balmaha *Central* 50 F7
Balmedie *Gramp* 65 D12
Balmerino *Fife* 58 F10
Balnacra *H'land* 62 D6
Balnahard *S'clyde* 55 F4
Balnapaling *H'land* 71 C8

Balquhidder *Central* 57 F8
Balsall *W Midlands* 30 O13
Balsham *Cambs* 24 O17
Balvicar *S'clyde* 55 F5
Bamburgh *Northum* 53 G13
Bamford *Derby* 37 M13
Bampton *Devon* 13 R10
Bampton *Oxon* 22 P13
Bampton *Cumb* 41 J11
Banavie *H'land* 56 E6
Banbury *Oxon* 22 O14
Banchory *Gramp* 65 D12
Banff *Gramp* 65 C11
Bangor *Gwyn* 34 M8
Bangor-is-y-Coed *Clwyd* 28 N11
Banham *Norfolk* 33 O19
Bankend *Dumf/Gal* 45 J9
Bankfoot *Tayside* 58 E9
Bankglen *S'clyde* 50 H8
Bankhead *S'clyde* 50 G7
Bankhead *Gramp* 65 D12
Banks *Lancs* 36 L11
Bankshill *Dumf/Gal* 46 J11
Bannockburn *Central* 51 F9
Banstead *Surrey* 17 Q16
Banwell *Avon* 13 Q11
Baptiston *Central* 50 F8
Barassie *S'clyde* 50 G7
Barbaraville *H'land* 71 C8
Barbon *Cumb* 41 K11
Barby *Northants* 30 O14
Bardney *Lincs* 39 M16
Bardon Mill *Northum* 46 J12
Bardsea *Cumb* 40 K10
Bardsey *W Yorks* 42 L14
Barford *Warwick* 22 O13
Barford *Norfolk* 33 N19
Bargoed *Mid Glam* 20 P10
Bargrennan *Dumf/Gal* 44 H7
Barham *Kent* 11 Q19
Barkestone *Leics* 31 N15
Barking *Gtr Lon* 17 P17
Barkston *Lincs* 31 N15
Barkway *Herts* 24 O17
Barlaston *Staffs* 29 N12
Barlborough *Derby* 38 M14
Barlby *N Yorks* 38 L14
Barley *Herts* 24 O17
Barmby Moor *Humber* 43 L15
Barmoor *Northum* 53 G13
Barmouth *Gwyn* 26 N8
Barmston *Humber* 43 K16
Barnard Castle *Durham* 41 J13
Barnby Dun *S Yorks* 38 L14
Barnby Moor *Notts* 38 M14
Barnet *Gtr Lon* 17 P16
Barnetby le Wold *Humber* 39 L16
Barnham *Suffolk* 32 O18
Barnham *W Sussex* 9 R15
Barningham *Suffolk* 33 O18
Barningham *Durham* 41 K13
Barnoldswick *Lancs* 37 L13
Barnsley *S Yorks* 38 L14
Barnstaple *Devon* 12 Q8
Barnt Green *Heref/Worcs* 29 O13
Barnton *Ches* 36 M11
Barnwell *Northants* 31 O16
Barr *S'clyde* 44 H7
Barrhead *S'clyde* 50 G8
Barrhill *S'clyde* 44 H7
Barrmill *S'clyde* 50 G7

Barrock *H'land* 70 A10
Barrow upon Humber
  Humber 39 L16
Barrow upon Soar *Leics* 30 N14
Barrowby *Lincs* 31 N15
Barrow-in-Furness *Cumb* 40 K10
Barry *S Glam* 20 Q10
Barry *Tayside* 59 F11
Barthol Chapel *Gramp* 65 D12
Bartley *Hants* 8 R13
Barton *Lancs* 41 L11
Barton *N Yorks* 42 K13
Barton Mills *Suffolk* 32 O18
Barton Stacey *Hants* 15 Q14
Barton under Needwood
  Staffs 30 N13
Barton upon Humber
  Humber 39 L16
Barton-le-Clay *Beds* 23 P16
Barton-le-Street *N Yorks* 44 K15
Barvas *W Isles* 66 B3
Barve *W Isles* 67 C2
Barwell *Leics* 30 N14
Barwick in Elmet *W Yorks* 42 L14
Baschurch *Shrops* 28 N11
Basildon *Essex* 17 P17
Basing *Hants* 16 Q14
Basingstoke *Hants* 15 Q14
Baslow *Derby* 37 M13
Bassenthwaite *Cumb* 45 J10
Bassingbourn *Cambs* 23 O16
Baston *Lincs* 31 N16
Batcombe *Som'set* 14 Q12
Bath *Avon* 14 Q12
Bathford *Avon* 14 Q12
Bathgate *Lothian* 51 G9
Batley *W Yorks* 37 L13
Battle *E Sussex* 10 R17
Battlefield *Shrops* 28 N11
Baumber *Lincs* 39 M16
Bawburgh *Norfolk* 33 N19
Bawdeswell *Norfolk* 33 N19
Bawdsey *Suffolk* 25 O19
Bawtry *S Yorks* 38 M14
Bayble *W Isles* 66 B4
Baycliff *Cumb* 40 K10
Bayhead *W Isles* 60 C2
Bayton *Heref/Worcs* 29 O12
Beachley *Glos* 21 P11
Beaconsfield *Bucks* 16 P15
Beadnell *Northum* 53 G13
Beaford *Devon* 12 R8
Beaminster *Dorset* 6 R11
Bearsden *S'clyde* 50 G8
Beattock *Dumf/Gal* 45 H10
Beaufort *Gwent* 20 P10
Beaulieu *Hants* 8 R14
Beauly *H'land* 63 D8
Beaumaris *Gwyn* 34 M8
Bebington *Mersey* 36 M11
Beccles *Suffolk* 33 O20
Becconsall *Lancs* 36 L11
Beckingham *Notts* 38 M15
Beckermet *Cumb* 40 K10
Beckfoot *Cumb* 45 J10
Beckford *Heref/Worcs* 21 O12
Beckingham *Notts* 38 M15
Beckington *Som'set* 14 Q12
Beckley *E Sussex* 10 R18
Beckley *Oxon* 22 P14
Bedale *N Yorks* 42 K14
Beddgelert *Gwyn* 34 M8

Bedford Beds	23	O16
Bedlington Northum	47	H13
Bedrule Borders	52	H11
Bedstone Shrops	28	O11
Bedwas Mid Glam	20	P10
Bedworth Warwick	30	O13
Beech Hants	8	Q14
Beeford Humber	43	L16
Beeley Derby	37	M13
Beer Devon	5	R10
Beeston Notts	30	N14
Beeston Norfolk	32	N18
Beeswing Dumf/Gal	45	H9
Begelly Dyfed	18	P7
Beguildy Powys	27	O10
Beighton S Yorks	38	M14
Beith S'clyde	50	G7
Belbroughton Heref/Worcs	29	O12
Belchford Lincs	39	M16
Belford Northum	53	G13
Bellerby N Yorks	41	K13
Bellingham Northum	46	H12
Bellochantuy S'clyde	49	G5
Belmont Lancs	36	L11
Belper Derby	30	M14
Belsay Northum	47	H13
Belstone Devon	4	R9
Belton Leics	30	N14
Belton Lincs	31	N15
Belton Norfolk	33	N20
Belton Humber	38	L15
Bembridge I of Wight	8	R14
Bemersyde Borders	52	G11
Bempton Humber	43	K16
Benenden Kent	10	Q18
Benfieldside Durham	47	J13
Benholm Gramp	59	E12
Benington Lincs	32	N17
Benllech Gwyn	34	M8
Benson Oxon	22	P14
Bentley Hants	16	Q15
Bentley S Yorks	38	L14
Bentpath Dumf/Gal	46	H10
Bentworth Hants	16	Q14
Benwick Cambs	31	O16
Beoley Heref/Worcs	29	O13
Bere Alston Devon	4	S8
Bere Ferrers Devon	4	S8
Bere Regis Dorset	6	R12
Berkeley Glos	21	P12
Berkhamsted Herts	16	P15
Berriedale H'land	61	D4
Berriew Powys	27	N10
Berryhillock Gramp	64	C11
Berrynarbor Devon	12	Q8
Berwick upon Tweed Northum	53	G12
Besthorpe Notts	38	M15
Bethersden Kent	10	Q18
Bethesda Gwyn	34	M8
Betley Staffs	29	M12
Betteshanger Kent	11	Q19
Bettyhill H'land	70	A8
Betws-y-Coed Gwyn	35	M9
Beulah Powys	19	O9
Beverley Humber	43	L16
Bewcastle Cumb	46	H11
Bewdley Heref/Worcs	29	O12
Bewerley N Yorks	42	K13
Bexhill E Sussex	10	R17
Bexley Gtr Lon	17	Q17
Beyton Suffolk	24	O18
Bibury Glos	21	P13
Bicester Oxon	22	P14
Bicker Lincs	31	N16
Bickington Devon	5	R9
Bickleigh Devon	4	S8
Bickleigh Devon	5	R10
Biddenden Kent	10	Q18
Biddulph Staffs	37	M12
Bideford Devon	12	Q8
Bidford-on-Avon Warwick	21	O13
Bielside Gramp	65	D12
Bigbury Devon	4	S9
Bigbury-on-Sea Devon	4	S9
Bigby Lincs	39	L16
Biggar Cumb	40	K10
Biggar S'clyde	51	G9
Biggin Hill Gtr Lon	17	Q17
Biggleswade Beds	23	O16
Bildeston Suffolk	25	O18
Billericay Essex	17	P17
Billesdon Leics	30	N15
Billingborough Lincs	31	N16
Billingham Clevl'd	47	J14
Billinghay Lincs	39	M16
Billingshurst W Sussex	9	Q16
Billington Leics	36	L12
Billy Row Durham	47	J13
Bilsby Lincs	39	M17
Bilsthorpe Notts	38	M14
Bilston W Midlands	29	N12
Bilton Humber	39	L16
Binbrook Lincs	39	M16
Binfield Berks	16	Q15
Bingham Notts	31	N15
Bingley W Yorks	41	L13
Binham Norfolk	33	N18
Birchington Kent	11	Q19
Birdham W Sussex	8	R15
Birdlip Glos	21	P12
Birdsall N Yorks	43	K15
Birgham Borders	52	G12
Birkenhead Mersey	36	M10
Birkhill Feus Tayside	58	F10
Birmingham W Midlands	29	O13
Birmington Derby	38	M14
Birnam Tayside	58	E9
Birtley Northum	46	H12
Birtley Northum	47	J13
Birtley Tyne/Wear	47	J13
Bishampton Heref/Worcs	21	O12
Bishop Auckland Durham	47	J13
Bishop Burton Humber	43	L15
Bishop Monkton N Yorks	42	K14
Bishop Norton Lincs	38	M15
Bishop's Castle Shrops	28	O11
Bishops Caundle Dorset	6	R12
Bishop's Cleeve Glos	21	P12
Bishops Frome Heref/Worcs	21	O12
Bishop's Itchington Warwick	22	O14
Bishop's Lydeard Som'set	13	Q10
Bishop's Nympton Devon	12	R9
Bishops Stortford Herts	24	P17
Bishop's Tachbrook Warwick	22	O13
Bishop's Tawton Devon	12	Q8
Bishop's Waltham Hants	8	R14
Bishopsteignton Devon	5	R9
Bishopstoke Hants	8	R14
Bishopston W Glam	19	P8
Bishopstone Wilts	15	Q13
Bishopstone Wilts	22	P13
Bishopthorpe N Yorks	42	L14
Bishopton Durham	42	J14
Bishopton S'clyde	50	G7
Bisley Glos	21	P12
Bispham Lancs	40	L10
Bitterley Shrops	29	O11
Black Torrington Devon	4	R8
Blackburn Lancs	36	L11
Blackburn Lothian	51	G9
Blackburn Gramp	65	D12
Blackfield Hants	8	R14
Blackford Tayside	57	F9
Blackhall Colliery Durham	47	J14
Blacklunans Tayside	58	E10
Blackmore Essex	17	P17
Blackpool Lancs	36	L10
Blackrod Gtr Man	36	L11
Blackthorn Oxon	22	P14
Blackwater Hants	16	Q15
Blackwater Foot S'clyde	49	G6
Blackwood Gwent	20	P10
Blackwood S'clyde	51	G9
Bladnoch Dumf/Gal	44	J8
Blaenau Ffestiniog Gwyn	35	N9
Blaenavon Gwent	20	P10
Blaengwrach W Glam	19	P9
Blaenporth Dyfed	18	O7
Blagdon Avon	14	Q11
Blaich H'land	55	E6
Blaina Gwent	20	P10
Blair Atholl Tayside	57	E9
Blairgowrie Tayside	58	E10
Blakedown Heref/Worcs	29	O12
Blakemere Heref/Worcs	20	O11
Blakeney Glos	21	P12
Blakeney Norfolk	33	N19
Blakesley Northants	22	O14
Blanchland Northum	47	J12
Blandford Forum Dorset	7	R12
Blankney Lincs	39	M16
Blaydon Tyne/Wear	47	J13
Bleadon Avon	13	Q11
Blean Kent	11	Q19
Bledington Glos	22	P13
Bletchingley Surrey	17	Q16
Bletchley Bucks	23	P15
Blewbury Oxon	22	P14
Blidworth Notts	38	M14
Blindley Heath Surrey	17	Q16
Blisworth Northants	22	O15
Blockley Glos	22	O13
Blofield Norfolk	33	N19
Bloxham Oxon	22	O14
Blubberhouses N Yorks	42	L13
Blundeston Suffolk	33	N20
Blunham Beds	23	O16
Blyth Notts	38	M14
Blyth Northum	47	H13
Blyth Bridge Borders	51	G10
Blythburgh Suffolk	33	O20
Blyton Lincs	38	M15
Boar's Hill Oxon	22	P14
Boat of Garten H'land	64	D9
Boddam Gramp	65	D13
Boddinick Cornw'l	3	S7
Bodedern Gwyn	34	M7
Bodelwyddan Clwyd	35	M9
Bodenham Heref/Worcs	20	O11
Bodfari Clwyd	35	M10
Bodiam E Sussex	10	Q18
Bodicote Oxon	22	O14
Bodmin Cornw'l	3	S7
Bognor Regis W Sussex	9	R15
Boldon Tyne/Wear	47	J14
Boldre Hants	8	R13
Bollington Ches	37	M12
Bolney W Sussex	9	R16

Bolsover *Derby* 38 M14
Bolton *Gtr Man* 36 L12
Bolton *Cumb* 41 J11
Bolton *Lothian* 52 G11
Bolton Abbey *N Yorks* 41 L13
Bolton by Bowland *Lancs* 41 L12
Bolton le Sands *Lancs* 40 K11
Bolton on Swale *N Yorks* 42 K13
Bolton upon Dearne *S Yorks* 38 L14
Bolventor *Cornw'l* 3 R7
Bonar Bridge *H'land* 71 C8
Bonawe Quarries *S'clyde* 56 F6
Bonby *Humber* 39 L16
Boncath *Dyfed* 18 O7
Bonchester Bridge *Borders* 52 H11
Bonchurch *I of Wight* 8 R14
Bo'ness *Central* 51 F9
Bonhill *S'clyde* 50 G7
Bonnybridge *Central* 51 F9
Bonnyrigg *Lothian* 52 G10
Bontddu *Gwyn* 27 N9
Bontnewydd *Gwyn* 34 M8
Boot *Cumb* 40 K10
Bootle *Mersey* 36 M11
Bootle *Cumb* 40 K10
Borden *Kent* 10 Q18
Bordon Camp *Hants* 8 Q15
Boreham *Essex* 24 P18
Borehamwood *Herts* 17 P16
Boreland *Dumf/Gal* 45 H10
Borgue *Dumf/Gal* 45 J8
Borough Green *Kent* 17 Q17
Boroughbridge *N Yorks* 42 K14
Borrowby *N Yorks* 42 K14
Borrowdale *Cumb* 40 J10
Borth *Dyfed* 26 O8
Borth-y-Gest *Gwyn* 34 N8
Borve *W Isles* 60 E1
Bosbury *Heref/Worcs* 21 O12
Boscastle *Cornw'l* 3 R7
Boscombe *Dorset* 7 R13
Bosham *W Sussex* 8 R15
Bosherston *Dyfed* 18 P7
Boston *Lincs* 31 N16
Boston Spa *W Yorks* 38 L14
Botesdale *Suffolk* 33 O18
Bothel *Cumb* 45 J10
Botley *Hants* 8 R14
Bottesford *Leics* 31 N15
Bottisham *Cambs* 24 O17
Bottwnnog *Gwyn* 34 N7
Boughton Street *Kent* 11 Q18
Boulmer *Northum* 53 H13
Bourne *Lincs* 31 N16
Bourne End *Bucks* 16 P15
Bournemouth *Dorset* 7 R13
Bourton *Dorset* 14 Q12
Bourton *Shrops* 29 N11
Bourton-on-the-Water *Glos* 22 P13
Bovey Tracey *Devon* 5 R9
Bovingdon *Herts* 16 P15
Bovington Camp *Dorset* 6 R12
Bow *Devon* 5 R9
Bow Street *Dyfed* 26 O8
Bowburn *Durham* 47 J13
Bower Chalke *Wilts* 15 Q13
Bowes *Durham* 41 J12
Bowgreave *Lancs* 40 L11
Bowling *S'clyde* 50 G8
Bowness-on-Solway *Cumb* 45 J10
Bowness-on-Windermere *Cumb* 40 K11

Bowsden *Northum* 53 G12
Bow *Wilts* 14 Q12
Boxford *Berks* 15 Q14
Boxford *Suffolk* 24 O18
Boxley *Kent* 10 Q18
Boxton *Humber* 43 K16
Boynton *Humber* 43 K16
Boyton *Suffolk* 25 O19
Bozeat *Northants* 23 O15
Brabourne Lees *Kent* 11 Q18
Bracadale *H'land* 61 D4
Bracebridge Heath *Lincs* 38 M15
Brackley *Northants* 22 O14
Bracknell *Berks* 16 Q15
Braco *Tayside* 57 F9
Bradfield *Essex* 25 P19
Bradford *W Yorks* 37 L13
Bradford Abbas *Dorset* 6 R11
Bradford-on-Avon *Wilts* 14 Q12
Bradford-on-Tone *Som'set* 13 R10
Brading *I of Wight* 8 R14
Bradley *Staffs* 29 N12
Bradninch *Devon* 5 R10
Bradpole *Dorset* 6 R11
Bradwell *Norfolk* 33 N20
Bradwell *Derby* 37 M13
Bradwell-on-Sea *Essex* 25 P18
Bradworthy *Devon* 12 R8
Braehead *S'clyde* 51 G9
Braemar *Gramp* 64 D10
Braemore *H'land* 69 C6
Bragar *W Isles* 66 B3
Braidwood *S'clyde* 51 G9
Brailes *Warwick* 22 O13
Brailsford *Derby* 30 N13
Braithwaite *Cumb* 45 J10
Bramber *W Sussex* 9 R16
Bramdean *Hants* 8 Q14
Bramfield *Suffolk* 33 O20
Bramford *Suffolk* 25 O19
Bramham *W Yorks* 42 L14
Bramhope *W Yorks* 42 L13
Bramley *Hants* 16 Q14
Bramley *Surrey* 16 Q15
Brampton *Cambs* 31 O16
Brampton *Cumb* 46 J11
Brampton Bryan *Heref/Worcs* 28 O11
Brampton Regis *Som'set* 13 Q10
Brancaster *Norfolk* 32 N18
Brancepeth *Durham* 47 J13
Branderburgh *Gramp* 64 C10
Brandesburton *Humber* 43 L16
Brandeston *Suffolk* 25 O19
Brandon *Suffolk* 32 O18
Brandon *Durham* 47 J13
Branston *Staffs* 30 N13
Branston *Lincs* 39 M16
Branthwaite *Cumb* 45 J10
Branton *S Yorks* 38 M14
Branxton *Northum* 53 G12
Brassington *Derby* 37 M13
Brasted *Kent* 17 Q17
Brattleby *Lincs* 38 M15
Bratton *Wilts* 14 Q12
Bratton Clovelly *Devon* 4 R8
Bratton Fleming *Devon* 12 Q9
Braughing *Herts* 24 P17
Braunston *Northants* 30 O14
Braunstone *Leics* 31 N15
Braunton *Devon* 12 Q8
Bray *Berks* 16 P15
Brayford *Devon* 12 Q9

Brayton *N Yorks* 38 L14
Breaclete *W Isles* 66 B3
Breadsall *Derby* 30 N14
Breage *Cornw'l* 2 S6
Breakish *H'land* 61 D5
Bream *Glos* 21 P11
Breamore *Hants* 7 R13
Breascleta *W Isles* 66 B3
Breaston *Derby* 30 N14
Brechfa *Dyfed* 19 P8
Brechin *Tayside* 59 E11
Brecon *Powys* 20 P10
Brede *E Sussex* 10 R18
Bredfield *Suffolk* 25 O19
Bredgar *Kent* 10 Q18
Bredon *Heref/Worcs* 21 O12
Breedon on the Hill *Leics* 30 N14
Brenchley *Kent* 17 Q17
Brendon *Devon* 12 Q9
Brenish *W Isles* 66 B2
Brent *Gtr Lon* 17 P16
Brent Knoll *Som'set* 13 Q11
Brent Pelham *Herts* 24 P17
Brentwood *Essex* 17 P17
Brenzett *Kent* 10 Q18
Brereton Green *Ches* 37 M12
Bretforton *Heref/Worcs* 21 O13
Brewood *Staffs* 29 N12
Bride *I of Man* 72 K8
Bridestowe *Devon* 4 R8
Bridge *Kent* 11 Q19
Bridge of Alford *Gramp* 64 D11
Bridge of Allan *Central* 51 F9
Bridge of Cally *Tayside* 58 E10
Bridge of Canny *Gramp* 65 D11
Bridge of Dee *Dumf/Gal* 45 J9
Bridge of Don *Gramp* 65 D12
Bridge of Earn *Tayside* 58 F10
Bridge of Forss *H'land* 70 A9
Bridge of Gairn *Gramp* 64 D10
Bridge of Gaur *Tayside* 56 E8
Bridge of Oich *H'land* 62 D7
Bridge of Orchy *S'clyde* 56 E7
Bridge of Weir *S'clyde* 50 G7
Bridgend *Mid Glam* 20 Q9
Bridgend *S'clyde* 48 G4
Bridgend *Tayside* 58 F10
Bridgend *Gramp* 64 D10
Bridgend of Linrathen *Tayside* 58 E10
Bridgetown *Som'set* 13 Q9
Bridgnorth *Shrops* 29 N12
Bridgwater *Som'set* 13 Q10
Bridlington *Humber* 43 K16
Bridport *Dorset* 6 R11
Brierfield *Lancs* 37 L12
Brierley *S Yorks* 38 L14
Brierley Hill *W Midlands* 29 O12
Brig o' Turk *Central* 57 F8
Brigg *Humber* 39 L16
Brighouse *W Yorks* 37 L13
Brighstone *I of Wight* 8 R14
Brightlingsea *Essex* 25 P19
Brighton *E Sussex* 9 R16
Brightwell *Oxon* 22 P14
Brignam *Cumb* 45 J10
Brigstock *Northants* 31 O15
Brill *Bucks* 22 P14
Brimfield *Heref/Worcs* 28 O11
Brindle *Lancs* 36 L11
Briningham *Norfolk* 33 N18
Brinklow *Warwick* 30 O14
Brinkworth *Wilts* 21 P13

Bristol *Avon*	14 Q11
Briston *Norfolk*	33 N19
Briton Ferry *W Glam*	19 P9
Brixham *Devon*	5 S9
Brixton *Devon*	4 S8
Brixworth *Northants*	31 O15
Brize Norton *Oxon*	22 P13
Broad Chalke *Wilts*	15 Q13
Broad Clyst *Devon*	5 R10
Broad Hinton *Wilts*	15 Q13
Bradford *H'land*	61 D5
Broadhembury *Devon*	5 R10
Broadmayne *Dorset*	6 R12
Broadstairs *Kent*	11 Q19
Broadwas *Heref/Worcs*	21 O12
Broadway *Heref/Worcs*	21 O13
Broadway *Som'set*	6 R11
Broadwindsor *Dorset*	6 R11
Brochel *H'land*	61 D4
Brockdish *Norfolk*	33 O19
Brockenhurst *Hants*	8 R13
Brocklesby *Lincs*	37 L13
Brocklesby *Lincs*	39 L16
Brodick *S'clyde*	49 G6
Bromborough *Mersey*	36 M11
Bromfield *Shrops*	28 O11
Bromfield *Cumb*	45 J10
Bromham *Wilts*	14 Q12
Bromham *Beds*	23 O15
Bromley *Gtr Lon*	17 Q17
Brompton *N Yorks*	42 K14
Brompton *N Yorks*	43 K15
Brompton on Swale *N Yorks*	42 K13
Bromsgrove *Heref/Worcs*	29 O12
Bromyard *Heref/Worcs*	21 O11
Brooke *Norfolk*	33 N19
Brookland *Kent*	10 R18
Brookmans Park *Herts*	17 P16
Brookwood *Surrey*	16 Q15
Broomfield *Essex*	17 P17
Broomhill *Northum*	47 H13
Brora *H'land*	71 B9
Broseley *Shrops*	29 N12
Brotton *Clevl'd*	42 J15
Brough *Humber*	38 L15
Brough *Cumb*	41 J12
Brough *H'land*	70 A10
Brough Sowerby *Cumb*	41 J12
Broughton *Hants*	15 Q13
Broughton *Northants*	31 O15
Broughton *Lancs*	36 L11
Broughton *Clwyd*	36 M10
Broughton *Humber*	38 L15
Broughton *N Yorks*	42 K14
Broughton *Borders*	51 G10
Broughton Gifford *Wilts*	14 Q12
Broughton in Furness *Cumb*	40 K10
Broughton Moor *Cumb*	45 J10
Broughty Ferry *Tayside*	58 F11
Brownhills *W Midlands*	29 N13
Broxbourne *Herts*	17 P16
Broxted *Essex*	24 P17
Brue *W Isles*	66 B3
Bruichladdich *S'clyde*	48 G4
Brundall *Norfolk*	33 N19
Brunton *Fife*	58 F10
Brushford *Som'set*	13 Q9
Bruton *Som'set*	14 Q12
Brydekirk *Dumf/Gal*	45 H10
Brymbo *Clwyd*	36 M10
Bryn *W Glam*	19 P9
Bryn *Gtr Man*	36 M11
Bryn Siencyn *Gwyn*	34 M8
Brynamman *Dyfed*	19 P10
Bryncethin *Mid Glam*	20 P9
Bryn-Crug *Gwyn*	26 N8
Bryneglwys *Clwyd*	35 M10
Brynmawr *Gwent*	20 P10
Brynteg *Clwyd*	36 M10
Bualintur *H'land*	61 D4
Bubwith *Humber*	38 L15
Buchlyvie *Central*	50 F8
Buckabank *Cumb*	46 J11
Buckden *Cambs*	31 O16
Buckden *N Yorks*	41 K12
Buckfast *Devon*	5 S9
Buckfastleigh *Devon*	5 S9
Buckhaven *Fife*	58 F10
Buckhurst Hill *Essex*	17 P17
Buckie *Gramp*	64 C11
Buckingham *Bucks*	22 P15
Buckland *Oxon*	22 P13
Buckland Brewer *Devon*	12 R8
Buckland Dinham *Som'set*	14 Q12
Buckland Monachorum *Devon*	4 S8
Buckland Newton *Dorset*	6 R12
Buckley *Clwyd*	36 M10
Bucknell *Shrops*	28 O11
Bucksburn *Gramp*	65 D12
Buckton *Humber*	43 K16
Bude *Cornw'l*	4 R7
Budleigh Salterton *Devon*	5 R10
Bugbrooke *Northants*	22 O14
Bugle *Cornw'l*	3 S7
Bugthorpe *Humber*	43 K15
Buildwas *Shrops*	29 N11
Builth Wells *Powys*	20 O10
Bulford *Wilts*	15 Q13
Bulkington *Warwick*	30 O14
Bulwell *Notts*	30 N13
Bulwell *Notts*	38 M14
Bunarkaig *H'land*	56 E7
Bunbury *Ches*	36 M11
Bunessan *S'clyde*	54 F4
Bungay *Suffolk*	33 O19
Bunnahabhainn *S'clyde*	48 G4
Bunny *Notts*	30 N14
Buntingford *Herts*	24 P16
Bunwell Street *Norfolk*	33 N19
Burbage *Wilts*	15 Q13
Burbage *Leics*	30 N14
Burbage *Derby*	37 M13
Bures *Essex*	24 P18
Burford *Oxon*	22 P13
Burgess Hill *W Sussex*	9 R16
Burgh by Sands *Cumb*	46 J10
Burgh Castle *Norfolk*	33 N20
Burgh Heath *Surrey*	17 Q16
Burgh le Marsh *Lincs*	39 M17
Burgh St. Margaret *Norfolk*	33 N20
Burghclere *Hants*	15 Q14
Burghead *Gramp*	64 C10
Burghfield Common *Berks*	16 Q14
Buriton *Hants*	8 R15
Burlesdon *Hants*	8 R14
Burley *Hants*	7 R13
Burley in Wharfedale *W Yorks*	42 L13
Burleydam *Ches*	29 N11
Burmarsh *Kent*	11 Q18
Burn *N Yorks*	38 L14
Burneside *Cumb*	41 K11
Burneston *N Yorks*	42 K13
Burnham *Bucks*	16 P15
Burnham Market *Norfolk*	32 N18
Burnham Thorpe *Norfolk*	32 N18
Burnham-on-Crouch *Essex*	24 P18
Burnham-on-Sea *Som'set*	13 Q11
Burnhaven *Gramp*	65 D13
Burnhope *Durham*	47 J13
Burniston *N Yorks*	43 K16
Burnley *Lancs*	37 L12
Burnmouth *Borders*	53 G12
Burnopfield *Durham*	47 J13
Burnsall *N Yorks*	41 K13
Burntisland *Fife*	51 F10
Burpham *W Sussex*	9 R15
Burrelton *Tayside*	58 E10
Burringham *Humber*	38 L15
Burrington *Devon*	12 R9
Burry Port *Dyfed*	19 P8
Burscough *Lancs*	36 L11
Burscough Bridge *Lancs*	36 L11
Burslem *Staffs*	37 M12
Burston *Norfolk*	33 O19
Burton *Ches*	36 M10
Burton *Lincs*	38 M15
Burton *Cumb*	41 K11
Burton Agnes *Humber*	43 K16
Burton Bradstock *Dorset*	6 R11
Burton Joyce *Notts*	30 N14
Burton Latimer *Northants*	31 O15
Burton Leonard *N Yorks*	42 K13
Burton on the Wolds *Leics*	30 N14
Burton upon Stather *Humber*	38 L15
Burton upon Trent *Staffs*	30 N13
Burwardsley *Ches*	36 M11
Burwarton *Shrops*	29 O11
Burwash *E Sussex*	10 R17
Burwell *Cambs*	32 O17
Burwell *Lincs*	39 M17
Bury *Cambs*	31 O16
Bury *Gtr Man*	37 L12
Bury *W Sussex*	9 R15
Bury St. Edmunds *Suffolk*	24 O18
Bushey *Herts*	16 P16
Butleigh *Som'set*	14 Q11
Buttermere *Cumb*	40 J10
Butterstone *Tayside*	58 E9
Butterton *Staffs*	37 M13
Butterwick *Lincs*	32 N17
Buxted *E Sussex*	10 R17
Buxton *Norfolk*	33 N19
Buxton *Derby*	37 M13
Bwlch *Powys*	20 P10
Byfield *Northants*	22 O14
Byfleet *Surrey*	16 Q16
Bylchau *Clwyd*	35 M9
Byrness *Northum*	46 H12
Bythorn *Cambs*	31 O16

C

Cabrach *Gramp*	64 D10
Caddington *Beds*	23 P16
Cadgwith *Cornw'l*	2 T6
Cadnam *Hants*	8 R13
Caerau *Mid Glam*	19 P9
Caergwrle *Clwyd*	36 M10
Caerleon *Gwent*	20 P11
Caernarfon *Gwyn*	34 M8
Caerphilly *Mid Glam*	20 P10
Caersws *Powys*	27 N10
Caerwent *Gwent*	20 P11
Caerwys *Clwyd*	35 M10

Cairnbaan *S'clyde* 49 F6
Cairndow *S'clyde* 56 F7
Cairneyhill *Fife* 51 F9
Cairnie *Gramp* 64 D11
Cairnryan *Dumf/Gal* 44 J7
Caister-on-Sea *Norfolk* 33 N20
Caistor *Lincs* 39 M16
Calbourne *I of Wight* 8 R14
Caldbeck *Cumb* 46 J10
Calder Bridge *Cumb* 40 K10
Caldercruix *S'clyde* 51 G9
Caldicot *Gwent* 20 P11
Caldwell *N Yorks* 42 J13
Calgary *S'clyde* 54 E4
Callander *Central* 57 F8
Callanish *W Isles* 66 B3
Callington *Cornw'l* 4 R8
Calne *Wilts* 14 Q12
Calow *Derby* 38 M14
Calshot *Hants* 8 R14
Calstock *Cornw'l* 4 S8
Calthwaite *Cumb* 46 J11
Calver *Derby* 37 M13
Calverton *Notts* 30 M14
Calvine *Tayside* 57 E9
Calzeat *Borders* 51 G10
Camastianavaig *H'land* 61 D4
Camberley *Surrey* 16 Q15
Cambo *Northum* 47 H13
Cambois *Northum* 47 H13
Camborne *Cornw'l* 2 S6
Cambridge *Cambs* 24 O17
Cambuslang *S'clyde* 50 G8
Camden *Gtr Lon* 17 P16
Camelford *Cornw'l* 3 R7
Cammachmore *Gramp* 65 D12
Campbeltown *H'land* 63 C8
Campbeltown *S'clyde* 49 H5
Camrose *Dyfed* 18 P6
Candlesby *Lincs* 39 M17
Canewdon *Essex* 24 P18
Cannich *H'land* 62 D7
Cannington *Som'set* 13 Q10
Cannock *Staffs* 29 N12
Canonbie *Dumf/Gal* 46 H11
Canonbridge *H'land* 63 C8
Canterbury *Kent* 11 Q19
Cantley *Norfolk* 33 N19
Canvey *Essex* 24 P18
Caol *H'land* 56 E6
Caoles *S'clyde* 54 E3
Capel *Surrey* 16 Q16
Capel Curig *Gwyn* 35 M9
Capel St. Mary *Suffolk* 25 O19
Capel-le-Ferne *Kent* 11 Q19
Capenhurst *Ches* 36 M11
Capheaton *Northum* 47 H13
Cappercleuch *Borders* 51 H10
Caputh *Tayside* 58 E10
Carbost *H'land* 61 D4
Cardenden *Fife* 51 F10
Cardiff *S Glam* 20 Q10
Cardigan *Dyfed* 18 O7
Cardington *Beds* 23 O16
Cardington *Shrops* 28 N11
Cardross *S'clyde* 50 G7
Cardurnock *Cumb* 45 J10
Carhampton *Som'set* 13 Q10
Carinish *W Isles* 60 C2
Carisbrooke *I of Wight* 8 R14
Cark *Cumb* 40 K11
Carleton Rode *Norfolk* 33 O19
Carlisle *Cumb* 46 J11

Carlops *Borders* 51 G10
Carloway *W Isles* 66 B3
Carlton *Notts* 30 N14
Carlton *N Yorks* 38 L14
Carlton *N Yorks* 41 K13
Carlton *N Yorks* 42 K14
Carlton Colville *Suffolk* 33 O20
Carlton in Lindrick *Notts* 38 M14
Carlton le Moorland *Notts* 38 M15
Carlton Miniott *N Yorks* 42 K14
Carlton on Trent *Notts* 38 M15
Carluke *S'clyde* 51 G9
Carmarthen *Dyfed* 19 P8
Carmel *Gwyn* 34 M8
Carmyllie *Tayside* 59 E11
Carnaby *Humber* 43 K16
Carnach *H'land* 62 D6
Carnforth *Lancs* 40 K11
Carno *Powys* 27 N9
Carnock *Fife* 51 F9
Carnon Downs *Cornw'l* 2 S6
Carnoustie *Tayside* 59 F11
Carnwath *S'clyde* 51 G9
Carr Shield *Northum* 46 J12
Carradale *H'land* 49 G6
Carrbridge *H'land* 63 D9
Carron *Gramp* 64 D10
Carronbridge *Dumf/Gal* 45 H9
Carrutherstown *Dumf/Gal* 45 H10
Carsaig *S'clyde* 55 F5
Carsington *Derby* 37 M13
Carsphairn *Dumf/Gal* 44 H8
Carstairs *S'clyde* 51 G9
Carstairs Junction *S'clyde* 51 G9
Cartmel *Cumb* 40 K11
Casterton *Cumb* 41 K11
Castle Acre *Norfolk* 32 N18
Castle Bolton *N Yorks* 41 K13
Castle Bromwich
  W Midlands 30 O13
Castle Bytham *Lincs* 31 N15
Castle Carrock *Cumb* 46 J11
Castle Cary *Som'set* 14 Q11
Castle Donington *Leics* 30 N14
Castle Eden *Durham* 47 J14
Castle Gresley *Derby* 30 N13
Castle Hedingham *Essex* 24 P18
Castle Kennedy *Dumf/Gal* 44 J7
Castle Rising *Norfolk* 32 N17
Castlebay *W Isles* 60 E2
Castleford *W Yorks* 38 L14
Castlemartin *Dyfed* 18 P6
Castleside *Durham* 47 J13
Castlethorpe *Bucks* 23 O15
Castleton *Derby* 37 M13
Castleton *N Yorks* 42 K15
Castletown *Tyne/Wear* 47 J14
Castletown *H'land* 70 A10
Castletown *I of Man* 72 K7
Caston *Norfolk* 33 N18
Castor *Cambs* 31 N16
Catcliffe *S Yorks* 38 M14
Caterham *Surrey* 17 Q16
Catfield *Norfolk* 33 N20
Catlowdy *Cumb* 46 H11
Caton *Lancs* 41 K11
Catrine *S'clyde* 50 G8
Catsfield *E Sussex* 10 R17
Catterall *Lancs* 40 L11
Catterick *N Yorks* 42 K13
Catterick Camp *N Yorks* 42 K13

Catterline *Gramp* 59 E12
Cattistock *Dorset* 6 R11
Catton *Northum* 46 J12
Catwick *Humber* 43 L16
Catworth *Cambs* 31 O16
Caulkerbush *Dumf/Gal* 45 J9
Cavendish *Suffolk* 24 O18
Caverswall *Staffs* 29 N12
Cawdor *H'land* 63 C9
Cawood *N Yorks* 42 L14
Cawston *Norfolk* 33 N19
Caxton *Cambs* 23 O16
Caythorpe *Lincs* 31 M15
Cayton *N Yorks* 43 K16
Cefn-Mawr *Clwyd* 28 N10
Cemaes Bay *Gwyn* 34 M8
Cemmaes *Powys* 27 N9
Cemmaes Road *Powys* 27 N9
Cenarth *Dyfed* 18 O7
Ceres *Fife* 58 F11
Cerne Abbas *Dorset* 6 R12
Cerrigydrudion *Clwyd* 35 M9
Chacewater *Cornw'l* 2 S6
Chacombe *Northants* 22 O14
Chadderton *Gtr Man* 37 L12
Chaddesley Corbett
  Heref/Worcs 29 O12
Chadlington *Oxon* 22 P13
Chadwell St. Mary *Essex* 17 Q17
Chagford *Devon* 5 R9
Chalfont St. Giles *Bucks* 16 P15
Chalfont St. Peter *Bucks* 16 P15
Chalford *Glos* 21 P12
Chalgrove *Oxon* 22 P14
Challacombe *Devon* 12 Q9
Challock Lees *Kent* 10 Q18
Chandler's Ford *Hants* 8 R14
Chapel en le Frith *Derby* 37 M13
Chapel of Garioch *Gramp* 65 D11
Chapel St. Leonards *Lincs* 39 M17
Chapel Stile *Cumb* 40 K10
Chapelhall *S'clyde* 51 G9
Chapelknowe *Dumf/Gal* 46 H11
Chapelton *S'clyde* 50 G8
Chapeltown *Lancs* 36 L12
Chapeltown *S Yorks* 38 M14
Chapeltown *Gramp* 64 D10
Chapmanslade *Wilts* 14 Q12
Chard *Som'set* 6 R11
Chardstock *Devon* 5 R11
Charing *Kent* 10 Q18
Charlbury *Oxon* 22 P14
Charleston *Tayside* 58 E11
Charlestown *Cornw'l* 3 S7
Charlestown *H'land* 69 C6
Charlestown of Aberlour
  Gramp 64 D10
Charlesworth *Derby* 37 M13
Charlton *Wilts* 21 P12
Charlton Kings *Glos* 21 P12
Charlton Marshall *Dorset* 7 R12
Charlwood *W Sussex* 9 Q16
Charminster *Dorset* 6 R11
Charmouth *Dorset* 6 R11
Chartham *Kent* 11 Q19
Chasetown *Staffs* 29 N12
Chatburn *Lancs* 41 L12
Chatham *Kent* 10 Q18
Chathill *Northum* 53 G14
Chatteris *Cambs* 32 O16
Chatton *Northum* 53 G14
Chawleigh *Devon* 12 R9
Cheadle *Staffs* 29 N12

headle *Gtr Man*	37 M12	
headle Hulme *Gtr Man*	37 M12	
heckley *Staffs*	29 N13	
hedburgh *Suffolk*	24 O18	
heddar *Som'set*	14 Q11	
heddington *Bucks*	23 P15	
heddleton *Staffs*	37 M12	
hedworth *Glos*	21 P13	
helford *Ches*	37 M12	
hellaston *Derby*	30 N14	
helmarsh *Shrops*	29 O12	
helmondiston *Suffolk*	25 P19	
helmorton *Derby*	37 M13	
helmsford *Essex*	24 P17	
heltenham *Glos*	21 P12	
hepstow *Gwent*	20 P11	
herhill *Wilts*	15 Q13	
heriton *Hants*	8 Q14	
heriton Bishop *Devon*	5 R9	
heriton Fitzpaine *Devon*	5 R9	
hertsey *Surrey*	16 Q15	
hesham *Bucks*	16 P15	
hesham Bois *Bucks*	16 P15	
heshunt *Herts*	17 P16	
heslyn Hay *Staffs*	29 N12	
hester *Ches*	36 M11	
hester le Street *Durham*	47 J13	
hesterfield *Derby*	37 M14	
hesters *Borders*	52 H11	
heswardine *Shrops*	29 N12	
heveley *Cambs*	24 O17	
hevington Drift *Northum*	47 H13	
hew Magna *Avon*	14 Q11	
hew Stoke *Avon*	14 Q11	
hewton Mendip *Som'set*	14 Q11	
hichester *W Sussex*	9 R15	
hickerell *Dorset*	6 R11	
hiddingfold *Surrey*	9 Q15	
hideock *Dorset*	6 R11	
hieveley *Berks*	15 Q14	
higwell *Essex*	17 P17	
hildrey *Oxon*	22 P14	
hild's Ercall *Shrops*	29 N11	
hilham *Kent*	11 Q18	
hillaton *Devon*	4 R8	
hillingham *Northum*	53 G13	
hillington *Devon*	5 S9	
hilmark *Wilts*	14 Q12	
hilton Buildings *Durham*	47 J13	
hinley *Derby*	37 M13	
hinnor *Oxon*	16 P15	
hippenham *Wilts*	14 Q12	
hippenham *Cambs*	32 O17	
hipping *Lancs*	41 L11	
hipping Campden *Glos*	22 O13	
hipping Norton *Oxon*	22 P13	
hipping Ongar *Essex*	17 P17	
hipping Sodbury *Avon*	21 P12	
hirbury *Shrops*	28 N10	
hirk *Clwyd*	28 N10	
hiselbourne *Borders*	53 G12	
hiseldon *Wilts*	15 P13	
hitterne *Wilts*	14 Q12	
hittlehampton *Devon*	12 Q9	
hollerton *Northum*	47 H12	
holsey *Oxon*	22 P14	
horley *Lancs*	36 L11	
horleywood *Herts*	16 P15	
hristchurch *Cambs*	32 N17	
hristchurch *Dorset*	7 R13	
hristleton *Ches*	36 M11	
hristow *Devon*	5 R9	

Chudleigh *Devon*	5 R9	
Chulmleigh *Devon*	12 R9	
Church Aston *Shrops*	29 N12	
Church Broughton *Derby*	30 N13	
Church Eaton *Staffs*	29 N12	
Church Lawford *Warwick*	30 O14	
Church Minshull *Ches*	36 M11	
Church Stoke *Powys*	28 N10	
Church Stretton *Shrops*	28 N11	
Churchend *Essex*	25 P18	
Churchill *Avon*	13 Q11	
Churchill *Oxon*	22 P13	
Churchtown *Lancs*	40 L11	
Churchtown *I of Man*	72 K8	
Churston Ferrers *Devon*	5 S9	
Churt *Surrey*	9 Q15	
Churton *Ches*	36 M11	
Cilcain *Clwyd*	35 M10	
Cilcennin *Dyfed*	19 O8	
Cilfynydd *Mid Glam*	20 P10	
Cilgerran *Dyfed*	18 O7	
Cilmery *Powys*	20 O10	
Cilycwm *Dyfed*	19 O9	
Cinderford *Glos*	21 P12	
Cirencester *Glos*	21 P13	
Clabhach *S'clyde*	54 E3	
Clachan *S'clyde*	49 G5	
Clachan *W Isles*	60 C2	
Clachan of Glendaruel *S'clyde*	49 F6	
Clachnaharry *H'land*	63 D8	
Clackmannan *Central*	51 F9	
Clacton-on-Sea *Essex*	25 P19	
Clanfield *Oxon*	22 P13	
Clanfield *Hants*	8 R14	
Clapham *Beds*	23 O16	
Clapham *N Yorks*	41 K12	
Clarbeston Road *Dyfed*	18 P7	
Clare *Suffolk*	24 O18	
Clashmore *H'land*	71 C8	
Clashnessie *H'land*	68 B6	
Clatt *Gramp*	64 D11	
Claughton *Lancs*	41 K11	
Claverdon *Warwick*	30 O13	
Clavering *Essex*	24 P17	
Claverley *Shrops*	29 N12	
Clawton *Devon*	4 R8	
Claxby *Lincs*	39 M16	
Clay Cross *Derby*	37 M14	
Claybrooke Magna *Leics*	30 O14	
Claydon *Suffolk*	25 O19	
Claypole *Lincs*	31 M15	
Clayton *Staffs*	29 N12	
Clayton West *W Yorks*	37 L13	
Clayton-le-Moors *Lancs*	36 L12	
Clayworth *Notts*	38 M15	
Cleadale *H'land*	61 E4	
Cleater *Cumb*	40 J9	
Cleator Moor *Cumb*	40 J9	
Clee St. Margaret *Shrops*	29 O11	
Cleethorpes *Humber*	39 L16	
Clent *Heref/Worcs*	29 O12	
Cleobury Mortimer *Shrops*	29 O12	
Clevedon *Avon*	13 Q11	
Cleveleys *Lancs*	40 L10	
Cley next the Sea *Norfolk*	33 N19	
Cliddesden *Hants*	16 Q14	
Cliffe *Kent*	10 Q17	
Cliffe *N Yorks*	38 L15	
Clifford *Heref/Worcs*	20 O10	
Clifford *W Yorks*	42 L14	
Clifton *Beds*	23 O16	
Clifton *Central*	56 F7	

Clifton Hampden *Oxon*	22 P14	
Clifton upon Dunsmore *Warwick*	30 O14	
Clifton-on-Teme *Heref/Worcs*	21 O12	
Cliftonville *Kent*	11 Q19	
Clipston *Northants*	30 O15	
Clitheroe *Lancs*	41 L12	
Clive *Shrops*	28 N11	
Clochan *Gramp*	64 C11	
Clophill *Beds*	23 O16	
Closeburn *Dumf/Gal*	45 H9	
Cloughton *N Yorks*	43 K16	
Clova *Tayside*	58 E10	
Clovelly *Devon*	12 R8	
Clovenfords *Borders*	52 G11	
Clovulin *H'land*	55 E6	
Clowne *Derby*	38 M14	
Clows Top *Heref/Worcs*	29 O12	
Clun *Shrops*	28 O10	
Clunes *H'land*	56 E7	
Clungunford *Shrops*	28 O11	
Clunton *Shrops*	28 O11	
Cluny *Cambs*	31 O16	
Clydach *W Glam*	19 P9	
Clydach *Gwent*	20 P10	
Clydebank *S'clyde*	50 G8	
Clynnogfawr *Gwyn*	34 M8	
Clyro *Powys*	20 O10	
Coalbrookdale *Shrops*	29 N11	
Coaltown of Wemyss *Fife*	58 F10	
Coalville *Leics*	30 N14	
Coatbridge *S'clyde*	50 G8	
Cobham *Surrey*	16 Q16	
Cobham *Kent*	22 P13	
Cockburnspath *Borders*	52 G12	
Cockenzie *Lothian*	52 G11	
Cockerham *Lancs*	40 L11	
Cockermouth *Cumb*	45 J10	
Cockfield *Durham*	47 J13	
Cocking *W Sussex*	9 R15	
Cockshutt *Shrops*	28 N11	
Coddenham *Suffolk*	25 O19	
Coddington *Notts*	38 M15	
Codford *Wilts*	14 Q12	
Codicote *Herts*	23 P16	
Codnor *Derby*	30 M14	
Codsall *Staffs*	29 N12	
Coedpoeth *Clwyd*	28 M10	
Coelbren *Powys*	19 P9	
Coggeshall *Essex*	24 P18	
Coillore *H'land*	61 D4	
Colaton Raleigh *Devon*	5 R10	
Colby *I of Man*	72 K7	
Colchester *Essex*	25 P18	
Cold Ash *Berks*	15 Q14	
Cold Norton *Essex*	24 P18	
Coldstream *Borders*	53 G12	
Colebrooke *Devon*	5 R9	
Coleford *Glos*	21 P11	
Colehill *Dorset*	7 R13	
Coleorton *Leics*	30 N14	
Colerne *Wilts*	14 Q12	
Coleshill *Bucks*	16 P15	
Coleshill *Warwick*	30 O13	
Colintraive *S'clyde*	49 G6	
Colkirk *Norfolk*	33 N18	
Coll *W Isles*	66 B4	
Collessie *Fife*	58 F10	
Colliston *Gramp*	65 D13	
Collin *Dumf/Gal*	45 H9	
Collingbourne Ducis *Wilts*	15 Q13	
Collingbourne Kingston *Wilts*	15 Q13	
Collingham *Notts*	38 M15	

Collingham *W Yorks* 42 L14
Colmonell *S'clyde* 44 H7
Colnbrook *Berks* 16 Q15
Colne *Cambs* 32 O17
Colne *Lancs* 41 L12
Colpy *Gramp* 65 D11
Colsterworth *Lincs* 31 N15
Coltishall *Norfolk* 33 N19
Colton *Staffs* 29 N13
Colwall *Northum* 47 H12
Colwich *Staffs* 29 N13
Colwyn *Clwyd* 35 M9
Colwyn Bay *Clwyd* 35 M9
Colyford *Devon* 5 R10
Colyton *Devon* 5 R10
Combe Martin *Devon* 12 Q8
Combe St. Nicholas *Som'set* 6 R11
Comberbach *Ches* 36 M11
Comberton *Cambs* 23 O17
Combwich *Som'set* 13 Q10
Compton *Berks* 15 P14
Compton *Hants* 15 Q14
Compton *Surrey* 16 Q15
Compton *W Sussex* 8 R15
Compton Martin *Avon* 14 Q11
Comrie *Tayside* 57 F9
Condover *Shrops* 28 N11
Congleton *Ches* 37 M12
Congresbury *Avon* 13 Q11
Coningsby *Lincs* 39 M16
Conisbrough *S Yorks* 38 M14
Coniston *Humber* 39 L16
Coniston *Cumb* 40 K10
Coniston Cold *N Yorks* 41 L12
Conistone *N Yorks* 41 K12
Connah's Quay *Clwyd* 35 M10
Connel *S'clyde* 55 F6
Connel Park *S'clyde* 50 H8
Consett *Durham* 47 J13
Constable Burton *N Yorks* 42 K13
Constantine *Cornw'l* 2 S6
Contin *H'land* 63 C7
Conwy *Gwyn* 35 M9
Conwyl Elfed *Dyfed* 19 P8
Cookham *Berks* 16 P15
Cookney *Gramp* 65 D12
Coombe Bissett *Wilts* 15 Q13
Cople *Beds* 23 O16
Copley *Durham* 47 J13
Copmanthorpe *N Yorks* 42 L14
Copplestone *Devon* 5 R9
Copt Hewick *N Yorks* 42 K14
Copthorne *W Sussex* 9 Q16
Copythorn *Hants* 8 R13
Corbridge *Northum* 47 J12
Corby *Lincs* 31 N15
Corby *Northants* 31 O15
Corfe *Som'set* 13 R10
Corfe Castle *Dorset* 7 R12
Corfe Mullen *Dorset* 7 R12
Corgarff *Gramp* 64 D10
Cornforth *Durham* 47 J13
Cornhill *Gramp* 65 C11
Cornhill on Tweed *Northum* 53 G12
Cornholme *W Yorks* 37 L12
Corpach *H'land* 56 E6
Corpusty *Norfolk* 33 N19
Corran *H'land* 55 E6
Corran *H'land* 62 D5
Corrie *S'clyde* 49 G6
Corrie Common *Dumf/Gal* 45 H10
Corringham *Essex* 17 P17

Corringham *Lincs* 38 M15
Corris *Gwyn* 27 N9
Corsham *Wilts* 14 Q12
Corsley *Wilts* 14 Q12
Corsock *Dumf/Gal* 45 H9
Corston *Wilts* 21 P12
Corstorphine *Lothian* 51 G10
Corton *Suffolk* 33 N20
Corwen *Clwyd* 35 N10
Coryton *Essex* 24 P18
Cosby *Leics* 30 N14
Coseley *W Midlands* 29 N12
Cosheston *Dyfed* 18 P7
Cossington *Som'set* 13 Q11
Costessey *Norfolk* 33 N19
Cotehill *Cumb* 46 J11
Cotgrave *Notts* 30 N14
Cotherstone *Durham* 41 J13
Cottam *Lancs* 36 L11
Cottenham *Cambs* 32 O17
Cottered *Herts* 23 P16
Cottesmore *Leics* 31 N15
Cottingham *Northants* 31 O15
Cottingham *Humber* 39 L16
Coulags *H'land* 62 D6
Coull *Gramp* 64 D11
Coulport *S'clyde* 50 F7
Coundon *Durham* 47 J13
Countesthorpe *Leics* 30 N14
Coupar Angus *Tayside* 58 E10
Cove *Hants* 16 Q15
Cove *S'clyde* 50 F7
Cove *H'land* 69 C5
Cove Bay *Gramp* 65 D12
Coventry *W Midlands* 30 O13
Coverack *Cornw'l* 2 S6
Cowbit *Lincs* 31 N16
Cowbridge *S Glam* 13 Q10
Cowdenbeath *Fife* 51 F10
Cowes *I of Wight* 8 R14
Cowfold *W Sussex* 9 R16
Cowley *Oxon* 22 P14
Cowling *N Yorks* 41 L12
Cowplain *Hants* 8 R14
Cowshill *Durham* 46 J12
Coxhoe *Durham* 47 J14
Coxley *Som'set* 14 Q11
Coxwold *N Yorks* 42 K14
Coylton *S'clyde* 50 H8
Crabbs Cross *Heref/Worcs* 29 O13
Crackenthorpe *Cumb* 41 J11
Cradley *Heref/Worcs* 21 O12
Cradhoe *Cornw'l* 4 S8
Craggie *H'land* 63 D8
Craigellachie *Gramp* 64 D10
Craigendoran *S'clyde* 50 G7
Craighouse *S'clyde* 48 G5
Craigie *S'clyde* 50 G8
Craigmillar *Lothian* 51 G10
Craignure *S'clyde* 55 F5
Craigo *Tayside* 59 E11
Craigton *Tayside* 58 E10
Craigtown *H'land* 70 B9
Crail *Fife* 59 F11
Cramlington *Northum* 47 H13
Cramond Bridge *Lothian* 51 G10
Cranborne *Dorset* 7 R13
Cranbrook *Kent* 10 Q18
Cranfield *Beds* 23 O15
Cranford *Northants* 31 O15
Cranleigh *Surrey* 9 Q16
Cranshaws *Borders* 52 G12

Crantock *Cornw'l* 2 S5
Crask of Aigas *H'land* 62 D7
Craster *Northum* 53 H13
Crathie *Gramp* 64 D10
Craven Arms *Shrops* 28 O11
Crawford *S'clyde* 51 H10
Crawfordjohn *S'clyde* 51 G10
Crawick *Dumf/Gal* 51 H10
Crawley *Hants* 9 Q14
Crawley *W Sussex* 9 Q16
Crawley Down *W Sussex* 9 Q16
Crawton *Gramp* 59 E11
Cray *Powys* 19 P9
Crayke *N Yorks* 42 K14
Crays Hill *Essex* 17 P17
Creagorry *W Isles* 60 D1
Creaton *Northants* 30 O14
Creca *Dumf/Gal* 45 H11
Credenhill *Heref/Worcs* 20 O11
Crediton *Devon* 5 R9
Creetown *Dumf/Gal* 44 J8
Creggans *S'clyde* 56 F7
Cregneish *I of Man* 72 K6
Cressage *Shrops* 29 N11
Creswell *Derby* 38 M14
Crewe *Ches* 36 M11
Crewkerne *Som'set* 6 R11
Crianlarich *Central* 56 F8
Cribyn *Dyfed* 19 O8
Criccieth *Gwyn* 34 N8
Crich *Derby* 37 M13
Crick *Northants* 30 O14
Crickhowell *Powys* 20 P11
Cricklade *Wilts* 21 P13
Crieff *Tayside* 57 F9
Crimond *Gramp* 65 C13
Crimplesham *Norfolk* 32 N17
Crinan *S'clyde* 49 F6
Cringleford *Norfolk* 33 N19
Croachy *H'land* 63 D8
Crocketford *Dumf/Gal* 45 H9
Crockham Hill *Kent* 17 Q17
Croft *N Yorks* 42 K13
Croftamie *Central* 50 F8
Croggan *S'clyde* 55 F6
Croglin *Cumb* 46 J11
Cromarty *H'land* 63 C8
Cromdale *H'land* 64 D10
Cromer *Norfolk* 33 N19
Cromford *Derby* 37 M13
Cromore *W Isles* 66 B3
Cromra *H'land* 63 E8
Cromwell *Notts* 38 M14
Crondall *Hants* 16 Q15
Crook *Durham* 47 J13
Crook of Alves *Gramp* 64 C10
Crook of Devon *Tayside* 58 F9
Crookham *Northum* 53 G11
Cropredy *Oxon* 22 O13
Cropton *N Yorks* 42 K15
Crosby *Mersey* 36 L10
Crosby *Cumb* 45 J10
Crosby *I of Man* 72 K6
Crosby Ravensworth *Cumb* 41 J11
Croscombe *Som'set* 14 Q11
Cross *W Isles* 66 B3
Cross Gates *Powys* 27 O10
Cross Hands *Dyfed* 19 P9
Crossbost *W Isles* 66 B3
Crossenny *Gwent* 21 P11
Crossens *Mersey* 36 L10
Crossgates *Fife* 51 F11

rosshill S'clyde	44	H7
rosshouse S'clyde	50	G7
rossmichael Dumf/Gal	45	J8
roston Lancs	36	L11
roughton Northants	22	P14
row Hill Heref/Worcs	21	P11
rowborough E Sussex	10	Q17
rowhurst E Sussex	10	R17
rowland Lincs	31	N16
rowle Heref/Worcs	21	O12
rowle Humber	38	L15
rowthorne Berks	16	Q15
roxton Norfolk	32	O18
roxton Kerrial Leics	31	N15
roy H'land	63	C8
royde Devon	12	Q8
roydon Gtr Lon	17	Q16
ruden Bay Gramp	65	D13
rudgington Shrops	29	N11
rudwell Wilts	21	P12
rumlin Gwent	20	P10
rymych Arms Dyfed	18	P7
rynant W Glam	19	P9
ruaig H'land	61	C5
rubbington Warwick	30	O13
rubert Cornw'l	2	S6
ruckfield W Sussex	9	Q16
ruckney Notts	38	M14
ruddington Bucks	16	P15
ruddington Ches	36	M11
rudworth S Yorks	38	L14
ruffley Herts	17	P16
rulbokie H'land	63	C8
rulcabock H'land	63	D8
rulgaith Cumb	46	J11
rulham Oxon	22	P14
rulkein H'land	68	B6
rulen Gramp	64	C11
rullercoats Tyne/Wear	47	H14
rullicudden H'land	63	C8
rullingworth W Yorks	37	L13
rullipool S'clyde	55	F5
rullompton Devon	5	R10
rulmington Shrops	28	O11
rulmstock Devon	13	R10
rulrain H'land	69	C8
rulross Fife	51	F9
rults Gramp	65	D12
rulworth Northants	22	O14
rumbernauld S'clyde	51	G9
ruminestown Gramp	65	C12
rummersdale Cumb	46	J11
rummertrees Dumf/Gal	45	J10
rummingstown Gramp	64	C10
rumnock S'clyde	50	H8
rumnor Oxon	22	P14
rumrew Cumb	46	J11
rumwhinton Cumb	46	J11
rupar Fife	58	F10
rurie Lothian	51	G10
rults Gramp	65	D12
rurry Rivel Som'set	13	Q10
rutnall Green Heref/Worcs	29	O12
ruxton Kent	17	Q17
rum Gwent	20	P10
rumrum W Glam	19	P9
rum-bach Mid Glam	20	P10
rumbran Gwent	20	P10
rumllynfell W Glam	19	P9
rumnak W Glam	27	N9
rurt-newydd Dyfed	19	O8
rumer W Glam	19	P9
rumwyd Clwyd	35	N10

D

Dacre Cumb	46	J11
Daddry Shield Durham	46	J12
Daglingworth Glos	21	P12
Dailly S'clyde	44	H7
Dairsie or Osnaburgh Fife	58	F11
Dalavich S'clyde	55	F6
Dalbeattie Dumf/Gal	45	J9
Dalby I of Man	72	K7
Dalchreichan H'land	62	D7
Dale Dyfed	18	P6
Dalginross Tayside	57	F9
Dalguise Tayside	57	E9
Dalhalvaig H'land	70	B9
Dalham Suffolk	24	O18
Daliburgh W Isles	60	D2
Dalkeith Lothian	52	G10
Dallas Gramp	64	C10
Dalmally S'clyde	56	F7
Dalmellington S'clyde	44	H8
Dalmeny Lothian	51	G10
Dalnacardoch Tayside	57	E8
Dalnaspidal Tayside	57	E8
Dalry Dumf/Gal	45	H8
Dalry S'clyde	50	G7
Dalrymple S'clyde	50	H7
Dalserf S'clyde	51	G9
Dalston Cumb	46	J11
Dalswinton Dumf/Gal	45	H9
Dalton N Yorks	41	K13
Dalton Dumf/Gal	45	H10
Dalton in Furness Cumb	40	K10
Dalwhinnie H'land	63	E8
Damerham Hants	7	R13
Danbury Essex	24	P18
Danby N Yorks	42	K15
Darfield S Yorks	38	L14
Darlaston W Midlands	29	N12
Darley Dale Derby	37	M13
Darlington Durham	42	J13
Darlton Notts	38	M15
Darnoch Durham	45	J10
Dartford Kent	17	Q17
Dartington Devon	5	S9
Dartmouth Devon	5	S9
Darton S Yorks	37	L13
Darvel S'clyde	50	G8
Darwen Lancs	36	L12
Datchet Berks	16	Q15
Davenham Ches	36	M11
Daventry Northants	22	O14
Davidson's Mains Lothian	51	G10
Davington Dumf/Gal	45	H10
Daviot H'land	63	D8
Daviot Gramp	65	D12
Dawley Shrops	29	N12
Dawlish Devon	5	R10
Deal Kent	11	Q19
Deanshanger Northants	23	O15
Dearham Cumb	45	J10
Debenham Suffolk	25	O19
Deddington Oxon	22	P14
Dedham Essex	25	P18
Deeping St. James Lincs	31	N16
Deeping St. Nicholas Lincs	31	N16
Defford Heref/Worcs	21	O12
Defynnog Powys	20	P9
Deiniolen Gwyn	34	M8
Delabole Cornw'l	3	R7
Delckirach Gramp	64	D10

Denbigh Clwyd	35	M10
Denby Dale W Yorks	37	L13
Denham Bucks	16	P15
Denholm Borders	52	H11
Denholme W Yorks	37	L13
Denmead Hants	8	R14
Dennington Suffolk	25	O19
Denny Central	51	F9
Denshaw Gtr Man	37	L12
Denston Suffolk	24	O18
Denstone Staffs	29	N13
Dent Cumb	41	K12
Denton E Sussex	10	R17
Denton Lincs	31	N15
Denton Gtr Man	37	M12
Denver Norfolk	32	N17
Denwick Northum	53	H13
Derby Derby	30	N13
Derbyhaven I of Man	72	K7
Dersingham Norfolk	32	N17
Dervaig S'clyde	54	E4
Derwen Clwyd	35	M10
Desborough Northants	31	O15
Desford Leics	30	N14
Detling Kent	10	Q18
Devil's Bridge Dyfed	27	O9
Devizes Wilts	14	Q12
Devonport Devon	4	S8
Devoran Cornw'l	2	S6
Dewsbury W Yorks	37	L13
Diabaig H'land	62	C5
Dibden Purlieu Hants	8	R14
Didcot Oxon	22	P14
Didmarton Glos	21	P12
Digby Lincs	39	M16
Dilham Norfolk	33	N19
Dilston Northum	47	J12
Dilton Marsh Wilts	14	Q12
Dilwyn Heref/Worcs	20	O11
Dinas Dyfed	18	O7
Dinas Mawddwy Gwyn	27	N9
Dinas Powis S Glam	13	Q10
Dingwall H'land	63	C8
Dinnington S Yorks	38	M14
Dinton Wilts	15	Q13
Dippin S'clyde	49	H6
Dirleton Lothian	52	F11
Dishforth N Yorks	42	K14
Disley Ches	37	M12
Diss Norfolk	33	O19
Distington Cumb	45	J9
Ditcheat Som'set	14	Q11
Ditchling E Sussex	9	R16
Dittisham Devon	5	S9
Ditton Priors Shrops	29	O11
Dobwalls Cornw'l	3	S7
Docking Norfolk	32	N18
Doddinghurst Essex	17	P17
Doddington Kent	10	Q18
Doddington Cambs	32	O17
Doddington Northum	53	G12
Dodworth S Yorks	37	L13
Dolanog Powys	27	N10
Dolfor Powys	27	O10
Dolgarrog Gwyn	35	M9
Dolgellau Gwyn	27	N9
Dollar Central	51	F9
Dolphinholme Lancs	41	L11
Dolphinton S'clyde	51	G10
Dolton Devon	5	R9
Dolwyddelan Gwyn	35	M9
Doncaster S Yorks	38	L14
Donington Lincs	31	N16

Donington on Bain *Lincs* 39 M16
Donisthorpe *Leics* 30 N13
Dorchester *Oxon* 22 P14
Dorchester *Dorset* 6 R12
Dordon *Warwick* 30 N13
Dore *S Yorks* 37 M13
Dores *H'land* 63 D8
Dorking *Surrey* 16 Q16
Dornie *H'land* 62 D5
Dornoch *H'land* 71 C8
Dorridge *W Midlands* 30 O13
Dorrington *Shrops* 28 N11
Dorstone *Heref/Worcs* 20 O10
Douglas *S'clyde* 51 G9
Douglas *I of Man* 72 K8
Douglastown *Tayside* 58 E11
Doulting *Som'set* 14 Q12
Doune *Central* 57 F8
Dounreay *H'land* 70 A9
Dove Holes *Derby* 37 M13
Dover *Kent* 11 Q19
Dovercourt *Essex* 25 P19
Dowlais *Mid Glam* 20 P10
Downham *Cambs* 32 O17
Downham Market *Norfolk* 32 N17
Downies *Gramp* 65 D12
Downton *Wilts* 7 R13
Draughton *N Yorks* 41 L13
Draycott *Som'set* 14 Q11
Draycott *Derby* 30 N14
Drayton *Oxon* 22 P14
Drayton *Norfolk* 33 N19
Drefach *Dyfed* 19 P8
Dreghorn *S'clyde* 50 G7
Drem *Lothian* 52 F11
Drimnin *H'land* 55 E5
Droitwich *Heref/Worcs* 21 O12
Dronfield *Derby* 38 M14
Drongan *S'clyde* 50 H8
Droxford *Hants* 8 R14
Drumbeg *H'land* 68 B6
Drumburgh *Cumb* 46 J10
Drumelzier *Borders* 51 G10
Drumfearn *H'land* 61 D5
Drumjohn *Dumf/Gal* 44 H8
Drumlithie *Gramp* 59 E12
Drummore *Dumf/Gal* 44 J7
Drumuir *Gramp* 64 D10
Drybridge *Gramp* 64 C11
Drymen *Central* 50 F8
Ducklington *Oxon* 22 P14
Duddingston *Lothian* 52 G10
Duddington *Northants* 31 N15
Duddo *Northum* 53 G12
Duddon *Ches* 36 M11
Dudley *W Midlands* 29 O12
Dudley *Tyne/Wear* 47 H13
Duffield *Derby* 30 N14
Dufftown *Gramp* 64 D10
Duffus *Gramp* 64 C10
Dufton *Cumb* 46 J12
Duggleby *N Yorks* 43 K15
Duirinish *H'land* 62 D5
Dull *Tayside* 57 E9
Dullingham *Cambs* 24 O17
Dulnain Bridge *H'land* 63 D9
Duloe *Cornw'l* 3 S8
Dulverton *Som'set* 13 Q9
Dumbarton *S'clyde* 50 G7
Dumbleton *Glos* 21 O13
Dumfries *Dumf/Gal* 45 H9
Duna *S'clyde* 49 G7

Dunan *H'land* 61 D5
Dunbar *Lothian* 52 F11
Dunbeath *H'land* 70 B10
Dunblane *Central* 57 F9
Dunchurch *Warwick* 30 O14
Dundee *Tayside* 58 F11
Dundonald *S'clyde* 50 G7
Dundonnell *Gramp* 65 D12
Dundrennan *Dumf/Gal* 45 J9
Dunecht *Gramp* 65 D12
Dunfermline *Fife* 51 F10
Dungavel *S'clyde* 51 G9
Dunham on the Hill *Ches* 36 M11
Dunholme *Lincs* 39 M16
Dunino *Fife* 59 F11
Dunipace *Central* 51 F9
Dunkeld *Tayside* 58 E9
Dunkeswell *Devon* 5 R10
Dunlop *S'clyde* 50 G7
Dunnet *H'land* 70 A10
Dunnington *N Yorks* 42 L15
Dunoon *S'clyde* 49 G7
Dunragit *Dumf/Gal* 44 J7
Duns *Borders* 52 G12
Dunsford *Surrey* 9 Q15
Dunsford *Devon* 5 R9
Dunstable *Beds* 23 P15
Dunster *Som'set* 13 Q10
Dunston *Staffs* 29 N12
Dunston *Lincs* 39 M16
Dunsyre *S'clyde* 51 G10
Dutocher *S'clyde* 50 G8
Dunton Bassett *Leics* 30 N14
Dunure *S'clyde* 50 H7
Dunvant *W Glam* 19 P8
Dunvegan *H'land* 61 D3
Dunwich *Suffolk* 33 O20
Durham *Durham* 47 J13
Durisdeer *Dumf/Gal* 45 H9
Durness *H'land* 68 A7
Durnford *Wilts* 15 Q13
Durrington *Wilts* 15 Q13
Dursley *Glos* 21 P12
Durweston *Dorset* 7 R12
Duston *Northants* 22 O15
Duthil *H'land* 63 D9
Dutton *Ches* 36 M11
Duxford *Cambs* 24 O17
Dwyran *Gwyn* 34 M8
Dyce *Gramp* 65 D12
Dyffryn *Gwyn* 26 N8
Dyke *Gramp* 63 C9
Dykehead *Tayside* 58 E10
Dymchurch *Kent* 11 Q18
Dymock *Glos* 21 P12
Dysart *Fife* 51 F10
Dyserth *Clwyd* 35 M10

E

Eaglesfield *Dumf/Gal* 45 H10
Eaglesfield *Cumb* 45 J10
Eaglesham *S'clyde* 50 G8
Eakring *Notts* 38 M15
Ealing *Gtr Lon* 16 P16
Earby *Lancs* 41 L12
Eardisland *Heref/Worcs* 20 O11
Eardisley *Heref/Worcs* 20 O10
Earith *Cambs* 32 O17
Earl Shilton *Leics* 30 N14
Earl Soham *Suffolk* 25 O19

Earl Stonham *Suffolk* 25 O19
Earls Barton *Northants* 23 O15
Earls Colne *Essex* 24 P17
Earlsferry *Fife* 58 F11
Earlston *Borders* 52 G11
Easdale *S'clyde* 55 F5
Easebourne *W Sussex* 9 R15
Easington *Humber* 39 L17
Easington *Durham* 47 J13
Easington Colliery *Durham* 47 J13
Easington Lane *Tyne/Wear* 47 J13
Easingwold *N Yorks* 42 K15
Eassie and Nevay *Tayside* 58 E11
East Aberthaw *S Glam* 13 Q10
East Allington *Devon* 5 S8
East Barkwith *Lincs* 39 M16
East Barming *Kent* 10 Q17
East Brent *Som'set* 13 Q10
East Budleigh *Devon* 5 R10
East Challow *Oxon* 22 P14
East Chinnock *Som'set* 6 R11
East Cowton *N Yorks* 42 K13
East Dean *E Sussex* 10 R9
East Dereham *Norfolk* 33 N18
East Garston *Berks* 15 Q14
East Grafton *Wilts* 15 Q13
East Grinstead *W Sussex* 10 Q16
East Haddon *Northants* 30 O14
East Hanney *Oxon* 22 P14
East Hanningfield *Essex* 24 P17
East Harling *Norfolk* 33 O18
East Harlsey *N Yorks* 42 K14
East Haven *Tayside* 59 E12
East Hendred *Oxon* 22 P14
East Hoathly *E Sussex* 10 R17
East Ilsley *Berks* 15 P14
East Keal *Lincs* 39 M17
East Kilbride *S'clyde* 50 G8
East Kirkby *Lincs* 39 M17
East Knoyle *Wilts* 14 Q12
East Leake *Notts* 30 N14
East Linton *Lothian* 52 G11
East Looe *Cornw'l* 3 S8
East Markham *Notts* 38 M15
East Meon *Hants* 8 R14
East Ord *Northum* 53 G12
East Peckham *Kent* 17 Q17
East Plean *Central* 51 F9
East Poringland *Norfolk* 33 N19
East Prawle *Devon* 5 S8
East Preston *W Sussex* 9 R15
East Retford *Notts* 38 M15
East Rudham *Norfolk* 32 N17
East Saltoun *Lothian* 52 G11
East Stour *Dorset* 14 Q12
East Wemyss *Fife* 58 F11
East Wittering *W Sussex* 8 R14
East Witton *N Yorks* 42 K13
East Wretham *Norfolk* 32 O18
Eastbourne *E Sussex* 10 R17
Eastchurch *Kent* 10 Q18
Eastergate *W Sussex* 9 R15
Eastgate *Durham* 47 J12
Eastleach Turville *Glos* 22 P13
Eastleigh *Hants* 8 R14
Eastnor *Heref/Worcs* 21 O12
Eastoft *Humber* 38 L15
Easton *Suffolk* 25 O19
Easton *Dorset* 6 S11
Easton on the Hill *Northants* 31 N15
Easton-in-Gordano *Avon* 14 Q11
Eastriggs *Dumf/Gal* 45 H10

Eastrington *Humber*	38	L15
Eastry *Kent*	11	Q19
Eastwood *Notts*	30	M14
Eaton *Leics*	31	N15
Eaton *Ches*	36	M11
Eaton Socon *Beds*	23	O16
Ebberston *N Yorks*	43	K15
Ebbw Vale *Gwent*	20	P10
Ecclefechan *Dumf/Gal*	45	H10
Eccles *Gtr Man*	36	M12
Eccles *Borders*	52	G12
Ecclesfield *S Yorks*	37	M14
Eccleshall *Staffs*	29	N12
Eccleston *Ches*	36	M11
Echt *Gramp*	65	D12
Eckington *Heref/Worcs*	21	O12
Eckington *Derby*	38	M14
Edale *Derby*	37	M13
Edderton *H'land*	71	C8
Eddleston *Borders*	52	G10
Edenbridge *Kent*	17	Q17
Edenfield *Lancs*	37	L12
Edenthorpe *S Yorks*	38	L14
Edern *Gwyn*	34	N7
Edgefield *Norfolk*	33	N19
Edgmond *Shrops*	29	N12
Edgworth *Lancs*	36	L12
Edinburgh *Lothian*	51	G10
Edington *Wilts*	14	Q12
Edlingham *Northum*	47	H13
Edmondbyers *Durham*	47	J13
Ednam *Borders*	52	G12
Edrom *Borders*	52	G12
Edwinstowe *Notts*	38	M14
Edzell *Tayside*	59	E11
Egglescliffe *Clevl'd*	42	J14
Eggleston *Durham*	47	J12
Egham *Surrey*	16	Q15
Eglingham *Northum*	53	H13
Egloskerry *Cornw'l*	4	R8
Eglwysbach *Gwyn*	35	M9
Eglwyswrw *Dyfed*	18	O7
Egremont *Cumb*	40	K9
Egton *N Yorks*	43	K15
Eldrig Village *Dumf/Gal*	44	J7
Elford *Staffs*	30	N13
Elgin *Gramp*	64	C10
Elgol *H'land*	61	D4
Elham *Kent*	11	Q19
Elie *Fife*	58	F11
Elishaw *Northum*	46	H12
Elkesley *Notts*	38	M15
Elland *W Yorks*	37	L13
Ellastone *Staffs*	30	N13
Eller Beck Bridge *N Yorks*	43	K15
Ellerby *N Yorks*	43	J15
Ellesmere *Shrops*	28	N11
Ellesmere Port *Ches*	36	M11
Ellingham *Northum*	53	G13
Ellington *Cambs*	31	O16
Ellington *Northum*	47	H13
Ellon *Gramp*	65	D12
Elloughton *Humber*	38	L15
Elm *Cambs*	32	N17
Elmore *Glos*	21	P12
Elmstead Market *Essex*	25	P18
Elmswell *Suffolk*	25	O18
Elrick *Gramp*	65	D12
Elsdon *Northum*	47	H12
Elsrickle *S'clyde*	51	G10
Elstead *Surrey*	16	Q15
Elsted *W Sussex*	9	R15
Elswick *Lancs*	40	L11
Elsworth *Cambs*	23	O16
Eltisley *Cambs*	23	O16
Elton *Cambs*	31	N16
Elton *Derby*	37	M13
Elvanfoot *S'clyde*	51	H9
Elveden *Suffolk*	32	O18
Elvington *N Yorks*	42	L15
Elwick *Clevl'd*	47	J14
Elworth *Ches*	36	M12
Ely *Cambs*	32	O17
Embleton *Northum*	53	G13
Embo *H'land*	71	C8
Embsay *N Yorks*	41	L13
Emneth *Norfolk*	32	N17
Empingham *Leics*	31	N15
Emsworth *Hants*	8	R15
Enderby *Leics*	30	N14
Endon *Staffs*	37	M12
Enfield *Gtr Lon*	17	P16
Enford *Wilts*	15	Q13
English Bicknor *Glos*	21	P11
Ennerdale *Cumb*	40	J10
Enstone *Oxon*	22	P14
Enville *Staffs*	29	O12
Epping *Essex*	17	P17
Epsom *Surrey*	17	Q16
Epworth *Humber*	38	L15
Erbusaig *H'land*	61	D5
Eriboll *H'land*	68	B7
Erlestoke *Wilts*	14	Q12
Erpingham *Norfolk*	33	N19
Errogie *H'land*	63	D8
Errol *Tayside*	58	F10
Ersary *W Isles*	60	E2
Escrick *N Yorks*	42	L14
Esher *Surrey*	16	Q16
Eskdale Green *Cumb*	40	K10
Essendine *Leics*	31	N15
Essington *Staffs*	29	N12
Eston *Clevl'd*	42	J14
Etal *Northum*	53	G12
Etchingham *E Sussex*	10	Q17
Eton *Berks*	16	Q15
Ettington *Warwick*	22	O13
Ettrickbridge End *Borders*	52	H11
Etwall *Derby*	30	N13
Euston *Suffolk*	32	O18
Euxton *Lancs*	36	L11
Evanton *H'land*	71	C8
Evenjobb *Powys*	20	O10
Evenwood *Durham*	47	J13
Evercreech *Som'set*	14	Q11
Everleigh *Wilts*	15	Q13
Evershot *Dorset*	6	R11
Evertown *Dumf/Gal*	46	H10
Evesham *Heref/Worcs*	21	O13
Ewell *Surrey*	17	Q16
Ewelme *Oxon*	22	P14
Ewenny *Mid Glam*	20	Q9
Ewerby *Lincs*	31	M16
Ewhurst *Surrey*	16	Q16
Ewyas Harold *Heref/Worcs*	20	P11
Exbourne *Devon*	4	R9
Exeter *Devon*	5	R9
Exford *Som'set*	12	Q9
Exminster *Devon*	5	R9
Exmouth *Devon*	5	R10
Exning *Suffolk*	32	O17
Exton *Leics*	31	N15
Exton *Devon*	5	R10
Eyam *Derby*	37	M13
Eydon *Northants*	22	O14
Eye *Cambs*	31	N16
Eye *Suffolk*	33	O19
Eyemouth *Borders*	53	G12
Eyke *Suffolk*	25	O19
Eynsford *Kent*	17	Q17
Eynsham *Oxon*	22	P14
Eythorne *Kent*	11	Q19

F

Failsworth *Gtr Man*	37	L12
Fair Oak *Hants*	8	R14
Fairbourne *Gwyn*	26	N8
Fairford *Glos*	21	P13
Fairlie *S'clyde*	50	G7
Fairlight *E Sussex*	10	R18
Fakenham *Norfolk*	32	N18
Faldingworth *Lincs*	39	M16
Falkirk *Central*	51	F9
Falkland *Fife*	58	F10
Fallin *Central*	51	F9
Falmer *E Sussex*	9	R16
Falmouth *Cornw'l*	2	S6
Falstone *Northum*	46	H12
Farcet *Cambs*	31	N16
Fareham *Hants*	8	R14
Faringdon *Oxon*	22	P13
Farington *Lancs*	36	L11
Farley *Wilts*	15	Q13
Farmborough *Avon*	14	Q12
Farnborough *Surrey*	16	Q15
Farnborough *Warwick*	22	O14
Farndon *Ches*	36	M11
Farndon *Notts*	38	M15
Farnell *Tayside*	59	E11
Farnham *Surrey*	16	Q15
Farnham *Suffolk*	25	O19
Farnham *N Yorks*	42	K14
Farnham *Dorset*	7	R12
Farningham *Kent*	17	Q17
Farnsfield *Notts*	38	M14
Farnworth *Gtr Man*	36	L12
Farr *H'land*	63	D8
Farr *H'land*	70	A8
Farringdon *Hants*	8	Q15
Farsley *W Yorks*	37	L13
Farthinghoe *Northants*	22	O14
Fauldhouse *Lothian*	51	G9
Faversham *Kent*	11	Q18
Fawley *Berks*	15	P14
Fawley *Hants*	8	R14
Fazeley *Staffs*	30	N13
Fearnan *Tayside*	57	E8
Featherstone *W Yorks*	38	L14
Feetham *N Yorks*	41	K12
Felbridge *Surrey*	9	Q16
Felixstowe *Suffolk*	25	P19
Felpham *W Sussex*	9	R15
Felsham *Suffolk*	24	O18
Felsted *Essex*	24	P17
Felton *Northum*	47	H13
Feltwell *Norfolk*	32	O18
Fen Drayton *Cambs*	23	O16
Fenny Compton *Warwick*	22	O14
Fenny Stratford *Bucks*	23	P15
Fenstanton *Cambs*	31	O16
Fenwick *S'clyde*	50	G8
Ferndale *Mid Glam*	20	P10
Ferndown *Dorset*	7	R13
Ferness *H'land*	63	D9
Fernhill Heath *Heref/Worcs*	21	O12

Fernhurst *W Sussex*	9	Q15
Fernilea *H'land*	61	D4
Ferring *W Sussex*	9	R16
Ferryden *Tayside*	59	E12
Ferryhill *Durham*	47	J13
Ferryside *Dyfed*	19	P8
Feshiebridge *H'land*	63	D9
Fetterangus *Gramp*	65	C12
Fettercairn *Gramp*	59	E11
Ffestiniog *Gwyn*	35	N9
Fife Keith *Gramp*	64	C11
Filby *Norfolk*	33	N20
Filey *N Yorks*	43	K16
Filkins *Oxon*	22	P13
Fillongley *Warwick*	30	O13
Filton *Avon*	14	Q11
Fimber *Humber*	43	K15
Fincham *Norfolk*	32	N17
Finchingfield *Essex*	24	P17
Findhorn *Gramp*	64	C9
Findochty *Gramp*	64	C11
Findon *Gramp*	65	D12
Findon *W Sussex*	9	R16
Finedon *Northants*	31	O15
Finnart *S'clyde*	50	F7
Finningham *Suffolk*	33	O19
Finningley *S Yorks*	38	M15
Finsbay *W Isles*	67	C3
Fintry *Central*	50	F8
Fionnphort *S'clyde*	54	F4
Fishbourne *I of Wight*	8	R14
Fishguard *Dyfed*	19	P7
Fishtoft *Lincs*	32	N17
Fittleworth *W Sussex*	9	R15
Fitzwilliam *W Yorks*	38	L14
Five Oaks *W Sussex*	9	Q16
Five Penny Borve *W Isles*	66	B4
Five Roads *Dyfed*	19	P8
Flagg *Derby*	37	M13
Flamborough *Humber*	43	K16
Fleckney *Leics*	30	N14
Fleet *Hants*	16	Q15
Fleetwood *Lancs*	40	L10
Fleming *Dumf/Gal*	46	H10
Fletching *E Sussex*	9	R17
Flimby *Cumb*	45	J9
Flimwell *E Sussex*	10	Q17
Flint *Clwyd*	35	M10
Flintham *Notts*	31	M15
Flitwick *Beds*	23	P16
Flixton *N Yorks*	43	K16
Flodden *Northum*	53	G12
Flookburgh *Cumb*	40	K11
Flore *Northants*	22	O14
Flynnon-groew *Clwyd*	35	M10
Fochabers *Gramp*	64	C10
Fodderty *H'land*	63	C8
Foggathorpe *Humber*	38	L15
Folkestone *Kent*	11	Q19
Folkingham *Lincs*	31	N16
Folly Gate *Devon*	4	R8
Fontmell Magna *Dorset*	7	R12
Ford *Shrops*	28	N11
Ford *Northum*	53	G12
Ford *S'clyde*	55	F6
Forden *Powys*	28	N10
Fordham *Cambs*	32	O17
Fordingbridge *Hants*	7	R13
Fordyce *Gramp*	64	C11
Forest Hill *Oxon*	22	P14
Forest Row *E Sussex*	10	Q17
Forfar *Tayside*	58	E11
Formby *Mersey*	36	L10
Fornham All Saints *Suffolk*	32	O18

Forres *Gramp*	64	C9
Forsbrook *Staffs*	29	N12
Forsinain *H'land*	70	B9
Forsinard *H'land*	70	B9
Fort Augustus *H'land*	63	D7
Fort George *H'land*	63	C8
Fort William *H'land*	56	E6
Forth *S'clyde*	51	G9
Fortingall *Tayside*	57	E8
Forton *Lancs*	40	L11
Fortrie *Gramp*	65	D11
Fortrose *H'land*	63	C8
Fortuneswell *Dorset*	6	R12
Forty Feet Bridge *Cambs*	31	O16
Fosdyke *Lincs*	32	N16
Fotherby *Lincs*	39	M16
Foulden *Gramp*	53	G12
Foulridge *Lancs*	41	L12
Foulsham *Norfolk*	33	N19
Fountainhall *Borders*	52	G11
Four Crosses *Gwyn*	34	N8
Four Lanes *Cornw'l*	2	S6
Four Marks *Hants*	8	Q14
Fovant *Wilts*	15	Q13
Fowey *Cornw'l*	3	S7
Fowlis *Tayside*	58	F10
Fowlis Wester *Tayside*	57	F9
Fowlmere *Cambs*	24	O17
Fownhope *Heref/Worcs*	21	P11
Foxdale *I of Man*	72	K7
Foxhole *Cornw'l*	3	S7
Foxholes *N Yorks*	43	K16
Foyers *H'land*	63	D8
Fraddon *Cornw'l*	3	S7
Framlingham *Suffolk*	25	O19
Frampton *Dorset*	6	R11
Frampton Cotterell *Avon*	21	P12
Frampton on Severn *Glos*	21	P12
Frant *E Sussex*	10	Q17
Fraserburgh *Gramp*	65	C12
Freckenham *Suffolk*	32	O17
Freckleton *Lancs*	36	L11
Freethorpe *Norfolk*	33	N20
Freiston *Lincs*	32	N17
Fremington *Devon*	12	Q8
Frensham *Surrey*	16	Q15
Freshwater *I of Wight*	8	R13
Fressingfield *Suffolk*	33	O19
Freswick *H'land*	70	A10
Freuchie *Fife*	58	F10
Friday Bridge *Cambs*	32	N17
Fridaythorpe *Humber*	43	K15
Frimley *Surrey*	16	Q15
Frinton-on-Sea *Essex*	25	P19
Friockheim *Tayside*	59	E11
Friskney *Lincs*	39	M17
Friston *Suffolk*	25	O20
Frithville *Lincs*	31	M16
Frittenden *Kent*	10	Q18
Fritwell *Oxon*	22	P14
Frizington *Cumb*	40	J10
Frodsham *Ches*	36	M11
Frome *Som'set*	14	Q12
Frosterley *Durham*	47	J13
Froxfield *Wilts*	15	Q13
Fulbeck *Lincs*	31	M15
Fulbourn *Cambs*	24	O17
Fulford *Staffs*	29	N12
Fulwood *Lancs*	36	L11
Furnace *S'clyde*	56	F6
Fyfield *Essex*	17	P17
Fyling Thorpe *N Yorks*	43	K15
Fyvie *Gramp*	65	D12

G

Gaddesby *Leics*	30	N15
Gaerwen *Gwyn*	34	M8
Gainford *Durham*	42	J13
Gainsborough *Lincs*	38	M15
Gairloch *H'land*	69	C5
Gairlochy *H'land*	56	E7
Galashiels *Borders*	52	G11
Galgate *Lancs*	40	L11
Galleywood *Essex*	24	P17
Galmisdale *H'land*	61	E4
Galmpton *Devon*	5	S9
Galston *S'clyde*	50	G8
Gamblesby *Cumb*	46	J11
Gamlingay *Cambs*	23	O16
Gamston *Notts*	38	M15
Ganton *N Yorks*	43	K16
Garboldisham *Norfolk*	33	O18
Gardenstown *Gramp*	65	C12
Garelochhead *S'clyde*	50	F7
Garforth *W Yorks*	38	L14
Garlieston *Dumf/Gal*	44	J8
Garlogie *Gramp*	65	D12
Garmouth *Gramp*	64	C10
Garn-Dolbenmaen *Gwyn*	34	N8
Garrabost *W Isles*	66	B4
Garreg *Gwyn*	34	N8
Garrigill *Cumb*	46	J12
Garsington *Oxon*	22	P14
Garstang *Lancs*	40	L11
Garth *Powys*	20	O9
Garthmyl *Powys*	27	N10
Gartly *Gramp*	64	D11
Garton-on-the-Wolds *Humber*	43	K16
Garvald *Lothian*	52	G11
Garve *H'land*	63	C7
Garvestone *Norfolk*	33	N18
Gatehouse of Fleet *Dumf/Gal*	44	J8
Gateshead *Tyne/Wear*	47	J13
Gateside *Fife*	58	F10
Gauldry *Fife*	58	F10
Gavinton *Borders*	52	G12
Gaydon *Warwick*	22	O14
Gayles *N Yorks*	41	K13
Gayton *Norfolk*	32	N18
Geddington *Northants*	31	O15
Gedney *Lincs*	32	N17
Gedney Hill *Lincs*	31	N16
Geldeston *Norfolk*	33	O20
Gelston *Dumf/Gal*	45	J9
George Nympton *Devon*	12	R9
Georgeham *Devon*	12	Q8
Germoe *Cornw'l*	2	S6
Gerrard's Cross *Bucks*	16	P15
Gifford *Lothian*	52	G11
Giggleswick *N Yorks*	41	K12
Gilberdyke *Humber*	38	L15
Gilcrux *Cumb*	45	J10
Gillamoor *N Yorks*	42	K13
Gilling *N Yorks*	42	K13
Gillingham *Kent*	10	Q18
Gillingham *Dorset*	14	Q12
Gilmerton *Tayside*	57	F9
Gilsland *Northum*	46	J11
Gilwern *Gwent*	20	P10
Girton *Cambs*	24	O17
Girvan *S'clyde*	44	H7
Gisburn *Lancs*	41	L12

Gisla W Isles	66	B3
Gislingham Suffolk	33	O19
Gladestry Powys	20	O10
Gladsmuir Lothian	52	G11
Glaisdale N Yorks	43	K15
Glamis Tayside	59	E11
Glanaman Dyfed	19	P9
Glanton Northum	53	H13
Glasbury Powys	20	O10
Glasgow S'clyde	50	G8
Glassford S'clyde	50	G8
Glasshouses N Yorks	42	K13
Glasson Lancs	40	L11
Glastonbury Som'set	14	Q11
Glemsford Suffolk	24	O18
Glen Auldyn I of Man	72	K8
Glen Barry Gramp	64	C11
Glen Mona I of Man	72	K8
Glenbarr S'clyde	49	G5
Glenbervie Gramp	59	E12
Glenboig S'clyde	50	G8
Glenbrittle H'land	61	D4
Glenbuck S'clyde	51	G9
Glencaple Dumf/Gal	45	H9
Glencarse Tayside	58	F10
Glencoe H'land	56	E6
Glendevon Tayside	58	F9
Gleneagles Tayside	57	F9
Glenelg H'land	62	D5
Glenfarg Tayside	58	F10
Glenfinnan H'land	55	E6
Glengarnock S'clyde	50	G7
Glenkindie Gramp	64	D11
Glenluce Dumf/Gal	44	J7
Glenmaye I of Man	72	K7
Glenrothes Fife	58	F10
Glentham Lincs	39	M16
Glentworth Lincs	38	M15
Glenuig H'land	55	E5
Glossop Derby	37	M13
Gloucester Glos	21	P12
Glusburn N Yorks	41	L12
Glyn Neath W Glam	19	P9
Glyncorrwg W Glam	19	P9
Glynde E Sussex	10	R17
Gnosall Staffs	29	N12
Goathland N Yorks	43	K15
Gobowen Shrops	28	N10
Godalming Surrey	16	Q15
Godmanchester Cambs	31	O16
Godshill I of Wight	8	R14
Godstone Surrey	17	Q16
Goginan Dyfed	27	O9
Golborne Gtr Man	36	M11
Goldsithney Cornw'l	2	S6
Golspie H'land	71	C9
Gooderstone Norfolk	32	N18
Goodmanham Humber	43	L15
Goodwick Dyfed	18	O7
Goodworth Clatford Hants	15	Q14
Goole Humber	38	L15
Goosnargh Lancs	41	L11
Goostrey Ches	37	M12
Gordon Borders	52	G11
Gordonstoun Gramp	64	C11
Gordonstown Gramp	65	D12
Gorebridge Lothian	52	G10
Goring Oxon	15	P14
Goring-by-Sea W Sussex	9	R16
Gorleston-on-Sea Norfolk	33	N20
Gorran Haven Cornw'l	3	S7
Gorseinon W Glam	19	P8
Gorslas Dyfed	19	P8
Gorsty Common		
Heref/Worcs	20	O11
Gosberton Lincs	31	N16
Gosforth Cumb	40	K10
Gosforth Tyne/Wear	47	H13
Gosport Hants	8	R14
Gotham Notts	30	N14
Gotherington Glos	21	P12
Goudhurst Kent	10	Q17
Goulceby Lincs	39	M16
Gourdon Gramp	59	E12
Gourock S'clyde	50	G7
Govilon Gwent	20	P10
Gowerton W Glam	19	P8
Goxhill Humber	39	L16
Grain Kent	10	Q18
Grainthorpe Lincs	39	M17
Gramisdale W Isles	60	D2
Grampound Cornw'l	3	S7
Grandborough Warwick	30	O14
Grandtully Tayside	57	E9
Grange Cumb	40	J10
Grange over Sands Cumb	40	K11
Grangemouth Central	51	F9
Grangetown Clevl'd	42	J14
Grantchester Cambs	24	O17
Grantham Lincs	31	N15
Granton Lothian	51	G10
Grantown-on-Spey H'land	64	D9
Grantshouse Borders	52	G12
Grasby Lincs	39	L16
Grasmere Cumb	40	K10
Grassington N Yorks	41	K13
Grateley Hants	15	Q13
Graveney Kent	11	Q18
Gravesend Kent	17	Q17
Gravir W Isles	67	B4
Grayrigg Cumb	41	K11
Grays Essex	17	Q17
Grayshott Hants	9	Q15
Great Altcar Lancs	36	L10
Great Asby Cumb	41	K12
Great Ayton N Yorks	42	K14
Great Baddow Essex	24	P17
Great Badminton Avon	21	P12
Great Bardfield Essex	24	O17
Great Barford Beds	23	O16
Great Barrington Glos	22	P13
Great Barton Suffolk	32	O18
Great Bedwyn Wilts	15	Q13
Great Bentley Essex	25	P19
Great Bircham Norfolk	32	N18
Great Bookham Surrey	16	Q16
Great Bowden Leics	30	O15
Great Broughton Cumb	45	J10
Great Chesterford Essex	24	O17
Great Cheverell Wilts	14	Q12
Great Chishill Cambs	24	O17
Great Clifton Cumb	45	J10
Great Coates Humber	39	L16
Great Comberton		
Heref/Worcs	21	O12
Great Cornard Suffolk	24	O18
Great Cressingham Norfolk	32	N18
Great Dalby Leics	31	N15
Great Doddington Northants	31	O15
Great Driffield Humber	43	K16
Great Dunmow Essex	24	P17
Great Easton Essex	24	P17
Great Eccleston Lancs	36	L11
Great Eccleston Lancs	40	L11
Great Ellingham Norfolk	33	N18
Great Finborough Suffolk	25	O18
Great Gidding Cambs	31	O16
Great Gonerby Lincs	31	N15
Great Gransden Cambs	23	O16
Great Harwood Lancs	36	L12
Great Hatfield Humber	43	L16
Great Haywood Staffs	29	N12
Great Haywood Staffs	30	N13
Great Hockham Norfolk	32	N18
Great Horkesley Essex	24	P18
Great Horwood Bucks	23	P15
Great Limber Lincs	39	L16
Great Malvern Heref/Worcs	21	O12
Great Massingham Norfolk	32	N18
Great Milton Oxon	22	P14
Great Missenden Bucks	16	P15
Great Mitton Lancs	41	L12
Great Musgrave Cumb	41	J12
Great Offley Herts	23	P16
Great Ormside Cumb	41	J12
Great Orton Cumb	46	J10
Great Paxton Cambs	23	O16
Great Ponton Lincs	31	N15
Great Rissington Glos	22	P13
Great Rollright Oxon	22	P13
Great Rowsley Derby	37	M13
Great Ryburgh Norfolk	33	N18
Great Salkeld Cumb	46	J11
Great Sampford Essex	24	P17
Great Sankey Ches	36	M11
Great Saughall Ches	36	M11
Great Shefford Berks	15	Q14
Great Shelford Cambs	24	O17
Great Smeaton N Yorks	42	K14
Great Tew Oxon	22	P14
Great Torrington Devon	12	R8
Great Totham Essex	24	P18
Great Wakering Essex	24	P18
Great Waltham Essex	17	P17
Great Wilbraham Cambs	24	O17
Great Wishford Wilts	15	Q13
Great Witley Heref/Worcs	29	O12
Great Wyrley Staffs	29	N12
Great Yarmouth Norfolk	33	N20
Great Yeldham Essex	24	O18
Greatham Clevl'd	47	J14
Green Hammerton N Yorks	42	K14
Greenhaugh Northum	46	H12
Greenhead Northum	46	J11
Greenholme S'clyde	50	G8
Greenlaw Borders	52	G12
Greenloaning Tayside	57	F9
Greenock S'clyde	50	G7
Greenodd Cumb	40	K10
Greens Norton Northants	22	O14
Greenway Dyfed	18	P7
Greenwich Gtr Lon	17	Q17
Greetham Leics	31	N15
Greetland W Yorks	37	L13
Gresford Clwyd	36	M11
Gress W Isles	66	B4
Gretna Dumf/Gal	46	J10
Gretna Green Dumf/Gal	46	J10
Gretton Northants	31	N15
Greystoke Cumb	46	J11
Grimsby Humber	39	L16
Grimshader W Isles	66	B4
Grimston Norfolk	32	N18
Grindale Humber	43	K16
Grindon Staffs	37	M13
Gringley on the Hill Notts	38	M15
Grinton N Yorks	41	K13
Gristhorpe N Yorks	43	K16
Grizebeck Cumb	40	K10
Groby Leics	30	N14

Groombridge E Sussex 10 Q17
Grosmont Gwent 20 P11
Grosmont N Yorks 43 K15
Gruinard H'land 69 C6
Grundisburgh Suffolk 25 O19
Guard Bridge Fife 58 F11
Guestling Green E Sussex 10 R18
Guildford Surrey 16 Q15
Guildtown Tayside 58 F10
Guilsborough Northants 30 O14
Guilsfield Powys 27 N10
Guisborough Clev'd 42 J14
Guiseley W Yorks 42 L13
Guist Norfolk 33 N18
Gullane Lothian 52 F11
Gunnerside N Yorks 41 K12
Gunnerton Northum 47 H12
Gunness Humber 38 L15
Gunnislake Cornw'l 4 R8
Gurnard I of Wight 8 R14
Guthrie Tayside 59 E11
Guyhirn Cambs 32 N12
Gwalchmai Gwyn 34 M8
Gwaun-Cae-Gurwen W Glam 19 P9
Gweek Cornw'l 2 S6
Gwennap Cornw'l 2 S6
Gwyddelwern Clwyd 35 M10
Gyffin Gwyn 35 M9
Gyffylliog Clwyd 35 M10

H

Hackness N Yorks 43 K15
Hackney Gtr Lon 17 P16
Hackthorpe Cumb 41 J11
Haconby Lincs 31 N16
Haddenham Bucks 16 P15
Haddenham Cambs 32 O17
Haddington Lothian 52 G11
Hadleigh Essex 24 P18
Hadleigh Suffolk 25 O18
Hadley Shrops 29 N12
Hadlow Kent 17 Q17
Hadnall Shrops 28 N11
Hagley Heref/Worcs 29 O12
Hagworthingham Lincs 39 M17
Hailsham E Sussex 10 R17
Hainton Lincs 39 M16
Halam Notts 38 M15
Halberton Devon 13 R10
Halbeton Devon 4 S9
Hale Lincs 31 N16
Hale Ches 36 M11
Hale Gtr Man 36 M12
Hales Norfolk 33 N20
Halesowen W Midlands 29 O12
Halesworth Suffolk 33 O19
Halford Warwick 22 O13
Halifax W Yorks 37 L13
Halkirk H'land 70 A10
Hallaton Leics 31 N15
Hallin H'land 61 C3
Halling Kent 17 Q17
Hallow Heref/Worcs 21 O12
Halsall Lancs 36 L11
Halse Som'set 13 Q10
Halsham Humber 39 L16
Halstead Essex 24 P18
Halton Ches 36 M11
Halton Lincs 39 M17

Halton Lancs 41 K11
Halton Northum 47 H12
Halton Gill N Yorks 41 K12
Haltwhistle Northum 46 J12
Halvergate Norfolk 33 N20
Hambledon Hants 8 R14
Hambledon Surrey 9 Q15
Hambleton N Yorks 38 L14
Hambleton Lancs 40 L11
Hamilton S'clyde 50 G8
Hammersmith Gtr Lon 17 Q16
Hampstead Norris Berks 15 Q14
Hampton in Arden W Midlands 30 O13
Hamsterley Durham 47 J13
Hamstreet Kent 10 Q18
Handcross W Sussex 9 Q16
Handforth Ches 37 M12
Hankelow Ches 29 M12
Hanley Staffs 29 M12
Hanmer Clwyd 28 N11
Hanslope Bucks 23 O15
Happisburgh Norfolk 33 N20
Harbottle Northum 46 H12
Harbury Warwick 22 O14
Harby Leics 31 N15
Harden W Yorks 41 L13
Hardrow N Yorks 41 K12
Harewood W Yorks 42 L14
Haringey Gtr Lon 17 P16
Harlech Gwyn 34 N8
Harleston Norfolk 33 O19
Harlington Beds 23 P15
Harlow Essex 17 P17
Harmston Lincs 38 M15
Harpenden Herts 16 P16
Harper Town Northum 46 J11
Harpley Norfolk 32 N18
Harrietsham Kent 10 Q18
Harrington Cumb 45 J9
Harrogate N Yorks 42 L13
Harrold Beds 23 O15
Harrow Gtr Lon 16 P16
Harston Cambs 24 O17
Hart Clev'd 47 J14
Hartburn Northum 47 H13
Hartest Suffolk 24 O18
Hartfield E Sussex 10 Q17
Hartford Ches 36 M11
Hartington Derby 37 M13
Hartland Devon 12 R8
Hartlebury Heref/Worcs 29 O12
Hartlepool Clev'd 47 J14
Hartley Northum 47 H14
Hartley Wintney Hants 16 Q15
Hartpury Glos 21 P12
Hartshill Warwick 30 N13
Hartshorne Derby 30 N13
Haverfordwest Dyfed 19 P7
Harvington Heref/Worcs 21 O13
Harwell Oxon 22 P14
Harwich Essex 25 P19
Harwood Dale N Yorks 43 K15
Haselbury Plucknett Som'set 6 R11
Haslemere Surrey 9 Q15
Haslingden Lancs 37 L12
Haslingfield Cambs 24 O17
Haslington Ches 36 M12
Hassocks W Sussex 9 R16
Hastigrow H'land 70 A10
Hastings E Sussex 10 R18
Haswell Durham 47 J14
Hatch Beauchamp Som'set 6 R11

Hatfield Herts 17 P16
Hatfield S Yorks 38 L15
Hatfield Broad Oak Essex 24 P17
Hatfield Heath Essex 24 P17
Hatfield Peverel Essex 24 P18
Hatherleigh Devon 4 R8
Hathern Leics 30 N14
Hathersage Derby 37 M13
Hatton Gramp 65 D13
Haugh of Urr Dumf/Gal 45 J9
Haughley Suffolk 25 O18
Haughton Staffs 29 N12
Hauxley Northum 47 H13
Havant Hants 8 R15
Haverhill Suffolk 24 O17
Haverigg Cumb 40 K10
Havering Gtr Lon 17 P17
Hawarden Clwyd 36 M10
Hawes N Yorks 41 K12
Hawick Borders 52 H11
Hawkchurch Devon 6 R11
Hawkesbury Upton Avon 21 P12
Hawkhurst Kent 10 Q18
Hawkshead Cumb 40 K10
Hawksworth Notts 31 N15
Hawkwell Essex 24 P18
Hawley Hants 16 Q15
Hawnby N Yorks 42 K14
Haworth W Yorks 42 L13
Hawkser N Yorks 43 K15
Haxby N Yorks 42 K14
Haydock Mersey 36 M11
Haydon Bridge Northum 46 J12
Hayfield Derby 37 M13
Hayle Cornw'l 2 S6
Hay-on-Wye Powys 20 O10
Hayton Notts 38 M15
Hayton Cumb 45 J10
Hayton Cumb 46 J11
Hayward's Heath W Sussex 9 R16
Hazel Grove Gtr Man 37 M12
Hazelbury Bryan Dorset 6 R12
Hazleton Glos 21 P13
Heacham Norfolk 32 N17
Headcorn Kent 10 Q18
Headington Oxon 22 P14
Headley Hants 8 Q15
Healey N Yorks 42 K13
Heanor Derby 30 M14
Heast H'land 61 D5
Heath Derby 38 M14
Heath & Reach Beds 23 P15
Heath End Hants 15 Q14
Heath Hayes Staffs 29 N13
Heathfield E Sussex 10 R17
Hebburn Tyne/Wear 47 J13
Hebden N Yorks 41 K13
Hebden Bridge W Yorks 37 L13
Hebron Northum 47 H13
Heckington Lincs 31 N16
Heckmondwike W Yorks 37 L13
Hedge End Hants 8 R14
Hednesford Staffs 29 N13
Hedon Humber 39 L16
Heighington Durham 47 J13
Helensburgh S'clyde 50 F7
Helford Cornw'l 2 S6
Helions Bumpstead Essex 24 O17
Hellesdon Norfolk 33 N19
Hellidon Northants 22 O14
Hellifield N Yorks 41 L12
Hellingly E Sussex 10 R17
Helmdon Northants 22 O14

Helmsdale *H'land*	71	B9
Helmsley *N Yorks*	42	K14
Helperby *N Yorks*	42	K14
Helpringham *Lincs*	31	N16
Helpstone *Cambs*	31	N16
Helsby *Ches*	36	M11
Helston *Cornw'l*	2	S6
Helstone *Cornw'l*	3	R7
Hemel Hempstead *Herts*	16	P15
Hemingbrough *N Yorks*	38	L15
Hempnall *Norfolk*	33	N19
Hempton *Norfolk*	32	N18
Hemsby *Norfolk*	33	N20
Hemsworth *W Yorks*	38	L14
Hemyock *Devon*	13	R10
Hendy *Dyfed*	19	P8
Henfield *W Sussex*	9	R16
Henley-in-Arden *Warwick*	30	O13
Henley-on-Thames *Oxon*	16	P15
Henllan *Clwyd*	35	M10
Henlow *Beds*	23	O16
Henshaw *Northum*	46	J12
Hensingham *Cumb*	40	J9
Henstridge *Som'set*	6	R12
Hepple *Northum*	47	H12
Hepscott *Northum*	47	H13
Hepworth *W Yorks*	37	L13
Herbrandston *Dyfed*	18	P6
Hereford *Heref/Worcs*	20	O11
Heriot *Borders*	52	G11
Hermitage *Berks*	15	Q14
Herne *Kent*	11	Q19
Herne Bay *Kent*	11	Q19
Hersden *Kent*	11	Q19
Herstmonceux *E Sussex*	10	R17
Hertford *Herts*	17	P16
Hesketh Bank *Lancs*	36	L11
Hessett *Suffolk*	24	O18
Hessle *Humber*	39	L16
Heswall *Mersey*	36	M10
Hethersett *Norfolk*	33	N19
Hetton-le-Hole *Tyne/Wear*	47	J14
Heveningham *Suffolk*	33	O19
Heversham *Cumb*	40	K11
Hevingham *Norfolk*	33	N19
Hexham *Northum*	47	J12
Heybridge *Essex*	24	P18
Heysham *Lancs*	40	K11
Heytesbury *Wilts*	14	Q12
Heywood *Gtr Man*	37	L12
Hibaldstow *Humber*	38	L15
Hickling Green *Norfolk*	33	N20
High Bentham *N Yorks*	41	K11
High Bickington *Devon*	12	R9
High Blantyre *S'clyde*	50	G8
High Coniscliffe *Durham*	42	J13
High Ercall *Shrops*	29	N11
High Etherley *Durham*	47	J13
High Garrett *Essex*	24	P18
High Halden *Kent*	10	Q18
High Halstow *Kent*	10	Q18
High Ham *Som'set*	13	Q11
High Hesket *Cumb*	46	J11
High Legh *Ches*	36	M12
High Lorton *Cumb*	45	J10
High Newton *Cumb*	40	K11
High Ongar *Essex*	17	P17
High Roding *Essex*	24	P17
High Spen *Tyne/Wear*	47	J13
High Valleyfield *Fife*	51	F9
High Wycombe *Bucks*	16	P15
Higham *Lancs*	37	L12
Higham *Derby*	37	M14
Higham Ferrers *Northants*	31	O15
Higham Upshire *Kent*	17	Q17
Highampton *Devon*	4	R8
Highbridge *Som'set*	13	Q11
Highclere *Hants*	15	Q14
Highley *Shrops*	29	O12
Hightae *Dumf/Gal*	45	H10
Hightown *Mersey*	36	L10
Highworth *Wilts*	22	P13
Hilborough *Norfolk*	32	N18
Hildenborough *Kent*	17	Q17
Hilderstone *Staffs*	29	N12
Hilgay *Norfolk*	32	N17
Hill Brow *W Sussex*	8	Q15
Hill of Fearn *H'land*	71	C9
Hillingdon *Gtr Lon*	16	P16
Hilmarton *Wilts*	15	Q13
Hilperton *Wilts*	14	Q12
Hilton *Derby*	30	N13
Hilton *Cambs*	31	O16
Hilton of Cadboll *H'land*	71	C9
Hinckley *Leics*	30	N14
Hinderwell *N Yorks*	43	J15
Hindhead *Surrey*	9	Q15
Hindley *Gtr Man*	36	L11
Hindolveston *Norfolk*	33	N19
Hindon *Wilts*	14	Q12
Hingham *Norfolk*	33	N18
Hinstock *Shrops*	29	N12
Hintlesham *Suffolk*	25	O19
Hirnant *Powys*	27	N10
Hirwaun *Mid Glam*	20	P9
Histon *Cambs*	24	O17
Hitcham *Suffolk*	25	O18
Hitchin *Herts*	23	P16
Hoarwithy *Heref/Worcs*	21	P11
Hobkirk *Borders*	52	H11
Hockering *Norfolk*	33	N19
Hockley *Essex*	24	P18
Hockley Heath *W Midlands*	29	O13
Hockwold cum Wilton *Norfolk*	32	O18
Hoddesdon *Herts*	17	P16
Hodnet *Shrops*	29	N11
Hoff *Cumb*	41	J11
Hogsthorpe *Lincs*	39	M17
Holbeach *Lincs*	32	N17
Holbeach St. Marks *Lincs*	32	N17
Holbrook *Suffolk*	25	P19
Holcombe Rogus *Devon*	13	R10
Holegate *Lincs*	39	M17
Holford *Som'set*	13	Q10
Holkham *Norfolk*	32	N18
Holland-on-Sea *Essex*	25	P19
Hollesley *Suffolk*	25	O19
Hollingbourne *Kent*	10	Q18
Hollington *Derby*	30	N13
Hollingworth *Derby*	37	M13
Hollym *Humber*	39	L17
Holme *Cambs*	31	O16
Holme *W Yorks*	37	L13
Holme *Cumb*	41	K11
Holme Hale *Norfolk*	32	N18
Holme next the Sea *Norfolk*	32	N18
Holme upon Spalding Moor *Humber*	43	L15
Holmer *Heref/Worcs*	20	O11
Holmer Green *Bucks*	16	P15
Holmes Chapel *Ches*	36	M12
Holmesfield *Derby*	37	M13
Holmewood *Derby*	38	M14
Holmfirth *W Yorks*	37	L13
Holmhead *S'clyde*	50	H8
Holmrook *Cumb*	40	K10
Holne *Devon*	5	R9
Holsworthy *Devon*	4	R8
Holt *Wilts*	14	Q12
Holt *Norfolk*	33	N19
Holt *Clwyd*	36	M11
Holt Heath *Heref/Worcs*	21	O12
Holton *Som'set*	14	Q12
Holwick *Durham*	47	J12
Holy Island *Northum*	53	G13
Holybourne *Hants*	16	Q15
Holyhead *Gwyn*	34	M7
Holymoorside *Derby*	37	M14
Holystone *Northum*	46	H12
Holywell *Clwyd*	35	M10
Holywood *Dumf/Gal*	45	H9
Honeybourne *Heref/Worcs*	21	O13
Honing *Norfolk*	33	N19
Honington *Suffolk*	32	O18
Honiton *Devon*	5	R10
Honley *W Yorks*	37	L13
Hoo *Kent*	10	Q18
Hook *Hants*	16	Q15
Hook Norton *Oxon*	22	P14
Hope *Clwyd*	36	M10
Hope *Derby*	37	M13
Hopeman *Gramp*	64	C10
Hopesay *Shrops*	28	O11
Hopton *Norfolk*	33	N20
Hopton *Suffolk*	33	O18
Horam *E Sussex*	10	R17
Horbling *Lincs*	31	N16
Horbury *W Yorks*	37	L13
Horden *Durham*	47	J14
Horley *Surrey*	17	Q16
Horncastle *Lincs*	39	M16
Horncliffe *Northum*	53	G12
Horndean *Hants*	8	R15
Horning *Norfolk*	33	N19
Horningsham *Wilts*	14	Q12
Hornsea *Humber*	43	L16
Horrabridge *Devon*	4	S8
Horse House *N Yorks*	41	K13
Horsebridge *E Sussex*	10	R17
Horsey *Norfolk*	33	N20
Horsforth *W Yorks*	42	L13
Horsham *Norfolk*	33	N19
Horsham *W Sussex*	9	Q16
Horsington *Lincs*	39	M16
Horsley *Northum*	47	J13
Horsmonden *Kent*	10	Q17
Horstead *Norfolk*	33	N19
Horsted Keynes *W Sussex*	9	Q16
Horton in Ribblesdale *N Yorks*	41	K12
Horwich *Gtr Man*	36	L11
Hothfield *Kent*	10	Q18
Hough on the Hill *Lincs*	31	N15
Hougharry *W Isles*	60	C1
Houghton *Hants*	15	Q13
Houghton *Cumb*	46	J11
Houghton on the Hill *Leics*	30	N15
Houghton Regis *Beds*	23	P15
Houghton-le-Spring *Tyne/Wear*	47	J14
Hounslow *Gtr Lon*	16	Q16
Houston *S'clyde*	50	G7
Hove *E Sussex*	9	R16
Hoveringham *Notts*	30	M15
Hoveton *Norfolk*	33	N19
Hovingham *N Yorks*	42	K15
Howden *Humber*	38	L15
Howick *Northum*	53	H13
Howmore *W Isles*	60	D2
Hownam *Borders*	46	H12

Howwood *S'clyde*	50	G7
Hoxne *Suffolk*	33	O19
Hoylake *Mersey*	36	M10
Huby *N Yorks*	42	K14
Huby *N Yorks*	42	L13
Hucclecote *Glos*	21	P12
Hucknall *Notts*	30	M14
Huddersfield *W Yorks*	37	L13
Hudswell *N Yorks*	41	K13
Huggate *Humber*	43	L15
Hullavington *Wilts*	21	P12
Hullbridge *Essex*	24	P18
Humberston *Humber*	39	L16
Hume *Borders*	52	G12
Humshaugh *Northum*	47	H12
Hundleby *Lincs*	39	M17
Hundon *Suffolk*	24	O18
Hungerford *Berks*	15	Q13
Hunmanby *N Yorks*	43	K16
Hunstanton *Norfolk*	32	N17
Hunstanworth *Durham*	47	J12
Hunter's Quay *S'clyde*	49	G7
Hunterston *S'clyde*	50	G7
Huntingdon *Cambs*	31	O16
Huntington *Heref/Worcs*	20	O10
Huntington *Staffs*	29	N12
Huntington *N Yorks*	42	L14
Huntley *Glos*	21	P12
Huntly *Gramp*	64	D11
Huntspill *Som'set*	13	Q11
Hurley *Berks*	16	P15
Hurlford *S'clyde*	50	G8
Hursley *Hants*	15	Q14
Hurst Green *E Sussex*	10	Q17
Hurst Green *Lancs*	41	L12
Hurstbourne Priors *Hants*	15	Q14
Hurstbourne Tarrant *Hants*	15	Q14
Hurstpierpoint *W Sussex*	9	R16
Hurworth *N Yorks*	42	K13
Husbands Bosworth *Leics*	30	O14
Husthwaite *N Yorks*	42	K14
Huthwaite *Notts*	38	M14
Huttoft *Lincs*	39	M17
Hutton *Lancs*	36	L11
Hutton *Humber*	43	L16
Hutton *Borders*	53	G12
Hutton le Hole *N Yorks*	42	K15
Hutton Rudby *N Yorks*	42	K14
Huxley *Ches*	36	M11
Hyde *Gtr Man*	37	M12
Hynish *S'clyde*	54	F3
Hythe *Kent*	11	Q19
Hythe *Hants*	8	R14

I

Ibstock *Leics*	30	N14
Ickleford *Herts*	23	P16
Icklesham *E Sussex*	10	R18
Icklingham *Suffolk*	32	O18
Ide *Devon*	5	R9
Ideford *Devon*	5	R9
Idle *W Yorks*	42	L13
Idmiston *Wilts*	15	Q13
Ifield *W Sussex*	9	Q16
Ightfield *Shrops*	29	N11
Ightham *Kent*	17	Q17
Ilam *Staffs*	37	M13
Ilchester *Som'set*	6	R11
Ilderton *Northum*	53	H13

Ilfracombe *Devon*	12	Q8
Ilkeston *Derby*	30	N14
Ilkley *W Yorks*	42	L13
Illogan *Cornw'l*	2	S6
Ilmington *Warwick*	22	O13
Ilminster *Som'set*	6	R11
Ilsington *Devon*	5	R9
Ilton *Som'set*	6	R11
Immingham *Humber*	39	L16
Immingham Dock *Humber*	39	L16
Ince *Ches*	36	M11
Ince Blundell *Mersey*	36	L10
Inchnadamph *H'land*	69	B7
Inchture *Tayside*	58	F10
Ingatestone *Essex*	24	P17
Ingham *Suffolk*	32	O18
Ingleby Arncliffe *N Yorks*	42	K14
Ingleton *N Yorks*	41	K12
Ingoldmells *Lincs*	39	M17
Ingoldsby *Lincs*	31	N15
Ingrave *Essex*	17	P17
Ingworth *Norfolk*	33	N19
Inkberrow *Heref/Worcs*	21	O13
Inkpen *Berks*	15	Q14
Innellan *S'clyde*	49	G7
Innerleithen *Borders*	52	G10
Innerwick *Lothian*	52	G12
Innerwick *Tayside*	57	E8
Insch *Gramp*	65	D11
Insh *H'land*	63	D9
Inskip *Lancs*	40	L11
Instow *Devon*	12	Q8
Inver *H'land*	71	C9
Inver Alligin *H'land*	62	C5
Inverallochy *Gramp*	65	C13
Inveran *H'land*	69	C8
Inverarity *S'clyde*	56	F6
Inverbervie *Gramp*	59	E12
Inverboyndie *Gramp*	65	C11
Inverdruie *H'land*	63	D9
Inveresk *Lothian*	52	G10
Inverey *Gramp*	64	E9
Inverfarigaig *H'land*	63	D8
Invergarry *H'land*	62	D7
Invergordon *H'land*	71	C8
Invergowrie *Tayside*	58	F10
Inverie *H'land*	62	D5
Inverinate *H'land*	62	D6
Inverkeilor *Tayside*	59	E11
Inverkeithing *Fife*	51	F10
Inverkeithny *Gramp*	65	C11
Inverkip *S'clyde*	50	G7
Inverkirkaig *H'land*	69	B6
Invermoriston *H'land*	63	D7
Inverness *H'land*	63	D8
Invershiel *H'land*	62	D6
Invershin *H'land*	71	C8
Inversnaid *Central*	56	F7
Inveruglas *S'clyde*	56	F7
Inverurie *Gramp*	65	D12
Invervar *Tayside*	57	E8
Ipplepen *Devon*	5	S9
Ipsden *Oxon*	22	P14
Ipstones *Staffs*	37	M13
Ipswich *Suffolk*	25	O19
Irby *Mersey*	36	M10
Irby in the Marsh *Lincs*	39	M17
Irchester *Northants*	31	O15
Ireby *Cumb*	45	J10
Ireleth *Cumb*	40	K10
Irlam *Gtr Man*	36	M12
Iron Acton *Avon*	21	P12
Ironbridge *Shrops*	29	N12
Ironville *Derby*	38	M14

Irthington *Cumb*	46	J1
Irthlingborough *Northants*	31	O1
Irvine *S'clyde*	50	G
Isfield *E Sussex*	10	R1
Isle of Whithorn *Dumf/Gal*	44	J
Isleham *Cambs*	32	O1
Isleornsay *H'land*	61	D
Islington *Gtr Lon*	17	P1
Islip *Oxon*	22	P1
Islivig *W Isles*	66	B
Itchen Abbas *Hants*	15	Q1
Iver *Bucks*	16	P1
Ivinghoe *Bucks*	23	P1
Ivybridge *Devon*	4	S
Iwerne Minster *Dorset*	7	R1
Ixworth *Suffolk*	32	O1

J

Jacobstowe *Devon*	4	R
Jarrow *Tyne/Wear*	47	J1
Jedburgh *Borders*	52	H1
Jemimaville *H'land*	63	C
John O'Groats *H'land*	70	A1
John O'Groats House Hotel *H'land*	70	A1
Johnshaven *Gramp*	59	E1
Johnston *Dyfed*	18	P
Johnstone *S'clyde*	50	G
Joppa *S'clyde*	50	H
Jurby *I of Man*	72	K

K

Kaimes *S'clyde*	50	G
Kames *S'clyde*	49	G
Kearsley *Gtr Man*	37	L1
Kedington *Suffolk*	24	O1
Keelby *Lincs*	39	L1
Kegworth *Leics*	30	N1
Keig *Gramp*	65	D1
Keighley *W Yorks*	41	L1
Keils *S'clyde*	48	G
Keinton Mandeville *Som'set*	14	Q1
Keir Mill *Dumf/Gal*	45	H
Keiss *H'land*	70	A1
Keith *Gramp*	65	C1
Kelbrook *Lancs*	41	L1
Keld *N Yorks*	41	K1
Kelham *Notts*	38	M1
Kellas *Tayside*	58	E1
Kellas *Gramp*	64	C1
Kelly Bray *Cornw'l*	4	R
Kelsale *Suffolk*	25	O1
Kelsall *Ches*	36	M1
Kelso *Borders*	52	G1
Keltneyburn *Tayside*	57	E
Kelty *Fife*	51	F1
Kelvedon *Essex*	24	P1
Kemble *Glos*	21	P1
Kemnay *Gramp*	65	D1
Kempsey *Heref/Worcs*	21	O1
Kempsford *Glos*	22	P1
Kempston *Beds*	23	O1
Kendal *Cumb*	41	K1
Kenilworth *Warwick*	30	O1
Kenmore *Tayside*	57	E
Kennford *Devon*	5	R

Kenninghall Norfolk	33	O18
Kennington Kent	11	Q18
Kennington Oxon	22	P14
Kennoway Fife	58	F10
Kentford Suffolk	32	O17
Kentisbeare Devon	5	R10
Kentra H'land	55	E5
Kepwick N Yorks	42	K14
Kerry Powys	27	O10
Kerrysdale H'land	69	C5
Kershader W Isles	67	B3
Kershopefoot Borders	46	H11
Kesgrave Suffolk	25	O19
Kessingland Suffolk	33	O20
Keswick Cumb	40	J10
Kettering Northants	31	O15
Kettleshulme Ches	37	M12
Kettlewell N Yorks	41	K12
Ketton Leics	31	N15
Kewstoke Avon	13	Q11
Kexby Lincs	38	M15
Keyingham Humber	39	L16
Keymer W Sussex	9	R16
Keynsham Avon	14	Q12
Keysoe Beds	23	O16
Keyworth Notts	30	N14
Kibworth Beauchamp Leics	30	N14
Kibworth Harcourt Leics	30	N14
Kidderminster Heref/Worcs	29	O12
Kidlington Oxon	22	P14
Kidsgrove Staffs	37	M12
Kidwelly Dyfed	19	P8
Kielder Northum	46	H11
Kilbarchan S'clyde	50	G7
Kilberry S'clyde	49	G5
Kilbirnie S'clyde	50	G7
Kilbride S'clyde	55	F6
Kilbride W Isles	60	D2
Kilburn Derby	30	M14
Kilchattan S'clyde	49	G6
Kilchenzie S'clyde	49	H5
Kilchiaran S'clyde	48	G4
Kilchoan H'land	55	E4
Kilchoman S'clyde	48	G4
Kilchrenan S'clyde	56	F6
Kilconquhar Fife	58	F11
Kilcreggan S'clyde	50	G7
Kildale N Yorks	42	K14
Kildonan S'clyde	49	H6
Kildonan H'land	70	B9
Kildrummy Gramp	64	D11
Kilfinan S'clyde	49	G6
Kilgetty Dyfed	18	P7
Kilham Humber	43	K16
Kilkhampton Cornw'l	4	R8
Killamarsh Derby	38	M14
Killay W Glam	19	P8
Killean S'clyde	49	G5
Killearn Central	50	F8
Killichronan S'clyde	55	F5
Killilan H'land	62	D6
Killin Central	57	F8
Killinghall N Yorks	42	K13
Kilmacolm S'clyde	50	G7
Kilmaluag H'land	67	C4
Kilmarnock S'clyde	50	G8
Kilmartin S'clyde	55	F6
Kilmaurs S'clyde	50	G7
Kilmelford S'clyde	55	F6
Kilmichael Glassary S'clyde	49	F6
Kilmoluag H'land	5	R10
Kilmorack H'land	63	D7
Kilmory H'land	55	E4
Kilmun S'clyde	49	G7
Kilnhurst S Yorks	38	M14
Kilninian S'clyde	54	E4
Kilninver S'clyde	55	F6
Kiloran S'clyde	54	F4
Kilrenny Fife	59	F11
Kilsby Northants	30	O14
Kilsyth S'clyde	50	G8
Kiltarlity H'land	63	D8
Kilve Som'set	13	Q10
Kilwinning S'clyde	50	G7
Kimberley Notts	30	N14
Kimbolton Heref/Worcs	20	O11
Kimbolton Cambs	31	O16
Kimmeridge Dorset	7	R12
Kinbrace H'land	70	B9
Kincardine Fife	51	F9
Kincardine Gramp	65	D11
Kincraig H'land	63	D9
Kindallachan Tayside	58	E9
Kineton Warwick	22	O13
Kinfauns Tayside	58	F10
Kingarth S'clyde	49	G6
Kinghorn Fife	51	F10
Kingerswell Devon	5	S9
King's Caple Heref/Worcs	21	P11
Kimberley Notts	31	N16
Kings Langley Herts	16	P16
King's Lynn Norfolk	32	N17
King's Norton W Midlands	29	O13
King's Nympton Devon	12	R9
King's Pyon Heref/Worcs	20	O11
Kings Somborne Hants	15	Q14
King's Sutton Northants	22	O14
King's Worthy Hants	15	Q14
Kingsand Cornw'l	4	S8
Kingsbarns Fife	59	F11
Kingsbridge Devon	5	S9
Kingsbury Warwick	30	N13
Kingsclere Hants	15	Q14
Kingscross S'clyde	49	G6
Kingsdon Som'set	6	Q11
Kingsdown Kent	11	Q19
Kingsdown Kent	17	Q17
Kingskettle Fife	58	F10
Kingsland Heref/Worcs	20	O11
Kingsley Staffs	29	M13
Kingsley Ches	36	M11
Kingsmuir Tayside	58	E11
Kingsnorth Kent	10	Q18
Kingsteignton Devon	5	R9
Kingston Surrey	17	Q16
Kingston Oxon	64	C10
Kingston Bagpuize Oxon	22	P14
Kingston Seymour Som'set	13	Q10
Kingston upon Hull Humber	39	L16
Kingston Heref/Worcs	20	O11
Kingstone Staffs	29	N13
Kingswear Devon	5	S9
Kingswinford W Midlands	29	O12
Kingswood Avon	14	Q11
Kingswood Surrey	17	Q16
Kingswood Glos	21	P12
Kington Heref/Worcs	20	O10
Kingussie H'land	63	D8
Kinloch Tayside	58	E10
Kinloch Castle H'land	61	D4
Kinloch Rannoch Tayside	57	E8
Kinlochbervie H'land	68	B6
Kinlocheil H'land	55	E6
Kinlochewe H'land	62	C6
Kinlochleven H'land	56	E7
Kinlochmoidart H'land	55	E5
Kinloss Gramp	64	C9
Kinnaird Tayside	58	F10
Kinnerley Shrops	28	N11
Kinnesswood Tayside	58	F10
Kinross Tayside	58	F10
Kinrossie Tayside	58	F10
Kintaravay W Isles	67	B3
Kintbury Berks	15	Q14
Kinveachy H'land	63	D9
Kippax W Yorks	38	L14
Kippen Central	50	F8
Kirby Moorside N Yorks	42	K15
Kirby Thore Cumb	46	J11
Kirk Deighton N Yorks	42	L14
Kirk Ella Humber	39	L16
Kirk Ireton Derby	30	M13
Kirk Langley Derby	30	N13
Kirk Merrington Durham	47	J13
Kirk Michael I of Man	72	K7
Kirk of Mochrum Dumf/Gal	44	J7
Kirk Smeaton N Yorks	38	L14
Kirk Yetholm Borders	53	G12
Kirkbampton Cumb	46	J10
Kirkbean Dumf/Gal	45	J9
Kirkbride Cumb	45	J10
Kirkburn Humber	43	L15
Kirkburton W Yorks	37	L13
Kirkby Mersey	36	M11
Kirkby Hill N Yorks	42	K14
Kirkby in Ashfield Notts	38	M14
Kirkby Lonsdale Cumb	41	K11
Kirkby Malham N Yorks	41	K12
Kirkby Malzeard N Yorks	42	K13
Kirkby Muxloe Leics	30	N14
Kirkby on Bain Lincs	39	M16
Kirkby Stephen Cumb	41	K12
Kirkcaldy Fife	51	F10
Kirkconnel Dumf/Gal	51	H9
Kirkcowan Dumf/Gal	44	J7
Kirkcudbright Dumf/Gal	45	J8
Kirkfieldbank S'clyde	51	G9
Kirkgunzeon Dumf/Gal	45	J9
Kirkham Lancs	36	L11
Kirkheaton W Yorks	37	L13
Kirkheaton Northum	47	H13
Kirkhill H'land	63	D8
Kirkhill of Kennethmont Gramp	65	D11
Kirkibost W Isles	60	C2
Kirkinner Dumf/Gal	44	J8
Kirkintilloch S'clyde	50	G8
Kirkland Dumf/Gal	45	H9
Kirkleatham Clev'd	42	J14
Kirkliston Lothian	51	G10
Kirkmaiden Dumf/Gal	44	J7
Kirkmichael S'clyde	44	H7
Kirkmichael Tayside	58	E9
Kirkmuirhill S'clyde	51	G9
Kirknewton Lothian	51	G10
Kirknewton Borders	53	G12
Kirkolm Dumf/Gal	44	J6
Kirkoswald S'clyde	44	H7
Kirkoswald Cumb	46	J10
Kirkpatrick Dumf/Gal	46	H10
Kirkpatrick Durham Dumf/Gal	45	H9
Kirksanton Cumb	40	K10
Kirkstile Dumf/Gal	46	H11
Kirkton Dumf/Gal	45	H9
Kirkton Borders	52	H11
Kirkton Gramp	65	D11
Kirkton of Auchterhouse Tayside	58	E10
Kirkton of Craig Tayside	59	E12
Kirkton of Culsalmond Gramp	65	D11

Kirkton of Durris *Gramp* 65 D12
Kirkton of Glenbuchat *Gramp* 64 D10
Kirkton of Glenisla *Tayside* 58 E10
Kirkton of Kingoldrum
Tayside 58 E10
Kirkton of Menmuir *Tayside* 59 E11
Kirkton of Rayne *Gramp* 65 D12
Kirkton of Skene *Gramp* 65 D12
Kirkton of Strathmartine
Tayside 58 E10
Kirktown of Alvah *Gramp* 65 C11
Kirktown of Auchterless
Gramp 65 D12
Kirktown of Fetteresso
Gramp 59 E12
Kirkwhelpington *Northum* 47 H12
Kirn *S'clyde* 49 G7
Kirriemuir *Tayside* 58 E10
Kirtlebridge *Dumf/Gal* 45 H10
Kirtlington *Oxon* 22 P14
Kirtomy *H'land* 70 A8
Kirton *Suffolk* 25 O19
Kirton *Lincs* 31 N16
Kirton *Notts* 38 M15
Kirton in Lindsey *Humber* 38 M15
Kislingbury *Northants* 22 O15
Knaphill *Surrey* 16 Q15
Knapton *Norfolk* 33 N19
Knaresborough *N Yorks* 42 K14
Knayton *N Yorks* 42 K14
Knebworth *Herts* 23 P16
Kneesall *Notts* 38 M15
Knighton *Powys* 28 O10
Kniveton *Derby* 37 M13
Knock *Cumb* 46 J12
Knock *Cumb* 64 C11
Knock *W Isles* 66 B4
Knockandhu *Gramp* 64 D10
Knockarthur *H'land* 71 B8
Knockin *Shrops* 28 N10
Knossington *Leics* 31 N15
Knottingley *N Yorks* 38 L14
Knowle *Devon* 12 Q8
Knowle *W Midlands* 30 O13
Knowsley *Mersey* 36 M11
Knowstone *Devon* 12 R9
Knucklas *Powys* 28 O10
Knutsford *Ches* 36 M12
Koose *W Isles* 66 B4
Kyle of Lochalsh *H'land* 61 D5
Kyleakin *H'land* 61 D5
Kylerhea *H'land* 62 D5
Kyles Stockinish *W Isles* 67 C3
Kylestrome *H'land* 68 B6

L

Laceby *Humber* 39 L16
Lacock *Wilts* 14 Q12
Ladbroke *Warwick* 22 O14
Ladock *Corn'l* 3 S7
Ladybank *Fife* 58 F10
Ladykirk *Borders* 53 G12
Lagavulin *S'clyde* 48 G4
Lagg *S'clyde* 48 G5
Lagg *S'clyde* 49 H6
Laggan *H'land* 62 D7
Laggan *H'land* 63 D8
Laggan *Gramp* 64 D10
Laide *H'land* 69 C5

Lairg *H'land* 71 B8
Lakenheath *Suffolk* 32 O18
Laleston *Mid Glam* 19 P9
Lamberhurst *Kent* 10 Q17
Lambeth *Gtr Lon* 17 Q16
Lambourn *Berks* 15 P13
Lamerton *Devon* 4 R8
Lamington *S'clyde* 51 G9
Lamlash *S'clyde* 49 G6
Lampeter *Dyfed* 19 O8
Lamphey *Dyfed* 18 P7
Lanark *S'clyde* 51 G9
Lancaster *Lancs* 40 K11
Lanchester *Durham* 47 J13
Landewednack *Corn'l* 2 T6
Landkey *Devon* 12 Q8
Landrake *Corn'l* 4 S8
Lane End *Bucks* 16 P15
Langar *Notts* 31 N15
Langcliffe *N Yorks* 41 K12
Langford *Beds* 23 O16
Langham *Leics* 31 N15
Langham *Norfolk* 33 N18
Langholm *Dumf/Gal* 46 H10
Langley *Northum* 46 J12
Langold *Notts* 38 M14
Langport *Som'set* 13 Q11
Langtoft *Lincs* 31 N16
Langtoft *Humber* 43 K16
Langton *Lincs* 39 M16
Langton Green *Kent* 10 Q17
Langton Matravers *Dorset* 7 R12
Langton Matravers *Dorset* 7 R13
Langtree *Devon* 12 R8
Langwathby *Cumb* 46 J11
Lanivet *Corn'l* 3 S7
Lanner *Corn'l* 3 S7
Lanreath *Corn'l* 3 S7
Lanton *Borders* 52 H11
Lapford *Devon* 5 R9
Laphroaig *S'clyde* 48 G4
Larbert *Central* 51 F9
Largo Ward *Fife* 58 F11
Largs *S'clyde* 50 G7
Larkhall *S'clyde* 51 G9
Laroch *H'land* 56 E6
Lartington *Durham* 41 J13
Lasham *Hants* 16 Q14
Lasswade *Lothian* 51 G10
Lastingham *N Yorks* 42 K15
Latheron *H'land* 70 B10
Latheronwheel *H'land* 70 B10
Lauder *Borders* 52 G11
Laugharne *Dyfed* 19 P8
Laughton *Lincs* 38 M15
Launton *Oxon* 22 P14
Launceston *Corn'l* 4 R8
Laurencekirk *Gramp* 59 E12
Laurieston *Dumf/Gal* 45 J8
Laurieston *Dumf/Gal* 51 G9
Lavant *W Sussex* 9 R15
Lavendon *Bucks* 23 O15
Lavenham *Suffolk* 24 O18
Laverstoke *Hants* 15 Q14
Law *S'clyde* 51 G9
Lawers *Tayside* 57 E8
Lawrenny *Dyfed* 18 P7
Laxay *W Isles* 66 B3
Laxdale *W Isles* 66 B4
Laxey *I of Man* 72 K8
Laxfield *Suffolk* 33 O19
Laxford Bridge *H'land* 68 B6
Laxton *Humber* 38 L15

Laxton *Notts* 38 M15
Layer de la Haye *Essex* 24 P18
Lazonby *Cumb* 46 J11
Lea *Glos* 21 P12
Leadburn *Lothian* 51 G10
Leaden Roding *Essex* 17 P17
Leadenham *Lincs* 31 M15
Leadgate *Durham* 47 J13
Leadhills *S'clyde* 51 H9
Leafield *Oxon* 22 P13
Leake Common Side *Lincs* 39 M17
Lealholm *N Yorks* 43 K15
Leamington *Warwick* 30 O13
Leasingham *Lincs* 31 M16
Leatherhead *Surrey* 16 Q16
Leathley *N Yorks* 42 L13
Leavening *N Yorks* 43 K15
Lechlade *Glos* 22 P13
Leckford *Hants* 15 Q14
Leckhampstead *Berks* 15 Q14
Leconfield *Humber* 43 L16
Ledaig *S'clyde* 55 F6
Ledbury *Heref/Worcs* 21 O12
Ledmore *H'land* 69 B2
Leebotwood *Shrops* 28 N11
Leeds *Kent* 10 Q18
Leeds *W Yorks* 37 L13
Leek *Staffs* 37 M12
Leeming *N Yorks* 42 K13
Lee-on-the-Solent *Hants* 8 R14
Legbourne *Lincs* 39 M17
Legerwood *Borders* 52 G11
Leicester *Leics* 30 N14
Leigh *Gtr Man* 36 L11
Leigh *Dorset* 6 R11
Leigh *Kent* 17 Q16
Leigh *Heref/Worcs* 21 O12
Leighton *S'clyde* 55 F6
Leigh-on-Sea *Essex* 24 P18
Leighton Buzzard *Beds* 23 P15
Leintwardine *Heref/Worcs* 28 O11
Leirinmore *H'land* 68 A7
Leiston *Suffolk* 25 O20
Leith *Lothian* 51 G10
Leitholm *Borders* 53 G12
Lelant *Corn'l* 2 S6
Lemreway *W Isles* 67 B4
Lendalfoot *S'clyde* 44 H7
Lenham *Kent* 10 Q18
Lennoxtown *S'clyde* 50 G8
Lenzie *S'clyde* 50 G8
Leominster *Heref/Worcs* 20 O11
Lephin *H'land* 61 D3
Lesbury *Northum* 53 H12
Leslie *Gramp* 65 D11
Lesmahagow *S'clyde* 51 G9
Lessingham *Norfolk* 33 N20
Leswalt *Dumf/Gal* 44 J6
Letchworth *Herts* 23 P16
Letham *Fife* 58 F10
Letham *Tayside* 59 E11
Lethanhill *S'clyde* 44 H8
Letheringsett *Norfolk* 33 N19
Letterewe *H'land* 69 C6
Letterston *Dyfed* 18 P7
Lettoch *H'land* 64 D9
Leuchars *Fife* 58 F11
Leurbost *W Isles* 66 B4
Leven *Humber* 43 L16
Leven *Fife* 58 F11
Levens *Cumb* 40 K11
Leverburgh *W Isles* 67 C2
Leverington *Cambs* 31 N17
Leverton *Lincs* 32 N17

Levisham *N Yorks* 43 K15
Lewannick *Cornw'l* 4 R8
Lewdown *Devon* 4 R8
Lewes *E Sussex* 10 R17
Lewes *E Sussex* 10 R17
Lewisham *Gtr Lon* 17 Q16
Lewknor *Oxon* 16 P15
Leyburn *N Yorks* 42 K13
Leyland *Lancs* 36 L11
Leysdown-on-Sea *Kent* 11 Q18
Lhanbryde *Gramp* 64 C10
Libberton *S'clyde* 51 G9
Lichfield *Staffs* 30 N13
Liddington *Wilts* 15 P13
Lidgate *Suffolk* 24 O18
Lidlington *Beds* 23 O15
Lifton *Devon* 4 R8
Lightwater *Surrey* 16 Q15
Lilleshall *Shrops* 29 N12
Lilley *Herts* 23 P16
Lilliesleaf *Borders* 52 G11
Limpley Stoke *Avon* 14 Q12
Limpsfield *Surrey* 17 Q17
Lincluden *Dumf/Gal* 45 H9
Lincoln *Lincs* 38 M15
Lindale *Cumb* 40 K11
Lindfield *W Sussex* 9 Q16
Lindores *Fife* 58 F10
Lingen *Heref/Worcs* 28 O11
Lingfield *Surrey* 17 Q16
Linkenholt *Hants* 15 Q14
Linlithgow *Lothian* 51 G9
Linsidemore *H'land* 69 C8
Linslade *Beds* 23 P15
Lintmill *Gramp* 64 C11
Linton *Glos* 21 P12
Linton *Cambs* 24 O17
Linton *N Yorks* 41 K12
Linwood *S'clyde* 50 G8
Lionel *W Isles* 66 B4
Liphook *Hants* 9 Q15
Liskeard *Cornw'l* 4 S8
Liss *Hants* 8 Q15
Lissington *Lincs* 39 M16
Litcham *Norfolk* 32 N18
Litchborough *Northants* 22 O14
Litherland *Mersey* 36 M11
Litlington *Cambs* 23 O16
Little Ballinluig *Tayside* 57 E9
Little Barford *Beds* 23 O15
Little Budworth *Ches* 36 M11
Little Bytham *Lincs* 31 N15
Little Compton *Warwick* 22 P13
Little Eaton *Derby* 30 N14
Little Haven *Dyfed* 18 P6
Little Newcastle *Dyfed* 18 P7
Little Ribston *N Yorks* 42 L14
Little Snoring *Norfolk* 33 N18
Little Steeping *Lincs* 39 M17
Little Stretton *Shrops* 28 N11
Little Stukeley *Cambs* 31 O16
Little Sutton *Ches* 36 M11
Little Thurlow *Suffolk* 24 O17
Little Wakering *Essex* 24 P18
Little Waldingfield *Suffolk* 24 O18
Little Walsingham *Norfolk* 32 N18
Little Waltham *Essex* 24 P17
Little Wenlock *Shrops* 29 N11
Littleborough *Gtr Man* 37 L12
Littlebourne *Kent* 11 Q19
Littlebury *Essex* 24 O17
Littleferry *H'land* 71 C8
Littleham *Devon* 12 R8
Littleham *Devon* 5 R10

Littlehampton *W Sussex* 9 R15
Littlemill *H'land* 63 C9
Littlemore *Oxon* 22 P14
Littleover *Derby* 30 N13
Littleport *Cambs* 32 O17
Litton *Derby* 37 M13
Liverpool *Mersey* 36 M11
Liverton *Clevl'd* 42 J15
Livingston *Lothian* 51 G9
Lizard *Cornw'l* 2 T6
Llanaber *Gwyn* 26 N8
Llanaelhaearn *Gwyn* 34 N8
Llanafan *Dyfed* 27 O9
Llanarmon Dyffryn Ceiriog
Clwyd 28 N10
Llanarmon-yn-Ial *Clwyd* 35 M10
Llanarth *Dyfed* 18 O8
Llanarthney *Dyfed* 19 P8
Llanbadarnfawr *Dyfed* 26 O8
Llanbedr *Gwyn* 34 N8
Llanbedrog *Gwyn* 34 N8
Llanberis *Gwyn* 34 M8
Llanbister *Powys* 27 O10
Llanboidy *Dyfed* 18 P7
Llanbrynmair *Powys* 27 N9
Llandaf *S Glam* 20 Q10
Llandderfel *Gwyn* 35 N9
Llanddeusant *Gwyn* 34 M8
Llanddew *Powys* 20 P10
Llanddewi-Brefi *Dyfed* 19 O9
Llanddona *Gwyn* 34 M8
Llanddowror *Dyfed* 18 P7
Llanddulas *Clwyd* 35 M9
Llandegai *Gwyn* 34 M8
Llandeilo *Dyfed* 19 P9
Llandenny *Gwent* 20 P11
Llandewi-Ystradenny *Powys* 27 O10
Llandinam *Powys* 27 O10
Llandissilio *Dyfed* 18 P7
Llandogo *Gwent* 20 P11
Llandovery *Dyfed* 19 P9
Llandre *Dyfed* 26 O8
Llandrillo *Clwyd* 35 N10
Llandrindod Wells *Powys* 20 O10
Llandudno *Gwyn* 35 M9
Llandwrog *Gwyn* 34 M8
Llandybie *Dyfed* 19 P8
Llandyfriog *Dyfed* 19 O8
Llandygwydd *Dyfed* 18 O7
Llandyrnog *Clwyd* 35 M10
Llandyssil *Powys* 27 N10
Llandyssul *Dyfed* 19 O8
Llanegryn *Gwyn* 26 N8
Llanelli *Dyfed* 19 P8
Llanelltyd *Gwyn* 27 N9
Llanelwedd *Powys* 20 O10
Llanenddwyn *Gwyn* 26 N8
Llanengan *Gwyn* 34 N7
Llanerchymedd *Gwyn* 34 M8
Llanerfyl *Powys* 27 N10
Llanfachraeth *Gwyn* 34 M7
Llanfachreth *Gwyn* 27 N9
Llanfaelog *Gwyn* 34 M8
Llanfaethlu *Gwyn* 34 M7
Llanfair *Gwyn* 34 N8
Llanfair Caereinion *Powys* 27 N10
Llanfair Talhaiarn *Clwyd* 35 M9
Llanfairfechan *Gwyn* 34 M8
Llanfairpwll *Gwyn* 34 M8
Llanfarian *Dyfed* 26 O8
Llanfechell *Gwyn* 34 M8
Llanferres *Clwyd* 35 M10
Llanfihangel Llantarnam
Gwent 20 P10

Llanfihangel Tal-y-llyn *Powys* 20 P10
Llanfihangel-ar-arth *Dyfed* 19 O8
Llanfihangel-Ystrad *Dyfed* 19 O8
Llanfrynach *Powys* 20 P10
Llanfyllin *Powys* 27 N10
Llanfynydd *Dyfed* 19 P8
Llanfyrnach *Dyfed* 18 P7
Llangadog *Dyfed* 19 P9
Llangammarch Wells *Powys* 20 O9
Llangarron *Heref/Worcs* 20 P11
Llangattock *Powys* 20 P10
Llangefni *Gwyn* 34 M8
Llangeinor *Mid Glam* 19 P9
Llangeitho *Dyfed* 19 O8
Llangendeirne *Dyfed* 19 P8
Llangennech *Dyfed* 19 P8
Llangoed *Gwyn* 34 M8
Llangollen *Clwyd* 28 N10
Llangorse *Powys* 20 P10
Llangranog *Dyfed* 18 O7
Llangrove *Heref/Worcs* 20 P11
Llangunllo *Powys* 28 O10
Llangurig *Powys* 27 O9
Llangwm *Dyfed* 18 P7
Llangwyryfon *Dyfed* 26 O8
Llangybi *Dyfed* 19 O8
Llangyfelach *W Glam* 19 P9
Llangynidr *Powys* 20 P10
Llangynog *Powys* 35 N10
Llanharan *Mid Glam* 20 P10
Llanharry *Mid Glam* 20 P10
Llanhilleth *Gwent* 20 P10
Llanidloes *Powys* 27 O9
Llanilar *Dyfed* 26 O8
Llanllechid *Gwyn* 34 M8
Llanllyfni *Gwyn* 34 M8
Llanmadoc *W Glam* 19 P8
Llanefydd *Clwyd* 35 M9
Llannon *Dyfed* 19 P8
Llannor *Gwyn* 34 N8
Llanon *Dyfed* 26 O8
Llanpumpsaint *Dyfed* 19 P8
Llanrhaeadr-ym-Mochnant
Clwyd 35 N10
Llanrhidian *W Glam* 19 P8
Llanrhystyd *Dyfed* 26 O8
Llanrian *Dyfed* 18 P6
Llanrug *Gwyn* 34 M8
Llanrwst *Gwyn* 35 M9
Llansadwrn *Dyfed* 19 P9
Llansaint *Dyfed* 19 P8
Llansannan *Clwyd* 35 M9
Llansantffraid *Dyfed* 26 O8
Llansantffraid Glyn Ceiriog
Clwyd 28 N10
Llansantffraid-Glan-Conway
Gwyn 35 M9
Llansantffraid-ym-Mechain
Powys 27 N10
Llansawel *Dyfed* 19 O8
Llansilin *Clwyd* 35 N10
Llanstephan *Dyfed* 19 P8
Llantilio Crosseny *Gwent* 20 P10
Llantrisant *Mid Glam* 20 P10
Llantwit Major *S Glam* 13 Q10
Llanuwchllyn *Gwyn* 35 N9
Llanvetherine *Gwent* 20 P11
Llanwddyn *Powys* 27 N10
Llanwnda *Dyfed* 18 P6
Llanwnnen *Dyfed* 19 O8
Llanwnog *Powys* 27 N10
Llanwrda *Dyfed* 19 P9
Llanwrin *Powys* 27 N9
Llanwrtyd Wells *Powys* 19 O9
Llanyblodwel *Shrops* 27 N10

Llanybri *Dyfed* 19 P8
Llanybydder *Dyfed* 19 O8
Llanymynech *Shrops* 28 N10
Llanystumdwy *Gwyn* 34 N8
Llawhaden *Dyfed* 18 P7
Llay *Clwyd* 36 M10
Llechryd *Dyfed* 18 O7
Lledrod *Dyfed* 27 O9
Llithfaen *Gwyn* 34 N8
Llowes *Powys* 20 O10
Llwydcoed *Mid Glam* 20 P10
Llwyngwril *Gwyn* 26 N8
Llwyn-hendy *Dyfed* 19 P8
Llydbrook *Glos* 21 P11
Llyswen *Powys* 20 O10
Loanhead *Lothian* 51 G10
Loans *S'clyde* 50 G7
Lobain *H'land* 61 C5
Loch Laggan Hotel *H'land* 63 E8
Lochailort *H'land* 61 C5
Lochaline *H'land* 55 E5
Lochans *Dumf/Gal* 44 J6
Locharbriggs *Dumf/Gal* 45 H9
Lochawe *S'clyde* 56 F6
Lochboisdale *W Isles* 60 D2
Lochbuie *S'clyde* 55 F5
Lochdon *S'clyde* 55 F5
Lochearnhead *Central* 57 F8
Locheport *W Isles* 60 C2
Lochgarthside *H'land* 63 D8
Lochgelly *Fife* 51 F10
Lochgilphead *S'clyde* 49 F6
Lochgoilhead *S'clyde* 56 F7
Lochinver *H'land* 69 B6
Lochluichart *H'land* 62 C7
Lochmaben *Dumf/Gal* 45 H10
Lochmaddy *W Isles* 60 C2
Lochportain *W Isles* 60 C2
Lochranza *S'clyde* 49 G6
Lochwinnoch *S'clyde* 50 G7
Lockerbie *Dumf/Gal* 45 H10
Lockton *N Yorks* 43 K15
Loddiswell *Devon* 5 S9
Loddon *Norfolk* 33 N19
Lodsworth *W Sussex* 9 R15
Lofthouse *W Yorks* 37 L14
Lofthouse *N Yorks* 42 K13
Loftus *Clevl'd* 43 J15
Logierait *Tayside* 57 E9
London *Gtr Lon* 17 P16
London Colney *Herts* 17 P16
Long Ashton *Avon* 14 Q11
Long Bennington *Lincs* 31 N15
Long Buckby *Northants* 30 O14
Long Burton *Dorset* 6 R12
Long Clawson *Leics* 30 N15
Long Compton *Warwick* 22 O13
Long Crendon *Bucks* 22 P15
Long Eaton *Notts* 30 N14
Long Hanborough *Oxon* 22 P14
Long Itchington *Warwick* 30 O14
Long Marston *N Yorks* 42 L14
Long Marton *Cumb* 46 J12
Long Melford *Suffolk* 24 O18
Long Newton *Clevl'd* 42 J14
Long Preston *N Yorks* 41 K12
Long Preston *N Yorks* 41 K12
Long Riston *Humber* 43 L16
Long Stratton *Norfolk* 33 O19
Long Sutton *Som'set* 14 Q11
Long Sutton *Lincs* 32 N17
Long Yester *Lothian* 52 G11
Longborough *Glos* 22 P13
Longden *Shrops* 28 N11

Longfield *Kent* 17 Q17
Longford *Glos* 21 P12
Longforgan *Tayside* 58 F10
Longformacus *Borders* 52 G12
Longframlington *Northum* 47 H13
Longhirst *Northum* 47 H13
Longhorsley *Northum* 47 H13
Longhoughton *Northum* 53 H13
Longmanhill *Gramp* 65 C12
Longmoor Camp *Hants* 8 Q15
Longmorn *Gramp* 64 C10
Longniddry *Lothian* 52 G11
Longridge *Lancs* 41 L11
Longside *Gramp* 65 C13
Longton *Staffs* 29 N12
Longtown *Heref/Worcs* 20 P11
Longtown *Cumb* 46 H11
Longwick *Bucks* 16 P15
Loose *Kent* 10 Q18
Loosley Row *Bucks* 16 P15
Lossiemouth *Gramp* 64 C10
Lostwithiel *Cornw'l* 3 S7
Lothmore *H'land* 71 B9
Loudwater *Bucks* 16 P15
Loughborough *Leics* 30 N14
Loughor *W Glam* 19 P8
Loughton *Essex* 17 P17
Louth *Lincs* 39 M16
Low Crosby *Cumb* 46 H11
Low Eggborough *N Yorks* 38 L14
Low Hutton *N Yorks* 43 K15
Low Mill *N Yorks* 42 K15
Low Row *Cumb* 46 J11
Lowca *Cumb* 40 J9
Lowdham *Notts* 30 M14
Lower Cam *Glos* 21 P12
Lower Heyford *Oxon* 22 P14
Lower Killeyan *S'clyde* 48 G4
Lower Largo *Fife* 58 F11
Lower Mayland *Essex* 24 P18
Lower Nazeing *Essex* 17 P17
Lower Shader *W Isles* 66 B4
Lower Slaughter *Glos* 21 P13
Lower Stoke *Kent* 10 Q18
Lowestoft *Suffolk* 33 O20
Loweswater *Cumb* 40 J10
Lowgill *Cumb* 41 K11
Lowick *Northum* 53 G13
Lowick Green *Cumb* 40 K10
Loxton *Avon* 9 Q15
Loxwood *W Sussex* 9 R15
Lubcroy *H'land* 69 C7
Lubenham *Leics* 30 O15
Luccombe *Som'set* 13 Q9
Lucker *Northum* 53 G13
Luckington *Wilts* 21 P12
Ludborough *Lincs* 39 M16
Ludenham *Humber* 38 L15
Ludgershall *Wilts* 15 Q13
Ludgershall *Bucks* 22 P14
Ludgvan *Cornw'l* 2 S6
Ludham *Norfolk* 33 N20
Ludlow *Shrops* 28 O11
Lugwardine *Heref/Worcs* 21 O11
Luib *H'land* 61 D4
Lumphanan *Gramp* 65 D11
Lumsden *Gramp* 64 D11
Lunan *Tayside* 59 E12
Lunanhead *Tayside* 58 E11
Luncarty *Tayside* 58 F10
Lundie *Tayside* 58 E10
Lundin Links *Fife* 58 F11
Luss *S'clyde* 50 F7

Lustleigh *Devon* 5 R9
Luston *Heref/Worcs* 20 O11
Luthermuir *Gramp* 59 E11
Luthrie *Fife* 58 F10
Luton *Beds* 23 P16
Lutterworth *Leics* 30 O14
Lutton *Lincs* 32 N17
Luxulyan *Cornw'l* 3 S7
Lybster *H'land* 70 B10
Lydbury North *Shrops* 28 O11
Lydd *Kent* 11 Q18
Lydd *Kent* 11 R18
Lydden *Kent* 11 Q19
Lydeard St. Lawrence *Som'set* 13 Q10
Lydford *Devon* 4 R8
Lydiate *Mersey* 36 L11
Lydney *Glos* 21 P11
Lyme Regis *Dorset* 6 R11
Lyminge *Kent* 11 Q19
Lymington *Hants* 8 R13
Lymm *Ches* 36 M12
Lympne *Kent* 11 Q19
Lympsham *Som'set* 13 Q10
Lympstone *Devon* 5 R10
Lyndhurst *Hants* 8 R13
Lyneham *Wilts* 21 P13
Lynemouth *Northum* 47 H13
Lyng *Som'set* 13 Q11
Lyng *Norfolk* 33 N19
Lynmouth *Devon* 12 Q9
Lynton *Devon* 12 Q9
Lyonshall *Heref/Worcs* 20 O11
Lytchett Matravers *Dorset* 7 R12
Lyth *H'land* 70 A10
Lytham *Lancs* 36 L10
Lythe *N Yorks* 43 J15

M

Mablethorpe *Lincs* 39 M17
Macclesfield *Ches* 37 M12
Macduff *Gramp* 65 C12
Machynlleth *Powys* 27 N9
Madeley *Shrops* 29 N12
Madeley *Staffs* 29 N12
Madley *Heref/Worcs* 20 O11
Madron *Cornw'l* 2 S6
Maenclochog *Dyfed* 18 P7
Maentwrog *Gwyn* 35 N9
Maerdy *Mid Glam* 20 P10
Maerdy *Clwyd* 35 N10
Maesteg *Mid Glam* 19 P9
Maghull *Mersey* 36 L11
Magor *Gwent* 20 P11
Maiden Bradley *Wilts* 14 Q12
Maiden Newton *Dorset* 6 R11
Maidenhead *Berks* 16 P15
Maidens *S'clyde* 44 H7
Maids Moreton *Bucks* 22 O15
Maidstone *Kent* 10 Q17
Malborough *Devon* 5 S9
Malden *Essex* 24 P18
Malham *N Yorks* 41 K12
Mallaig *H'land* 61 E5
Mallwyd *Gwyn* 27 N9
Malmesbury *Wilts* 21 P12
Malpas *Gwent* 20 P11
Malpas *Ches* 28 M11
Maltby *S Yorks* 38 M14
Maltby le Marsh *Lincs* 39 M17

alton N Yorks	43	K15
alvern Link Heref/Worcs	21	Q12
alvern Wells Heref/Worcs	21	Q12
amble Heref/Worcs	29	O12
ancetter Warwick	30	N13
anchester Gtr Man	37	M12
anea Cambs	32	O17
angotsfield Avon	14	Q11
anning's Heath W Sussex	9	Q16
anningtree Essex	25	P19
anorbier Dyfed	18	P7
ansfield Notts	38	M14
ansfield Woodhouse Notts	38	M14
anton Leics	31	N15
anuden Essex	24	P17
appleton Derby	30	M13
appleton Humber	43	L16
arazion Cornw'l	2	S6
arch Cambs	32	N17
archam Oxon	22	P13
archington Staffs	29	N12
archwood Hants	8	R14
arden Kent	10	Q18
ardy Gwent	20	P10
aredham le Fen Lincs	39	M16
aresfield E Sussex	10	R17
argam W Glam	19	P9
argate Kent	11	Q19
argnaheglish S'clyde	49	G6
arham Norfolk	32	N18
arhamchurch Cornw'l	4	R7
ariveg W Isles	67	B4
ark Som'set	13	Q11
arket Bosworth Leics	30	N14
arket Deeping Lincs	31	N16
arket Drayton Shrops	29	N12
arket Harborough Leics	30	O15
arket Lavington Wilts	15	Q13
arket Rasen Lincs	39	M16
arket Weighton Humber	43	L15
arkfield Leics	30	N14
arkinch Fife	58	F10
arkington N Yorks	42	K13
arkyate Herts	24	P18
arlborough Wilts	15	Q13
arloes Dyfed	18	P6
arlow Bucks	16	P15
arnhull Dorset	6	R12
arnoch Gramp	65	C11
arple Gtr Man	37	M12
arsh Gibbon Bucks	22	P14
arsham Norfolk	33	N19
arshchapel Lincs	39	M17
arshfield Avon	14	Q11
arshfield Gwent	20	P10
arshwood Dorset	6	R11
arske N Yorks	41	K13
arske-by-the-Sea Clevl'd	42	J14
arston Oxon	22	P14
arston Ches	37	M12
arston Magna Som'set	6	R11
arsworth Bucks	16	P15
artham Norfolk	33	N20
artin Lincs	39	M16
artin Hants	7	R13
artlesham Suffolk	25	O19
artletwy Dyfed	18	P7
artley Heref/Worcs	21	O12
artock Som'set	6	R11
arton Warwick	30	O14
arton Ches	37	M12
arton Lincs	38	M15
arton Clevl'd	42	J14
Mary Tavy Devon	4	R8
Marybank H'land	63	C7
Maryburgh H'land	63	C8
Maryculter Gramp	65	D12
Marykirk Gramp	59	E11
Marypark Gramp	64	D10
Maryport Cumb	45	J10
Masham N Yorks	42	K13
Mastin Moor Derby	38	M14
Matfen Northum	47	H13
Mathry Dyfed	18	P6
Matlock Derby	37	M13
Matlock Bath Derby	37	M13
Mattishall Norfolk	33	N19
Mauchline S'clyde	50	G8
Maud Gramp	65	C12
Maughold I of Man	72	K8
Maulden Beds	23	O16
Mawnan Smith Cornw'l	2	S6
Maxwellheugh Borders	52	G12
Maxwelltown Dumf/Gal	45	H9
Maybole S'clyde	44	H7
Mayfield E Sussex	10	Q17
Mayfield Staffs	29	M13
Mealsgate Cumb	45	J10
Meare Som'set	14	Q11
Measham Leics	30	N13
Medbourne Leics	31	N15
Medstead Hants	8	Q14
Meeth Devon	4	R8
Meidrim Dyfed	19	P8
Meifod Powys	27	N10
Meigle Tayside	58	E10
Meikle Wartle Gramp	65	D12
Meillteyrn Gwyn	34	N7
Melbost W Isles	66	B4
Melbourn Cambs	24	O17
Melbourne Derby	30	N14
Melbourne Humber	43	L15
Meldreth Cambs	24	O17
Meliden Clwyd	35	M10
Melkridge Northum	46	J12
Melksham Wilts	14	Q12
Melling Lancs	41	K11
Mellis Suffolk	33	O19
Mellon Charles H'land	69	C5
Mellor Lancs	36	L11
Melmerby N Yorks	42	K14
Melmerby Cumb	46	J11
Melrose Borders	52	G11
Melsonby N Yorks	42	K13
Meltham W Yorks	37	L13
Meltheringham Lincs	39	M16
Melton Constable Norfolk	33	N19
Melton Mowbray Leics	31	N15
Melvaig H'land	69	C5
Melvich H'land	70	A9
Memsie Gramp	65	C12
Menai Bridge Gwyn	34	M8
Mendlesham Suffolk	25	O19
Menheniot Cornw'l	4	S8
Menstrie Central	51	F9
Meopham Kent	17	Q17
Mepal Cambs	32	O17
Mere Wilts	14	Q12
Mere Ches	36	M12
Meriden W Midlands	30	O13
Merriott Som'set	6	R11
Merrow Surrey	16	Q15
Mersham Kent	11	Q18
Merstham Surrey	17	Q16
Merthyr Tydfil Mid Glam	20	P10
Merthyr Vale Mid Glam	20	P10
Merton Devon	12	R8
Merton Gtr Lon	17	Q16
Meshaw Devon	12	R9
Messingham Humber	38	L15
Metfield Suffolk	33	O19
Methil Fife	58	F10
Methley W Yorks	38	L14
Methlick Gramp	65	D12
Methven Tayside	58	F10
Methwold Norfolk	32	N18
Mevagissey Cornw'l	3	S7
Mexborough S Yorks	38	M14
Mey H'land	70	A10
Miavaig W Isles	66	B3
Michael Muir Gramp	65	D12
Micheldever Hants	15	Q14
Micklefield W Yorks	38	L14
Mickleover Derby	30	N13
Mickleton Glos	22	O13
Mickleton Durham	41	J12
Middle Barton Oxon	22	P14
Middle Rasen Lincs	39	M16
Middle Wallop Hants	15	Q13
Middlebie Dumf/Gal	45	H10
Middleham N Yorks	42	K13
Middlemarsh Dorset	6	R12
Middlesbrough Clevl'd	42	J14
Middlestown W Yorks	37	L13
Middleton Suffolk	25	O20
Middleton Gtr Man	37	L12
Middleton Derby	37	M13
Middleton Cumb	40	K11
Middleton Lancs	41	K11
Middleton Northum	47	H13
Middleton S'clyde	54	F3
Middleton Cheney Northants	22	O14
Middleton in Teesdale Durham	47	J12
Middleton on the Wolds Humber	43	L15
Middleton St. George Durham	42	J14
Middleton Tyas N Yorks	42	K13
Middleton-on-Sea W Sussex	9	R15
Middlewich Ches	36	M12
Middlezoy Som'set	13	Q11
Midhurst W Sussex	9	R15
Midlem Borders	52	G11
Midsomer Norton Avon	14	Q12
Midtown Brae H'land	69	C5
Milborne Port Som'set	6	R12
Milborne St. Andrew Dorset	6	R12
Milbourne Northum	47	H13
Milburn Cumb	46	J11
Mildenhall Suffolk	32	O17
Milfield Northum	53	G12
Milford Surrey	16	Q15
Milford Derby	30	M14
Milford Haven Dyfed	18	P6
Milford-on-Sea Hants	8	R13
Millbrook Cornw'l	4	S8
Millers Dale Derby	37	M13
Millhouse S'clyde	49	G6
Millom Cumb	40	K10
Millport S'clyde	50	G7
Milltown H'land	62	C7
Milltown Gramp	65	C11
Milnathort Tayside	58	F10
Milngavie S'clyde	50	G8
Milnrow Gtr Man	37	L12
Milnthorpe Cumb	40	K11
Milton Northants	22	O15

Milton *Cambs*	24	O17
Milton *S'clyde*	44	H7
Milton *H'land*	63	D8
Milton *H'land*	71	C8
Milton Abbas *Dorset*	6	R12
Milton Abbot *Devon*	6	Q14
Milton Ernest *Beds*	23	O15
Milton Keynes *Bucks*	23	O15
Milton of Campsie *S'clyde*	50	G8
Milton under Wychwood *Oxon*	22	P13
Milverton *Som'set*	13	Q10
Milwich *Staffs*	29	N12
Minchinhampton *Glos*	21	P12
Minehead *Som'set*	13	Q10
Minera *Clwyd*	36	M10
Minety *Wilts*	21	P13
Minishant *S'clyde*	50	H7
Minnigaff *Dumf/Gal*	44	J8
Minskip *N Yorks*	42	K14
Minster *Kent*	11	Q19
Minsterley *Shrops*	28	N11
Minster-on-Sea *Kent*	10	Q18
Minsterworth *Glos*	21	P12
Mintlaw *Gramp*	65	C13
Minto *Borders*	52	H11
Mirfield *W Yorks*	37	L13
Miserden *Glos*	21	P12
Misterton *Notts*	38	M15
Misterton *Som'set*	6	R11
Mistley *Essex*	25	P19
Mitcheldean *Glos*	21	P12
Mitchell *Cornw'l*	2	S6
Mobberley *Ches*	37	M12
Modbury *Devon*	4	S9
Moelfre *Gwyn*	34	M8
Moffat *Dumf/Gal*	45	H10
Moira *Dumf/Gal*	45	H10
Mold *Clwyd*	36	M10
Molescroft *Humber*	43	L16
Mollington *Oxon*	22	O14
Monaive *Dumf/Gal*	45	H9
Monifieth *Tayside*	58	F11
Monikie *Tayside*	58	E11
Monk Fryston *N Yorks*	38	L14
Monkland *Heref/Worcs*	20	O11
Monkleigh *Devon*	12	R8
Monks Eleigh *Suffolk*	24	O18
Monks Kirby *Warwick*	30	O14
Monkton *Kent*	11	Q19
Monkton *S'clyde*	50	G7
Monmouth *Gwent*	20	P11
Montacute *Som'set*	6	R11
Montgarrie *Gramp*	65	D11
Montgomery *Powys*	28	N10
Montrose *Tayside*	59	E12
Monyash *Derby*	37	M13
Monymusk *Gramp*	65	D11
Monzie *Tayside*	57	F9
Moor Ends *S Yorks*	38	L15
Moore *Ches*	36	M11
Moorlinch *Som'set*	13	Q11
Moorsholm *Clevl'd*	42	J15
Morchard Bishop *Devon*	5	R9
Morcombelake *Dorset*	6	R11
Morcott *Leics*	31	N15
Morda *Shrops*	28	N10
Mordiford *Heref/Worcs*	21	O11
Morebath *Devon*	13	Q10
Morebattle *Borders*	52	G12
Morecambe *Lancs*	40	K11
Moreton *Mersey*	36	M10
Moreton *Dorset*	6	R12
Moretonhampstead *Devon*	5	R9
Moreton-in-Marsh *Glos*	22	P13

Morfa Nefyn *Gwyn*	34	N7
Morland *Cumb*	41	J11
Morley *W Yorks*	37	L13
Morpeth *Northum*	47	H13
Mortehoe *Devon*	12	Q8
Mortimer Common *Berks*	16	Q14
Morton *Lincs*	31	N16
Morton *Derby*	38	M14
Morton *Lincs*	38	M15
Morville *Shrops*	29	N11
Mosbrough *Derby*	38	M14
Moss *Clwyd*	36	M10
Mossat *Gramp*	64	D11
Mossblown *S'clyde*	50	H7
Mossley *Gtr Man*	37	L12
Mosstodloch *Gramp*	64	C10
Mosterton *Dorset*	6	R11
Mostyn *Clwyd*	35	M10
Motcombe *Dorset*	14	Q12
Motherwell *S'clyde*	51	G9
Mottisfont *Hants*	15	Q13
Moulin *Tayside*	57	E9
Moulsford *Oxon*	22	P14
Moulton *Suffolk*	24	O17
Moulton *Lincs*	31	N16
Moulton *Northants*	31	O15
Moulton *Ches*	36	M11
Moulton *N Yorks*	42	K13
Mount Hawke *Cornw'l*	2	S6
Mountain Ash *Mid Glam*	19	P10
Mountnessing *Essex*	17	P17
Mountsorrel *Leics*	30	N14
Mousehole *Cornw'l*	2	S5
Mouswald *Dumf/Gal*	45	H10
Moy *H'land*	63	D8
Moylgrove *Dyfed*	18	O7
Muasdale *S'clyde*	49	G5
Much Dewchurch *Heref/Worcs*	20	P11
Much Hadham *Herts*	24	P17
Much Hoole *Lancs*	36	L11
Much Marcle *Glos*	21	P12
Much Wenlock *Shrops*	29	N11
Muchalls *Gramp*	65	D12
Mucklestone *Staffs*	29	N12
Muddiford *Devon*	12	Q8
Mudford *Som'set*	6	R11
Muir of Fowlis *Gramp*	64	D11
Muir of Ord *H'land*	63	C8
Muirdrum *Tayside*	59	E11
Muirhead *Tayside*	58	F10
Muirkirk *S'clyde*	50	G8
Muker *N Yorks*	41	K12
Mulbarton *Norfolk*	33	N19
Mulben *Gramp*	64	C10
Mullaigvaig *H'land*	61	D5
Mullion *Cornw'l*	2	S6
Mumbles *W Glam*	19	P9
Mumby *Lincs*	39	M17
Mundesley *Norfolk*	33	N19
Mundford *Norfolk*	32	N18
Munlochy *H'land*	63	C8
Munslow *Shrops*	28	O11
Murton *Durham*	47	J14
Musbury *Devon*	5	R10
Musselburgh *Lothian*	51	G10
Muston *N Yorks*	43	K16
Muthill *Tayside*	57	F9
Mybster *H'land*	70	B10
Myddfai *Dyfed*	19	P9
Myddle *Shrops*	28	N11
Mydroilyn *Dyfed*	19	O8
Mylor Bridge *Cornw'l*	2	S6
Mytholmroyd *W Yorks*	37	L13

N

Naburn *N Yorks*	42	L
Nacton *Suffolk*	25	O
Nafferton *Humber*	43	K
Nailsea *Avon*	14	Q
Nailsworth *Glos*	21	P
Nairn *H'land*	63	
Nantgarw *Mid Glam*	20	P
Nantlle *Gwyn*	34	N
Nantwich *Ches*	36	M
Nantyglo *Gwent*	20	P
Napton on the Hill *Warwick*	22	O
Narberth *Dyfed*	18	
Narborough *Leics*	30	N
Naseby *Northants*	30	O
Nash *Bucks*	23	C
Nassington *Northants*	31	N
Nateby *Cumb*	41	K
Natland *Cumb*	41	K
Naunton *Glos*	21	P
Navenby *Lincs*	38	M
Nawton *N Yorks*	42	K
Nayland *Suffolk*	24	P
Neath *W Glam*	19	
Necton *Norfolk*	32	N
Needham Market *Suffolk*	25	O
Nefyn *Gwyn*	34	
Neilston *S'clyde*	50	
Nelson *Lancs*	41	L
Nenthead *Cumb*	46	J
Nenthorn *Borders*	52	G
Nesscliff *Shrops*	28	N
Neston *Ches*	36	M
Nether Broughton *Leics*	30	N
Nether Langwith *Notts*	38	M
Nether Poppleton *N Yorks*	42	L
Nether Stowey *Som'set*	13	Q
Netheravon *Wilts*	15	Q
Netherbury *Dorset*	6	R
Netherthird *S'clyde*	50	
Netherton *Northum*	47	H
Netherwitton *Northum*	47	H
Nethy Bridge *H'land*	64	
Netley *Hants*	8	R
Netley Marsh *Hants*	16	P
Nettlebed *Oxon*	16	P
Nettleham *Lincs*	39	M
Nevern *Dyfed*	18	
New Abbey *Dumf/Gal*	45	
New Aberdour *Gramp*	65	C
New Alresford *Hants*	8	Q
New Alyth *Tayside*	58	E
New Blyth *Gramp*	65	C
New Brighton *Mersey*	36	M
New Buckenham *Norfolk*	33	C
New Clipstone *Notts*	38	M
New Coylton *S'clyde*	50	
New Cumnock *S'clyde*	50	
New Deer *Gramp*	65	C
New Donnington *Shrops*	29	N
New Earswick *N Yorks*	42	L
New Galloway *Dumf/Gal*	45	
New Hey *Gtr Man*	37	L
New Holland *Humber*	39	L
New Hutton *Cumb*	41	K
New Leeds *Gramp*	65	C
New Luce *Dumf/Gal*	44	
New Mill *W Yorks*	37	L
New Mills *Derby*	37	M
New Pitsligo *Gramp*	65	C

ew Quay *Dyfed* 19 O8
ew Radnor *Powys* 20 O10
ew Romney *Kent* 11 R18
ew Sauchie *Central* 51 F9
ew Selma *S'clyde* 55 F6
ew Tredegar *Mid Glam* 20 P10
ewark-on-Trent *Notts* 38 M15
ewbiggin *Cumb* 46 J11
ewbiggin *Cumb* 46 J11
ewbiggin *Durham* 47 J12
ewbiggin-by-the-Sea *Northum* 47 H13
ewbigging *S'clyde* 51 G9
ewbigging *Tayside* 58 E11
ewbiggin-on-Lune *Cumb* 41 K12
ewbold Verdon *Leics* 30 N14
ewborough *Staffs* 30 N13
ewborough *Cambs* 31 N16
ewborough *Gwyn* 34 M8
ewbourn *Suffolk* 25 O19
ewbridge *Gwent* 20 P10
ewbridge on Wye *Powys* 20 O10
ewbrough *Northum* 46 H12
ewburgh *Fife* 58 F10
ewburgh *Grampian* 65 D12
ewburn *Tyne/Wear* 47 J13
ewbury *Berks* 15 Q14
ewby *Cumb* 41 J11
ewby *N Yorks* 41 K12
ewby *N Yorks* 43 K16
ewby Bridge *Cumb* 40 K11
ewby Wiske *N Yorks* 42 K14
ewcastle *Shrops* 28 O13
ewcastle *Tyne/Wear* 47 J13
ewcastle Emlyn *Dyfed* 19 O8
ewcastleton *Borders* 46 H11
ewcastle-under-Lyme *Staffs* 29 M12
ewchurch *Powys* 20 O10
ewdigate *Surrey* 17 Q16
ewent *Glos* 21 P12
ewhall *Ches* 29 M11
ewhall *Derby* 30 N13
ewhallpoint *H'land* 63 C8
ewham *Gtr Lon* 17 P17
ewhaven *E Sussex* 9 R17
ewholm *N Yorks* 43 K15
ewick *E Sussex* 10 R17
ewington *Kent* 10 Q18
ewkirk *Grampian* 64 D11
ewland *Glos* 21 P11
ewlyn *Cornw'l* 2 S5
ewlyn East *Cornw'l* 2 S6
ewmachar *Grampian* 65 D12
ewmains *S'clyde* 51 G9
ewmarket *Suffolk* 24 O17
ewmarket *W Isles* 66 B4
ewmill *Borders* 46 H11
ewmill *Grampian* 64 C11
ewmilns *S'clyde* 50 G8
ewnham *Kent* 10 Q18
ewnham *Glos* 21 P12
ewnham *Heref/Worcs* 29 O11
ewport *Dyfed* 18 O7
ewport *Gwent* 20 P11
ewport *Essex* 24 O17
ewport *Shrops* 29 N12
ewport *H'land* 70 B10
ewport *I of Wight* 8 R14
ewport Pagnell *Bucks* 23 O15
ewport-on-Tay *Fife* 58 F11
ewquay *Cornw'l* 2 S6

Newsham *N Yorks* 41 K13
Newstead *Notts* 38 M14
Newton *Mid Glam* 19 Q9
Newton *Cambs* 32 N17
Newton *Lancs* 41 L12
Newton *Dumf/Gal* 45 H10
Newton *Cumb* 45 J10
Newton Abbot *Devon* 5 R9
Newton Arlosh *Cumb* 45 J10
Newton Aycliffe *Durham* 47 J13
Newton Ferrers *Devon* 4 S8
Newton Mearns *S'clyde* 50 G8
Newton on the Moor *Northum* 47 H13
Newton Poppleford *Devon* 5 R10
Newton Reigny *Cumb* 46 J11
Newton St. Cyres *Devon* 5 R9
Newton Stewart *Dumf/Gal* 45 J8
Newton-by-the-Sea *Northum* 53 G13
Newtongrange *Lothian* 52 G10
Newton-le-Willows *Mersey* 36 M11
Newtonmore *H'land* 63 D8
Newton-on-Trent *Lincs* 38 M15
Newton-upon-Ouse *N Yorks* 42 K14
Newtown *Powys* 27 N10
Newtown St. Boswells *Borders* 52 G11
Newtyle *Tayside* 58 E10
Neyland *Dyfed* 18 P7
Nigg *Gramp* 65 D12
Nigg *H'land* 71 C9
Nine Mile Burr *Lothian* 51 G10
Ninfield *E Sussex* 10 R17
Niton *I of Wight* 8 R14
Narborough *Norfolk* 32 N18
Nocton *Lincs* 39 M16
Nolton *Dyfed* 18 P6
Nonington *Kent* 11 Q19
Nordelph *Norfolk* 32 N17
Norham *Northum* 53 G12
Normanby *N Yorks* 43 K15
Normandy *Surrey* 16 Q15
Normanton *W Yorks* 37 L14
Normanton on Trent *Notts* 38 M15
North Ballachulish *H'land* 56 E6
North Berwick *Lothian* 52 F11
North Boisdale *W Isles* 60 D2
North Bovey *Devon* 5 R9
North Bradley *Wilts* 14 Q12
North Brentor *Devon* 4 R8
North Burton *Humber* 43 K16
North Cadbury *Som'set* 14 Q11
North Cave *Humber* 38 L15
North Cerney *Glos* 21 P13
North Charlton *Northum* 53 H13
North Cheriton *Som'set* 14 Q12
North Creake *Norfolk* 32 N18
North Curry *Som'set* 13 Q11
North Dalton *Humber* 43 L15
North Duffield *N Yorks* 42 L15
North Elmham *Norfolk* 33 N18
North Erradale *H'land* 69 C5
North Ferriby *Humber* 38 L15
North Frodingham *Humber* 43 L16
North Grimston *N Yorks* 43 K15
North Hill *Cornw'l* 4 R8
North Hinksey *Oxon* 22 P14
North Hykeham *Lincs* 38 M15
North Kelsey *Lincs* 39 L16
North Kelsey *Lincs* 39 M16
North Kessock *H'land* 63 C8
North Kyme *Lincs* 39 M16

North Leigh *Oxon* 22 P14
North Lopham *Norfolk* 33 O18
North Luffenham *Leics* 31 N15
North Marston *Bucks* 23 P15
North Middleton *Lothian* 52 G10
North Molton *Devon* 12 Q9
North Muskham *Notts* 38 M15
North Newbald *Humber* 38 L15
North Petherton *Som'set* 13 Q10
North Queensferry *Fife* 51 F10
North Scarle *Lincs* 38 M15
North Shawbost *W Isles* 66 B3
North Shields *Tyne/Wear* 47 H14
North Somercotes *Lincs* 39 M17
North Stainley *N Yorks* 42 K13
North Sunderland *Northum* 53 G13
North Tawton *Devon* 4 R9
North Thoresby *Lincs* 39 M16
North Tidworth *Wilts* 15 Q13
North Tolsta *W Isles* 66 B4
North Walsham *Norfolk* 33 N19
North Waltham *Hants* 15 Q14
North Weald Basset *Essex* 17 P17
North Wheatley *Notts* 38 M15
North Willingham *Lincs* 39 M16
North Wingfield *Derby* 37 M14
Northallerton *N Yorks* 42 K14
Northam *Devon* 12 Q8
Northampton *Northants* 23 O15
Northbourne *Kent* 11 Q19
Northchapel *W Sussex* 9 Q15
Northfleet *Kent* 17 Q17
Northiam *E Sussex* 10 R18
Northleach *Glos* 21 P13
Northlew *Devon* 4 R8
Northmuir *Tayside* 58 E11
Northop *Clwyd* 35 M10
Northton *W Isles* 67 C2
Northwich *Ches* 36 M11
Northwold *Norfolk* 32 N18
Norton *Kent* 11 Q19
Norton *Powys* 28 O10
Norton *Glos* 21 P13
Norton *Suffolk* 32 O18
Norton *N Yorks* 43 K15
Norton Fitzwarren *Som'set* 13 Q10
Norton in Hales *Shrops* 29 N12
Norton St. Philip *Som'set* 14 Q12
Norwich *Norfolk* 33 N19
Noss Mayo *Devon* 4 S8
Nottingham *Notts* 30 N14
Nuneaton *Warwick* 30 N14
Nunney *Som'set* 14 Q12
Nunnington *N Yorks* 42 K15
Nunthorpe *Clevl'd* 42 J14
Nuthall *Notts* 30 N14
Nybster *H'land* 70 A10

O

Oadby *Leics* 30 N14
Oakenclough *Lancs* 41 L11
Oakengates *Shrops* 29 N12
Oakford *Devon* 13 R9
Oakham *Leics* 31 N15
Oakhill *Som'set* 14 Q11
Oakington *Cambs* 24 O17
Oakley *Hants* 15 Q14
Oakley *Bucks* 22 P14
Oakley *Beds* 23 O15
Oakley *Fife* 51 F9

Oakworth W Yorks 41 L13
Oathlaw Tayside 58 E11
Oban S'clyde 55 F6
Ockley Surrey 16 Q16
Odcombe Som'set 6 R11
Odiham Hants 16 Q15
Offord Cambs 31 O16
Ogbourne St. George Wilts 15 Q13
Ogmore Vale Mid Glam 20 P9
Ogmore-by-Sea Mid Glam 19 Q9
Okeford Fitzpaine Dorset 6 R12
Okehampton Devon 4 R8
Old Bolingbroke Lincs 39 M17
Old Buckenham Norfolk 33 O19
Old Burghclere Hants 15 Q14
Old Cleeve Som'set 13 Q10
Old Dailly S'clyde 44 H7
Old Dalby Leics 30 N14
Old Deer Gramp 65 C12
Old Fletton Cambs 31 N16
Old Kilpatrick S'clyde 50 G7
Old Leake Lincs 32 M17
Old Mawbray Cumb 45 J10
Old Rayne Gramp 65 D11
Old Windsor Berks 16 Q15
Oldbury-upon-Severn Avon 21 P11
Oldcoates Notts 38 M14
Oldham Gtr Man 37 L12
Oldhamstocks Lothian 52 G12
Oldmeldrum Gramp 65 D12
Olgrinmore H'land 70 B9
Ollerton Ches 37 M12
Ollerton Notts 38 M15
Olney Bucks 23 O15
Olveston Avon 14 P11
Ombersley Heref/Worcs 29 O12
Onchan I of Man 72 K8
O'Neil Gramp 65 D11
Onich H'land 56 E6
Onllwyn W Glam 19 P9
Opinan H'land 69 C5
Ord H'land 61 D5
Ord of Caithness H'land 71 B9
Ordhead Gramp 65 D11
Ordie Gramp 64 D11
Orford Suffolk 25 O20
Orleton Heref/Worcs 28 O11
Ormesby Clevl'd 42 J14
Ormesby St. Margaret Norfolk 33 N20
Ormskirk Lancs 36 L11
Orton Cumb 41 K11
Orwell Cambs 24 O16
Osbournby Lincs 31 N16
Osmington Dorset 6 R12
Osmotherley N Yorks 42 K14
Ossett W Yorks 37 L13
Oswaldkirk N Yorks 42 K14
Oswaldtwistle Lancs 36 L12
Oswestry Shrops 28 N10
Otford Kent 17 Q17
Othery Som'set 13 Q11
Otley Suffolk 25 O19
Otley W Yorks 42 L13
Otter Ferry S'clyde 49 F6
Otterbourne Hants 15 Q14
Otterburn Northum 46 H12
Otterburn Camp Northum 46 H12
Otterton Devon 5 R10
Ottery St. Mary Devon 5 R10
Ottringham Humber 39 L16
Oughtibridge S Yorks 37 M13
Oulton Staffs 29 N12

Oulton Suffolk 33 N20
Oulton Cumb 45 J10
Oundle Northants 31 O16
Ousby Cumb 46 J11
Ousdale H'land 71 B9
Outhgill Cumb 41 K12
Outwell Norfolk 32 N17
Over Cambs 32 O17
Over Wallop Hants 15 Q13
Overseal Derby 30 N13
Overstrand Norfolk 33 N19
Overton Hants 15 Q14
Overton Clwyd 28 N11
Overton Lancs 40 K11
Overy Staithe Norfolk 32 N18
Ovingham Northum 47 J13
Ovington Northum 47 J13
Owermoigne Dorset 6 R12
Owston Ferry Humber 38 M15
Oxenhope W Yorks 37 L13
Oxford Oxon 22 P14
Oxnam Borders 46 H12
Oxted Surrey 17 Q16
Oxton Notts 38 M14
Oxton Borders 52 G11
Oykel Bridge H'land 69 C7
Oyne Gramp 65 D11

P

Padanaram Tayside 58 E11
Padbury Bucks 22 P15
Paddock Wood Kent 17 Q17
Padstow Cornw'l 3 R7
Pagham W Sussex 9 R15
Paignton Devon 5 S9
Pailton Warwick 30 O14
Painscastle Powys 20 O10
Painshawfield Northum 47 J13
Painswick Glos 21 P12
Paisley S'clyde 50 G8
Palgrave Suffolk 33 O19
Palnackie Dumf/Gal 45 J9
Pandy Gwent 20 P11
Pangbourne Berks 15 Q14
Pant Shrops 28 N10
Papworth Everard Cambs 23 O16
Par Cornw'l 3 S7
Parbold Lancs 36 L11
Parham Suffolk 25 O19
Park Gramp 65 D12
Parkham Devon 12 R8
Parracombe Devon 12 Q9
Parson Drove Cambs 32 N17
Partney Lincs 39 M17
Parton Cumb 40 J9
Parton Dumf/Gal 45 H8
Partridge Green W Sussex 16 Q15
Parwich Derby 37 M13
Patcham E Sussex 9 R16
Pateley Bridge N Yorks 42 K13
Patna S'clyde 44 H8
Patrick Brompton N Yorks 42 K13
Patrick I of Man 72 K7
Patrington Humber 39 L16
Patterdale Cumb 40 J11
Paulerspury Northants 22 O15
Paull Humber 39 L16
Paulton Avon 14 Q11
Pawlett Som'set 13 Q11

Payhembury Devon 5 R10
Peacehaven E Sussex 9 R16
Peak Forest Derby 37 M13
Peakirk Cambs 31 N16
Peasedown St. John Avon 14 Q11
Peasenhall Suffolk 33 O19
Peaslake Surrey 16 Q16
Peat Inn Fife 58 F11
Pebworth Heref/Worcs 21 O12
Pecket Well W Yorks 37 L13
Peebles Borders 52 G10
Peel I of Man 72 K7
Pegswood Northum 47 H13
Pelynt Cornw'l 3 S7
Pemberton Gtr Man 36 L11
Pembrey Dyfed 19 P8
Pembridge Heref/Worcs 20 O10
Pembroke Dyfed 18 P7
Pembroke Dock Dyfed 18 P7
Pembury Kent 17 Q17
Pen y cae Clwyd 28 N10
Pen y Groes Gwyn 34 M9
Penally Dyfed 18 P7
Penarth S Glam 13 Q10
Pencader Dyfed 19 P8
Pencaitland Lothian 52 G11
Penclawdd W Glam 19 P8
Pencoed Mid Glam 20 P9
Pencombe Heref/Worcs 21 O11
Pendeen Cornw'l 2 S5
Pendine Dyfed 18 P7
Pendle Hill Lancs 41 L12
Penegoes Powys 27 N9
Penicuik Lothian 51 G10
Penistone S Yorks 37 L13
Penkridge Staffs 29 N12
Penmachno Gwyn 35 M9
Penmaenmawr Gwyn 35 M9
Penn Bucks 16 P15
Pennal Gwyn 27 N9
Pennan Gramp 65 C12
Penpont Dumf/Gal 45 H9
Penrhyndeudraeth Gwyn 34 N9
Penrith Cumb 46 J11
Penruddock Cumb 46 J11
Penryn Cornw'l 2 S6
Pensarn Clwyd 35 M10
Pensford Avon 14 Q11
Penshaw Tyne/Wear 47 J13
Penshurst Kent 17 Q17
Pensilva Cornw'l 4 R7
Pentire Cornw'l 2 S6
Pentraeth Gwyn 34 M9
Pentre Mid Glam 20 P9
Pentrefoelas Clwyd 35 M10
Pentyrch Mid Glam 20 P9
Penwithick Stents Cornw'l 3 S7
Penybont Powys 27 O10
Pen-y-bont-fawr Powys 35 N10
Pen-y-Groes Dyfed 19 P8
Penysarn Gwyn 34 M9
Penzance Cornw'l 2 S5
Peopleton Heref/Worcs 21 O12
Perranporth Cornw'l 2 S6
Perranuthnoe Cornw'l 2 S6
Perranzabuloe Cornw'l 2 S6
Pershore Heref/Worcs 21 O12
Perth Tayside 58 F10
Peter Tavy Devon 4 R8
Peterborough Cambs 31 N16
Peterchurch Heref/Worcs 20 O10
Peterhead Gramp 65 C13
Peterlee Durham 47 J13

etersfield Hants	8	Q15
eterstow Heref/Worcs	21	P11
etham Kent	11	Q19
etrockstow Devon	4	R8
ett E Sussex	10	R18
etworth W Sussex	9	R15
evensey E Sussex	10	R17
evensey Bay E Sussex	10	R17
ewsey Wilts	15	Q13
ickering N Yorks	43	K15
ickhill N Yorks	42	K14
iddlehinton Dorset	6	R12
iddletrenthide Dorset	6	R12
iercebridge Durham	42	J13
illing Lancs	40	L11
ilsley Derby	37	M13
ilsley Derby	38	M14
ilton Som'set	14	Q11
imperne Dorset	7	R12
inchbeck Lincs	31	N16
inhoe Devon	5	R10
inwherry S'clyde	44	H7
inxton Derby	38	M14
irbright Surrey	16	Q15
immill S'clyde	49	G6
irton Herts	23	P16
itcairngreen Tayside	58	F9
itlessie Fife	58	F10
itlochry Tayside	57	E9
itmedden Gramp	65	D12
itney Som'set	13	Q11
itscottie Fife	58	F11
ittenweem Fife	59	F11
itton Wilts	15	Q13
laistow W Sussex	9	Q15
laxtol Kent	17	Q17
laying Place Cornw'l	2	S6
leasington Lancs	36	L11
leasley Derby	38	M14
lenmeller Northum	46	J12
lockton H'land	62	D5
loughfield Heref/Worcs	20	O11
luckley Kent	10	Q18
lumbland Cumb	45	J10
lumpton Wall Cumb	46	J11
lungar Leics	31	N15
lymouth Devon	4	S8
lympton Devon	4	S8
lymstock Devon	4	S8
lymtree Devon	5	R10
ocklington Humber	43	L15
olain H'land	3	S7
olbain H'land	69	B6
olebrook Northants	31	O16
olegate E Sussex	10	R17
olesworth Warwick	30	N13
olglass H'land	69	B6
olpero Cornw'l	3	S7
olwarth Borders	52	G12
olzeath Cornw'l	3	R7
ondersbridge Cambs	31	N16
onsanooth Cornw'l	2	S6
ont Henry Dyfed	19	P8
ont Robert Powys	27	N10
ont Yates Dyfed	19	P8
ontardawe W Glam	19	P9
ontardulais W Glam	19	P8
ontefract N Yorks	38	L14
onteland Northum	47	H13
onterwyd Dyfed	27	O9
ontesbury Shrops	28	N11
ontfadog Clwyd	28	N10

Pont-llan-fraith Gwent	20	P10
Pontnewydd Gwent	20	P10
Pontrhydfendigard Dyfed	27	O9
Pontrilas Heref/Worcs	20	P11
Pontyberem Dyfed	19	P8
Pont-y-clun Mid Glam	20	P10
Pontycymmer Mid Glam	19	P9
Pontypool Gwent	20	P10
Pontypridd Mid Glam	20	P10
Pool W Yorks	42	L13
Pool of Muckhart Central	58	F9
Poole Dorset	7	R13
Poolewe H'land	69	C5
Pooley Bridge Cumb	46	J11
Porlock Som'set	13	Q9
Porlock Weir Som'set	12	Q9
Port Appin S'clyde	55	E6
Port Askaig S'clyde	48	G4
Port Bannatyne S'clyde	49	G6
Port Carlisle Cumb	45	J10
Port Charlotte S'clyde	48	G4
Port Dinorwic Gwyn	34	M8
Port Ellen S'clyde	48	G4
Port Elphinstone Gramp	65	D12
Port Errol Gramp	65	D13
Port Eynon W Glam	19	P8
Port Glasgow S'clyde	50	G7
Port Henderson H'land	69	C5
Port Isaac Cornw'l	3	R7
Port Logan Dumf/Gal	44	J7
Port na Long H'land	60	D4
Port of Ness W Isles	66	B4
Port St. Mary I of Man	72	K7
Port Talbot W Glam	19	P9
Port William Dumf/Gal	44	J7
Portbury Avon	14	Q11
Portchester Hants	8	R14
Portesham Dorset	6	R11
Portessie Gramp	64	C11
Portgordon Gramp	64	C10
Portgower H'land	71	B9
Porth Mid Glam	20	P10
Porthcawl Mid Glam	19	Q9
Porthcurno Cornw'l	2	S5
Porthleven Cornw'l	2	S6
Porthmadog Gwyn	34	N8
Porthscatho Cornw'l	3	S7
Porthtowan Cornw'l	2	S6
Porthyrryd Dyfed	19	P8
Portinnisherrich S'clyde	56	F6
Portishead Avon	14	Q11
Portknockie Gramp	64	C11
Portlethen Gramp	65	D12
Portloe Cornw'l	3	S7
Portmahomack H'land	71	C9
Portnacroish S'clyde	55	E6
Portnaguran W Isles	66	B4
Portnahaven S'clyde	48	G3
Portobello S'clyde	52	G10
Porton Wilts	15	Q13
Portpatrick Dumf/Gal	44	J6
Portreath Cornw'l	2	S6
Portree H'land	61	D4
Portskerra H'land	70	A9
Portslade E Sussex	9	R16
Portsmouth Hants	8	R14
Portsoy Gramp	65	C11
Portuairk H'land	55	E4
Postbridge Devon	4	R9
Potter Hanworth Lincs	39	M16
Potter Heigham Norfolk	33	N20
Potter Street Essex	17	P17
Potterne Wilts	14	Q12

Potters Bar Herts	17	P16
Potterspury Northants	22	O15
Potton Beds	23	O16
Poulton Glos	21	P13
Poulton-le-Fylde Lancs	40	L11
Poundstock Cornw'l	4	R7
Powerstock Dorset	6	R11
Powick Heref/Worcs	21	O12
Powmill Tayside	51	F9
Poynings W Sussex	9	R16
Poynton Ches	37	M12
Praze-an-Beeble Cornw'l	2	S6
Prees Shrops	29	N11
Preesall Lancs	40	L11
Prescot Mersey	36	M11
Preshute Wilts	15	Q13
Prestatyn Clwyd	35	M10
Prestbury Glos	21	P12
Prestbury Ches	37	M12
Presteigne Powys	27	O10
Preston Kent	11	Q19
Preston Lancs	36	L11
Preston Humber	39	L16
Preston Lothian	52	G11
Preston Borders	52	G11
Preston Dorset	6	R12
Preston Candover Hants	15	Q14
Prestonpans Lothian	52	G11
Prestwich Gtr Man	37	L12
Prestwick S'clyde	50	H7
Prickwillow Cambs	32	O17
Princes Risborough Bucks	16	P15
Princetown Devon	5	R9
Priors Marston Warwick	22	O14
Probus Cornw'l	3	S7
Prudhoe Northum	47	J13
Puckeridge Herts	23	P17
Pucklechurch Avon	14	Q12
Puddletown Dorset	6	R12
Pudsey W Yorks	37	L13
Pulborough W Sussex	9	R15
Pulford Ches	36	M11
Pulham Market Norfolk	33	O19
Pulham St. Mary Norfolk	33	O19
Pumpsaint Dyfed	19	O9
Puncheston Dyfed	18	P7
Purbrook Hants	8	R14
Purfleet Essex	17	Q17
Purleigh Essex	24	P18
Purley Berks	16	Q14
Purston Jaglin W Yorks	38	L14
Purton Wilts	21	P13
Pwllheli Gwyn	34	N8
Pyle Mid Glam	19	P9
Pytchley Northants	31	O15
Pyworthy Devon	4	R8

Q

Quadring Lincs	31	N16
Quainton Bucks	22	P15
Quarter S'clyde	50	G8
Quatford Shrops	29	N12
Queen Camel Som'set	14	Q11
Queenborough Kent	10	Q18
Queensbury W Yorks	37	L13
Queensferry Clwyd	36	M10
Queensferry Lothian	51	G10
Quendon Essex	24	P17
Quorndon Leics	30	N14

R

Place	Ref		Place	Ref		Place	Ref
Raasay *H'land*	61 D4		Reedham *Norfolk*	33 N20		Riverhead *Kent*	17 Q1
Rackenford *Devon*	12 R9		Reepham *Norfolk*	33 N19		Rivington *Lancs*	36 L1
Rackheath *Norfolk*	33 N19		Reepham *Lincs*	39 M16		Roade *Northants*	23 O1
Racks *Dumf/Gal*	45 H9		Reeth *N Yorks*	41 K13		Roadhead *Cumb*	46 H1
Radcliffe *Gtr Man*	37 L12		Reiff *H'land*	69 B6		Roadside *H'land*	70 A
Radcliffe *Northum*	47 H13		Reigate *Surrey*	17 Q16		Roadside of Kinneff *Gramp*	59 E
Radcliffe on Trent *Notts*	30 N14		Reighton *N Yorks*	43 K16		Roag *H'land*	61 D
Radford Semele *Warwick*	30 O14		Reiss *H'land*	70 B10		Roberton *S'clyde*	51 G
Radlett *Herts*	17 P16		Rempstone *Notts*	30 N14		Roberton *Borders*	52 H1
Radley *Oxon*	22 P14		Rendham *Suffolk*	25 O19		Robertsbridge *E Sussex*	10 R1
Radstock *Avon*	14 Q12		Renfrew *S'clyde*	50 G8		Robin Hood's Bay *N Yorks*	43 K1
Radyr *S Glam*	20 P10		Renishaw *Derby*	38 M14		Roborough *Devon*	12 F
Rafford *Gramp*	64 C9		Rennington *Northum*	53 H13		Rocester *Staffs*	30 N
Raglan *Gwent*	20 P11		Renton *S'clyde*	50 G7		Roch *Dyfed*	18 F
Rainford *Mersey*	36 M11		Renwick *Cumb*	46 J11		Rochdale *Gtr Man*	37 L1
Rainham *Kent*	10 Q18		Repton *Derby*	30 N13		Roche *Cornw'l*	3 S
Rainhill *Mersey*	36 M11		Resolven *W Glam*	19 P9		Rochester *Kent*	10 Q1
Rainow *Ches*	37 M12		Rhayader *Powys*	27 O9		Rochester *Northum*	47 H1
Rainworth *Notts*	38 M14		Rhewl *Clwyd*	35 M10		Rochford *Essex*	24 P1
Rait *Tayside*	58 F10		Rhiconich *H'land*	69 B7		Rockbourne *Hants*	7 R1
Rampside *Cumb*	40 K10		Rhiw *Gwyn*	34 N7		Rockcliffe *Dumf/Gal*	45 J
Rampton *Cambs*	32 O17		Rhonehouse *Dumf/Gal*	45 J9		Rockcliffe *Cumb*	46 H1
Rampton *Notts*	38 M15		Rhoose *S Glam*	13 Q10		Rockfield *H'land*	71 C
Ramsbottom *Gtr Man*	37 L12		Rhoscolyn *Gwyn*	34 M7		Rodborough *Glos*	21 P
Ramsbury *Wilts*	15 Q13		Rhosllanerchrugog *Clwyd*	28 M10		Roddington *Shrops*	29 N
Ramsden Heath *Essex*	24 P17		Rhosneigr *Gwyn*	34 M7		Rode *Som'set*	14 Q
Ramsey *Essex*	25 P19		Rhos-on-Sea *Clwyd*	35 M9		Rode Heath *Ches*	37 M
Ramsey *Cambs*	31 O16		Rhossilli *W Glam*	19 P8		Rodel *W Isles*	67 C
Ramsey *I of Man*	72 K8		Rhostyllen *Clwyd*	35 M10		Rodings *Essex*	17 P
Ramsey St. Mary's *Cambs*	31 O16		Rhosybol *Gwyn*	34 M8		Rodmell *E Sussex*	9 R
Ramsgate *Kent*	11 Q19		Rhu *S'clyde*	50 F7		Rogart *H'land*	71 B
Ramsgill *N Yorks*	41 K13		Rhuallt *Clwyd*	35 M10		Rogate *W Sussex*	8 Q1
Ranfurly *S'clyde*	50 G7		Rhuddlan *Clwyd*	35 M10		Rogerstone *Gwent*	20 P
Rangeworthy *Avon*	21 P12		Rhydcymerau *Dyfed*	19 O8		Rogiet *Gwent*	20 P
Rannoch Station *Tayside*	56 E7		Rhyd-ddu *Gwyn*	34 M8		Rollesby *Norfolk*	33 N2
Ranskill *Notts*	38 M14		Rhydlewis *Dyfed*	19 O8		Rolleston *Staffs*	30 N
Ratby *Leics*	30 N14		Rhyl *Clwyd*	35 M10		Rolvenden *Kent*	10 Q1
Rathen *Gramp*	65 C12		Rhymney *Mid Glam*	20 P10		Romaldkirk *Durham*	41 J
Ratho *Lothian*	51 G10		Rhynie *Gramp*	64 D11		Romanby *N Yorks*	42 K1
Rathven *Gramp*	64 C11		Ribchester *Lancs*	36 L11		Romannobridge *Borders*	51 G1
Rattray *Tayside*	58 E10		Riccall *N Yorks*	42 L14		Romiley *Gtr Man*	37 M1
Raunds *Northants*	31 O15		Riccarton *S'clyde*	50 G7		Romsey *Hants*	8 R1
Ravenglass *Cumb*	40 K10		Richards Castle *Shrops*	28 O11		Romsley *Heref/Worcs*	29 O1
Ravenscar *N Yorks*	43 K16		Richmond *Gtr Lon*	16 Q16		Rookhope *Durham*	47 J1
Ravenstonedale *Cumb*	41 K12		Richmond *N Yorks*	42 K13		Rookley *I of Wight*	8 R1
Ravensworth *N Yorks*	42 K13		Rickarton *Gramp*	59 E12		Roos *Humber*	39 L1
Rawcliffe *Humber*	38 L15		Rickinghall *Suffolk*	33 O18		Roose *Cumb*	40 K1
Rawdon *W Yorks*	42 L13		Rickmansworth *Herts*	17 P16		Ropley *Hants*	8 Q1
Rawmarsh *S Yorks*	38 M14		Ridgewell *Essex*	24 O18		Ropsley *Lincs*	31 N1
Rawtenstall *Lancs*	37 L12		Ridsdale *Northum*	47 H12		Rosedale Abbey *N Yorks*	43 K1
Rayleigh *Essex*	24 P18		Rievaulx *N Yorks*	42 K14		Rosehearty *Gramp*	65 C1
Rayne *Essex*	24 P18		Rigg *Dumf/Gal*	46 J10		Rosemarket *Dyfed*	18 F
Reading *Berks*	16 Q15		Rigton *N Yorks*	42 L13		Rosemarkie *H'land*	63 C
Rearsby *Leics*	30 N14		Rilla Mill *Cornw'l*	4 R8		Rosewell *Lothian*	51 F
Reay *H'land*	70 A9		Rillington *N Yorks*	43 K15		Roskhill *H'land*	61 D
Red Dial *Cumb*	46 J10		Ringford *Dumf/Gal*	45 J8		Roslin *Lothian*	51 G
Redbourn *Herts*	16 P16		Ringmer *E Sussex*	10 R17		Rosneath *S'clyde*	50 F
Redbourne *Humber*	38 M15		Ringstead *Northants*	31 O15		Rossett *Clwyd*	36 M1
Redbridge *Gtr Lon*	17 P17		Ringstead *Norfolk*	32 N18		Ross-on-Wye *Heref/Worcs*	21 P
Redcar *Clev'l'd*	42 J14		Ringwood *Hants*	7 R13		Rosyth *Fife*	51 F
Redditch *Heref/Worcs*	29 O13		Ringwould *Kent*	11 Q19		Rothbury *Northum*	47 H1
Redesdale Camp *Northum*	46 H12		Ripe *E Sussex*	10 R17		Rotherfield *E Sussex*	10 Q1
Redesmouth *Northum*	46 H12		Ripley *Surrey*	16 Q16		Rotherham *S Yorks*	38 M1
Redford *Tayside*	59 E11		Ripley *Derby*	37 M14		Rothes *Gramp*	64 C
Redgrave *Suffolk*	33 O18		Ripley *N Yorks*	42 K13		Rothesay *S'clyde*	49 G
Redhill *Surrey*	17 Q16		Ripon *N Yorks*	42 K13		Rothienorman *Gramp*	65 D1
Redlynch *Wilts*	7 R13		Rippingale *Lincs*	31 N16		Rothley *Leics*	30 N1
Redruth *Cornw'l*	2 S6		Ripponden *W Yorks*	37 L13		Rothwell *Northants*	31 O1
Redwick *Gwent*	20 P11		Risabus *S'clyde*	48 G4		Rothwell *W Yorks*	38 L1
			Risby *Suffolk*	32 O18		Rothwell *Lincs*	39 M1
			Risca *Gwent*	20 P10		Rottal *Tayside*	58 E1
			Risegate *Lincs*	31 N16		Rottingdean *E Sussex*	9 R1
			Riseley *Beds*	23 O16		Roughton *Norfolk*	33 N1
			Rishton *Lancs*	36 L12		Routh *Humber*	43 L1

owanburn *Dumf/Gal* 46 H11
owardennan *Central* 56 F7
owde *Wilts* 14 Q12
owhedge *Essex* 25 P18
owington *Warwick* 30 O13
owland's Castle *Hants* 8 R15
owlands Gill *Tyne/Wear* 47 J13
ownhams *Hants* 8 R14
owrah *Cumb* 40 J10
oxburgh *Borders* 52 G12
oxby *Humber* 38 L15
oxton *Beds* 23 O16
oxwell *Essex* 17 P17
oybridge *H'land* 56 E7
oydon *Herts* 17 P17
oyston *Herts* 23 O16
oyston *S Yorks* 37 L14
oyston *Gtr Man* 37 L12
uabon *Clwyd* 28 N10
uadh-phort Mor *S'clyde* 48 G4
uan Minor *Corn'l* 2 T6
uardean *Glos* 21 P11
ubery *Heref/Worcs* 29 O12
uddington *Notts* 30 N14
udgeway *Avon* 21 P11
udgwick *W Sussex* 9 Q16
udston *Humber* 43 K16
udyard *Staffs* 37 M12
ufford *Lancs* 36 L11
ufforth *N Yorks* 42 L14
ugby *Warwick* 30 O14
ugeley *Staffs* 29 N13
umburgh *Suffolk* 33 O19
umney *S Glam* 20 Q10
uncorn *Ches* 36 M11
uncton *Norfolk* 32 N17
unswick *N Yorks* 43 J15
ushden *Northants* 31 O15
ushton *Northants* 31 O15
uskington *Lincs* 31 M16
usper *W Sussex* 9 Q16
uspidge *Glos* 21 P11
uswarp *N Yorks* 43 K15
ustington *W Sussex* 9 R15
utherglen *S'clyde* 50 G8
uthin *Clwyd* 35 M10
uthven *Tayside* 58 E10
uthven *H'land* 63 D8
uthven *Gramp* 64 C11
uthwell *Dumf/Gal* 45 J10
uyton Eleven Towns *Shrops* 28 N11
ydal *Cumb* 40 K11
yde *I of Wight* 8 R14
ye *E Sussex* 10 R18
yhall *Leics* 31 N15
ylstone *N Yorks* 41 K12
yton-on-Dunsmore *Warwick* 30 O14

S

acriston *Durham* 47 J13
adberge *Durham* 42 J14
addell *S'clyde* 49 G5
affron Walden *Essex* 24 O17
ageston *Dyfed* 18 P7
t. Abb's *Borders* 53 G12
. Agnes *Corn'l* 2 S6
. Albans *Herts* 17 P16
. Andrews *Fife* 58 F11
. Anne's *Lancs* 36 L10

St. Ann's *Dumf/Gal* 45 H10
St. Aryans *Gwent* 20 P11
St. Asaph *Clwyd* 35 M10
St. Athan *S Glam* 13 Q10
St. Austell *Corn'l* 3 S7
St. Bees *Cumb* 40 K9
St. Blazey *Corn'l* 3 S7
St. Boswells *Borders* 52 G11
St. Briavels *Glos* 21 P11
St. Brides Major *Mid Glam* 13 Q9
St. Budeaux *Devon* 4 S8
St. Buryan *Corn'l* 2 S5
St. Catherine's *S'clyde* 56 F6
St. Clears *Dyfed* 19 P8
St. Cleer *Corn'l* 4 S8
St. Columb Major *Corn'l* 3 S7
St. Columb Road *Corn'l* 3 S7
St. Combs *Gramp* 65 C13
St. Cyrus *Gramp* 59 E12
St. Davids *Dyfed* 18 P6
St. Day *Corn'l* 2 S6
St. Dennis *Corn'l* 3 S7
St. Dogmaels *Dyfed* 18 O7
St. Enoder *Corn'l* 3 S7
St. Erth *Corn'l* 2 S6
St. Fagans *S Glam* 20 Q10
St. Faith *Norfolk* 33 N19
St. Fergus *Gramp* 65 C13
St. Fillans *Tayside* 57 F8
St. Florence *Dyfed* 18 P7
St. Germans *Corn'l* 4 S8
St. Harmon *Powys* 27 O10
St. Helen's *Mersey* 36 M11
St. Helen's *I of Wight* 8 R14
St. Hilary *S Glam* 13 Q10
St. Ishmael's *Dyfed* 18 P6
St. Issey *Corn'l* 3 R7
St. Ives *Corn'l* 2 S6
St. Ives *Cambs* 31 O16
St. Ives *Dorset* 7 R13
St. John's *I of Man* 72 K7
St. John's Chapel *Durham* 46 J12
St. John's Highway *Norfolk* 32 N17
St. Just *Corn'l* 2 S5
St. Just *Corn'l* 2 S6
St. Keverne *Corn'l* 2 S6
St. Kew *Corn'l* 3 R7
St. Lawrence *I of Wight* 8 R14
St. Leonards *E Sussex* 10 R18
St. Levan *Corn'l* 2 S5
St. Mabyn *Corn'l* 3 R7
St. Mairtin's *Shrops* 28 N11
St. Margaret's at Cliffe *Kent* 11 Q19
St. Mark's *I of Man* 72 K7
St. Mary Bourne *Hants* 15 Q14
St. Mary's Bay *Kent* 11 Q18
St. Mawes *Corn'l* 2 S6
St. Mawgan *Corn'l* 3 R7
St. Mellion *Corn'l* 4 S8
St. Mellions *S Glam* 20 P10
St. Merryn *Corn'l* 3 R7
St. Michaels *Kent* 10 Q18
St. Michael's on Wyre *Lancs* 40 L11
St. Minver *Corn'l* 3 R7
St. Monance *Fife* 59 F11
St. Neot *Corn'l* 3 S7
St. Neots *Cambs* 23 O16
St. Nicholas *Dyfed* 18 P6
St. Nicholas at Wade *Kent* 11 Q19
St. Osyth *Essex* 25 P19
St. Peters *Kent* 11 Q19
St. Quivox *S'clyde* 50 H7
St. Stephen *Corn'l* 3 S7
St. Stephens *Corn'l* 4 S8

St. Teath *Corn'l* 3 R7
St. Tudy *Corn'l* 3 R7
St. Vigeans *Tayside* 59 E11
Salcombe *Devon* 5 S9
Sale *Gtr Man* 37 M12
Salen *H'land* 55 E5
Salen *S'clyde* 55 E5
Salford *Beds* 23 O15
Salford *Gtr Man* 37 M12
Salford Priors *Warwick* 21 O13
Salfords *Surrey* 17 Q16
Salhouse *Norfolk* 33 N19
Saline *Fife* 51 F9
Salisbury *Wilts* 15 Q13
Sallachy *H'land* 62 D6
Saltash *Corn'l* 4 S8
Saltburn *Clevl'd* 42 J15
Saltburn *H'land* 71 C8
Saltcoats *S'clyde* 50 G7
Saltfleet *Lincs* 39 M17
Saltfleetby St. Peter *Lincs* 39 M17
Salford *Avon* 14 Q12
Salthouse *Norfolk* 33 N19
Saltney *Ches* 36 M11
Saltwood *Kent* 11 Q19
Sampford Brett *Som'set* 13 Q10
Sampford Courtenay *Devon* 4 R9
Sampford Peverell *Devon* 5 R10
Sancton *Humber* 43 L15
Sand Hutton *N Yorks* 42 K14
Sandbach *Ches* 36 M12
Sandbank *S'clyde* 49 G7
Sandford *Devon* 5 R9
Sandgate *Kent* 11 Q19
Sandhaven *Gramp* 65 C12
Sandhead *Dumf/Gal* 44 J7
Sandhurst *Berks* 10 Q18
Sandhurst *Hants* 16 Q15
Sandiacre *Derby* 30 N14
Sandown *I of Wight* 8 R14
Sandringham *Norfolk* 32 N18
Sandsend *N Yorks* 43 J15
Sandwell *W Midlands* 29 N13
Sandwich *Kent* 11 Q19
Sandwick *W Isles* 66 B4
Sandwith *Cumb* 40 J9
Sandy *Beds* 23 O16
Sanquhar *Dumf/Gal* 45 H9
Santon Bridge *Cumb* 40 K10
Santon Downham *Suffolk* 32 O18
Sarclet *H'land* 70 B10
Sarisbury *Hants* 8 R14
Sarn *Gwyn* 34 N7
Sarre *Kent* 11 Q19
Satley *Durham* 47 J13
Satterthwaite *Cumb* 40 K10
Sauchen *Gramp* 65 D12
Saundersfoot *Dyfed* 18 P7
Sawbridgeworth *Herts* 24 P17
Sawley *Lancs* 41 L12
Sawley *N Yorks* 42 K13
Sawrey *Cumb* 40 K11
Sawston *Cambs* 24 O17
Sawtry *Cambs* 31 O16
Saxby All Saints *Humber* 39 L16
Saxilby *Lincs* 38 M15
Saxlingham Nethergate *Norfolk* 33 N19
Saxmundham *Suffolk* 25 O19
Scagglethorpe *N Yorks* 43 K15
Scalasaig *S'clyde* 54 F4
Scalby *N Yorks* 43 K16
Scaleby *Cumb* 46 J11
Scalford *Leics* 31 N15

Scarastavore W Isles 67 C2
Scarborough N Yorks 43 K16
Scarcliffe Derby 38 M14
Scarfskerry H'land 70 A10
Scarinish S'clyde 54 F3
Scarisbrick Lancs 36 L11
Scarning Norfolk 33 N18
Scawby Humber 38 L15
Scole Norfolk 33 O19
Scopwick Lincs 39 M16
Scoraig H'land 69 C6
Scorton Lancs 40 L11
Scorton N Yorks 42 K13
Scotstown H'land 55 E5
Scotter Lincs 38 L15
Scotton Lincs 38 M15
Scotton N Yorks 42 K13
Scourie H'land 68 B6
Scrabster H'land 70 A9
Scremerston Northum 53 G13
Scruton N Yorks 42 K13
Sculthorpe Norfolk 32 N18
Scunthorpe Humber 38 L15
Sea Palling Norfolk 33 N20
Seaford E Sussex 9 R17
Seaforth Mersey 36 M10
Seaham Durham 47 J14
Seahouses Northum 53 G13
Seal Kent 17 Q17
Seamer N Yorks 42 K14
Seamer N Yorks 43 K16
Seasalter Kent 11 Q18
Seascale Cumb 40 K10
Seathwaite Cumb 40 K10
Seaton Leics 31 N15
Seaton Humber 43 L16
Seaton Cumb 45 J9
Seaton Devon 5 R10
Seaton Carew Clevl'd 47 J14
Seaton Delaval Northum 47 H13
Seave Green N Yorks 42 K14
Seaview I of Wight 8 R14
Seavington Som'set 6 R11
Sebergham Cumb 46 J11
Sedburgh Cumb 41 K11
Sedgeberrow Heref/Worcs 21 O13
Sedgefield Durham 47 J14
Sedgeford Norfolk 32 N18
Sedgley W Midlands 29 N12
Sedlescombe Street
   E Sussex 10 R18
Seend Wilts 14 Q12
Selattyn Shrops 28 N10
Selborne Hants 8 Q15
Selby N Yorks 38 L14
Selkirk Borders 52 G11
Selsey W Sussex 8 R15
Selston Notts 38 M14
Selworthy Som'set 13 Q9
Semington Wilts 14 Q12
Sennen Cornw'l 2 S5
Sennybridge Powys 20 P9
Settle N Yorks 41 K12
Seven Sisters W Glam 19 P9
Sevenoaks Kent 17 Q17
Severn Beach Avon 14 P11
Severn Stoke Heref/Worcs 21 O12
Shaftesbury Dorset 14 Q12
Shalbourne Wilts 15 Q13
Shalfleet I of Wight 8 R14
Shalford Surrey 16 Q15
Shalmsford Street Kent 11 Q18
Shandon S'clyde 50 F7

Shanklin I of Wight 8 R14
Shap Cumb 41 J11
Sharnbrook Beds 23 O15
Sharnford Leics 30 N14
Sharpness Glos 21 P12
Shavington Ches 36 M12
Shawbury Shrops 29 N11
Shawforth Lancs 37 L12
Shawhead Dumf/Gal 45 H9
Shawwood S'clyde 50 G8
Shebbear Devon 4 R8
Shedfield Hants 8 R14
Sheepwash Devon 4 R8
Sheerness Kent 10 Q18
Sheet Hants 8 Q15
Sheffield S Yorks 37 M13
Shefford Beds 23 O16
Shelf W Yorks 37 L13
Shelley W Yorks 37 L13
Shenfield Essex 17 P17
Shenstone Staffs 29 N13
Shepherdswell Kent 11 Q19
Shepley W Yorks 37 L13
Shepshed Leics 30 N14
Shepton Mallet Som'set 14 Q11
Sherborne Glos 22 P13
Sherborne Dorset 6 R11
Sherborne St. John Hants 15 Q14
Sherburn N Yorks 43 K15
Shere Surrey 16 Q15
Sherfield English Hants 7 R13
Sheriff Hutton N Yorks 42 K15
Sheriffhales Shrops 29 N12
Sheringham Norfolk 33 N19
Sherington Bucks 23 O15
Sherston Wilts 21 P12
Shiel Bridge H'land 62 D6
Shieldaig H'land 62 C5
Shifnal Shrops 29 N12
Shilbottle Northum 47 H13
Shildon Durham 47 J13
Shillingford Oxon 22 P14
Shillingstone Dorset 6 R12
Shillington Beds 23 P16
Shincliffe Durham 47 J13
Shinfield Berks 16 Q15
Shinner's Bridge Devon 5 S9
Shipdham Norfolk 33 N18
Shipham Som'set 14 Q11
Shiplake Oxon 16 Q15
Shipley W Yorks 37 L13
Shipston on Stour Warwick 22 O13
Shipton Shrops 29 N11
Shipton N Yorks 38 L14
Shipton Bellinger Hants 15 Q13
Shipton Thorpe Humber 43 L15
Shipton under Wychwood
   Oxon 22 P13
Shire Oak W Midlands 29 N13
Shirebrook Derby 38 M14
Shirland Derby 38 M14
Shirley W Midlands 30 O13
Shiskine S'clyde 49 G6
Shobdon Heref/Worcs 20 O11
Shoeburyness Essex 24 P18
Shoreham Kent 17 Q17
Shoreham-by-Sea W Sussex 9 R16
Shorwell I of Wight 8 R14
Shotesham Norfolk 33 N19
Shotley Bridge Durham 47 J13
Shotley Gate Suffolk 25 P19
Shotton Clwyd 36 M10
Shotton Colliery Durham 47 J14
Shotts S'clyde 51 G9

Shouldham Norfolk 32 N18
Shrawardine Shrops 28 N11
Shrewsbury Shrops 29 N11
Shrewton Wilts 15 Q12
Shrivenham Oxon 22 P14
Shulishader W Isles 66 B8
Shurdington Glos 21 P13
Shustoke Warwick 30 N13
Sibsey Lincs 32 M17
Sidbury Devon 5 R10
Sidford Devon 5 R10
Sidlesham W Sussex 8 R15
Sidmouth Devon 5 R10
Sigglesthorne Humber 43 L16
Silchester Hants 16 Q14
Sileby Leics 30 N14
Silecroft Cumb 40 K10
Silkstone S Yorks 37 L13
Silksworth Tyne/Wear 47 J14
Silloth Cumb 45 J9
Silsden W Yorks 37 L13
Silver End Essex 24 P18
Silverdale Lancs 40 K11
Silverstone Northants 22 O15
Silverton Devon 5 R10
Simonburn Northum 46 H12
Simonsbath Som'set 12 Q9
Singleton Lancs 40 L10
Singleton W Sussex 9 R15
Sissinghurst Kent 10 Q18
Sittingbourne Kent 10 Q18
Sixpenny Handley Dorset 7 R12
Skateraw Gramp 65 D15
Skeffling Humber 39 L18
Skegness Lincs 39 M18
Skelbo H'land 71 C13
Skelmanthorpe W Yorks 37 L13
Skelmersdale Lancs 36 L11
Skelmorlie S'clyde 50 G7
Skelton Clevl'd 42 J14
Skelton N Yorks 46 J12
Skelton Cumb 46 J11
Skelwith Bridge Cumb 40 K11
Skenfrith Gwent 20 P11
Skerray H'land 70 A11
Skewen W Glam 19 P8
Skidby Humber 39 L16
Skigersta W Isles 66 B8
Skillington Lincs 31 N16
Skipness S'clyde 49 G6
Skipsea Humber 43 L17
Skipton N Yorks 41 L12
Skipton-on-Swale N Yorks 42 K14
Skirling Borders 51 G10
Slaggyford Northum 46 J12
Slaidburn Lancs 41 L12
Slaithwaite W Yorks 37 L13
Slaley Northum 47 J13
Slamannan Central 51 G9
Sleaford Lincs 31 N16
Sledmere Humber 43 K16
Sleights N Yorks 43 K15
Sliddery S'clyde 49 G6
Slindon W Sussex 9 R15
Slinfold W Sussex 9 Q16
Slingsby N Yorks 42 K15
Slough Bucks 16 P16
Slyne Lancs 40 K11
Smailholm Borders 52 G12
Smallburn S'clyde 51 G9
Smalley Derby 38 M14
Smarden Kent 10 Q18
Smearisary H'land 55 E5
Smithfield Cumb 46 J11

Snailbeach *Shrops*	28	N11
Snainton *N Yorks*	43	K15
Snaith *Humber*	38	L14
Snake Inn *Derby*	37	M13
Snape *Suffolk*	25	O20
Snape *N Yorks*	42	K13
Sneaton *N Yorks*	43	K15
Snettisham *Norfolk*	32	N17
Snitter *Northum*	47	H13
Snitterfield *Warwick*	22	O13
Snodland *Kent*	17	Q17
Soham *Cambs*	32	O17
Solihull *W Midlands*	30	O13
Sollas *W Isles*	60	C2
Solva *Dyfed*	18	P6
Somercotes *Derby*	38	M14
Somerton *Som'set*	14	Q11
Somersham *Cambs*	31	O16
Sompting *W Sussex*	9	R16
Sonning *Berks*	16	Q15
Sonning Common *Oxon*	16	P15
Sopley *Hants*	7	R13
Sorbie *Dumf/Gal*	44	J8
Sordale *H'land*	70	A10
Sorisdale *S'clyde*	54	E4
Sorn *S'clyde*	50	G8
Sortat *H'land*	70	A10
Soulby *Cumb*	41	K12
Soutergate *Cumb*	40	K10
South Benfleet *Essex*	24	P18
South Brent *Devon*	5	S9
South Cave *Humber*	38	L15
South Cerney *Glos*	21	P13
South Chard *Som'set*	6	R11
South Creake *Norfolk*	32	N18
South Dell *W Isles*	66	B4
South Elkington *Lincs*	39	M16
South Elmstall *W Yorks*	38	L14
South Ferriby *Humber*	38	L15
South Harting *W Sussex*	8	R15
South Hayling *Hants*	8	R15
South Hetton *Durham*	47	J14
South Killingholme *Humber*	39	L16
South Kirkby *W Yorks*	38	L14
South Kyme *Lincs*	31	M16
South Lancing *W Sussex*	9	R16
South Lopham *Norfolk*	33	O18
South Luffenham *Leics*	31	N15
South Milford *N Yorks*	38	L14
South Molton *Devon*	12	Q9
South Muskham *Notts*	38	M15
South Normanton *Derby*	38	M14
South Normanton *Derby*	38	M14
South Otterington *N Yorks*	42	K14
South Perrott *Dorset*	6	R11
South Petherton *Som'set*	6	R11
South Pool *Devon*	5	S9
South Reston *Lincs*	39	M17
South Shawbost *W Isles*	66	B3
South Shields *Tyne/Wear*	47	J14
South Shore *Lancs*	36	L11
South Skirlaugh *Humber*	43	L16
South Stoke *Oxon*	22	P14
South Tidworth *Hants*	15	Q13
South Walsham *Norfolk*	33	N19
South Wingfield *Derby*	37	M14
South Witham *Lincs*	31	N15
South Woodham Ferrers *Essex*	24	P18
South Wootton *Norfolk*	32	N17
South Zeal *Devon*	4	R9
Southam *Warwick*	22	O14

Southampton *Hants*	8	R14
Southborough *Kent*	17	Q17
Southend *S'clyde*	49	H5
Southend-on-Sea *Essex*	24	P18
Southery *Norfolk*	32	N17
Southminster *Essex*	24	P18
Southport *Mersey*	36	L10
Southrepps *Norfolk*	33	N19
Southrop *Glos*	22	P13
Southsea *Hants*	8	R14
Southwaite *Cumb*	46	J11
Southwark *Gtr Lon*	17	Q16
Southwater *W Sussex*	9	Q16
Southwell *Notts*	38	M15
Southwell *Dorset*	6	R12
Southwick *Wilts*	14	Q12
Southwick *W Sussex*	9	R16
Southwold *Suffolk*	33	O20
Sowerby *N Yorks*	42	K14
Sowerby Bridge *W Yorks*	37	L13
Spalding *Lincs*	31	N16
Sparkford *Som'set*	14	Q11
Sparsholt *Hants*	15	Q14
Spean Bridge *H'land*	56	E7
Speen *Berks*	15	Q14
Speeton *N Yorks*	43	K16
Speke *Mersey*	36	M11
Speldhurst *Kent*	17	Q17
Spennymoor *Durham*	47	J13
Spetisbury *Dorset*	7	R12
Spey Bay *Gramp*	64	C10
Spilsby *Lincs*	39	M17
Spinningdale *H'land*	71	C8
Spital *H'land*	70	B10
Spitalburn *Gramp*	59	E11
Spittal *Dyfed*	18	P7
Spittal *Northum*	53	G12
Spittal of Glenshee *Tayside*	58	E10
Spittalfield *Tayside*	58	E10
Spixworth *Norfolk*	33	N19
Spofforth *N Yorks*	42	L14
Spondon *Derby*	30	N14
Spott *Lothian*	52	G11
Spratton *Northants*	30	O15
Spreyton *Devon*	4	R9
Spridlington *Lincs*	39	M16
Springfield *Dumf/Gal*	46	J10
Sproatley *Humber*	39	L16
Sprouston *Borders*	52	G12
Sproxton *N Yorks*	43	K14
Spurstow *Ches*	36	M11
Stadhampton *Oxon*	22	P14
Staffin *H'land*	61	C4
Stafford *Staffs*	29	N12
Stagsden *Beds*	23	O15
Staindrop *Durham*	41	J13
Staines *Surrey*	16	Q15
Stainforth *S Yorks*	38	L14
Stainforth *N Yorks*	41	K12
Stainland *W Yorks*	37	L13
Stainton *Lincs*	39	M16
Stainton *Cumb*	46	J11
Staintondale *N Yorks*	43	K15
Stair *S'clyde*	50	H8
Staithes *N Yorks*	43	J15
Stalbridge *Dorset*	6	R12
Stalham *Norfolk*	33	N20
Stalling Busk *N Yorks*	41	K12
Stallingborough *Humber*	39	L16
Stalmine *Lancs*	40	L11
Stalybridge *Gtr Man*	37	M12
Stamford *Lincs*	31	N16
Stamford Bridge *Humber*	43	L15
Standish *Gtr Man*	36	L11

Standlake *Oxon*	22	P14
Standon *Herts*	24	P17
Stane *S'clyde*	51	G9
Stanford in the Vale *Oxon*	22	P13
Stanford-le-Hope *Essex*	17	P17
Stanhoe *Norfolk*	32	N18
Stanhope *Durham*	47	J12
Stanley *Derby*	30	N14
Stanley *Durham*	47	J13
Stanley *Tayside*	58	F10
Stannington *S Yorks*	37	M13
Stannington *Northum*	47	H13
Stanstead Abbots *Herts*	17	P17
Stansted Mountfitchet *Essex*	24	P17
Stanton *Glos*	21	P13
Stanton *Suffolk*	32	O18
Stanton Fitzwarren *Wilts*	21	P13
Stanton Harcourt *Oxon*	22	P14
Stanton upon Hine Heath *Shrops*	29	N11
Stanwick *Northants*	31	O15
Stanwix *Cumb*	46	J11
Staple *Kent*	11	Q19
Stapleford *Cambs*	24	O17
Stapleford *Notts*	30	N14
Staplehurst *Kent*	10	Q18
Stapleton *Leics*	30	N14
Stapleton *N Yorks*	42	K13
Starbotton *N Yorks*	41	K12
Starcross *Devon*	5	R10
Startforth *Durham*	41	J13
Stathern *Leics*	31	N15
Staunton *Gwent*	21	P11
Staunton *Glos*	21	P12
Staunton on Wye *Heref/Worcs*	20	O11
Staveley *Derby*	38	M14
Staveley *Cumb*	40	K11
Staverton *Northants*	22	O14
Staxigoe *H'land*	70	B10
Staxton *N Yorks*	43	K16
Stebbing *Essex*	24	P17
Stedham *W Sussex*	9	R15
Steep *Hants*	8	Q15
Steeple *Essex*	24	P18
Steeple Aston *Oxon*	22	P14
Steeple Bumpstead *Essex*	24	O17
Steeple Claydon *Bucks*	16	P15
Steeple Morden *Cambs*	23	O16
Stenton *Lothian*	52	G11
Stepps *S'clyde*	50	G8
Stetchworth *Cambs*	24	O17
Stevenage *Herts*	23	P16
Stevenston *S'clyde*	50	G7
Steventon *Oxon*	22	P14
Stewartby *Beds*	23	O15
Stewarton *S'clyde*	50	G7
Stewkley *Bucks*	23	P15
Steyning *W Sussex*	9	R16
Stichill *Borders*	52	G12
Sticker *Cornw'l*	3	S7
Stickford *Lincs*	39	M17
Sticklepath *Devon*	4	R9
Stickney *Lincs*	39	M17
Stiffkey *Norfolk*	33	N18
Stillington *N Yorks*	42	K14
Stillington *Clevl'd*	47	J14
Stilton *Cambs*	31	O16
Stirling *Central*	51	F9
Stisted *Essex*	24	P18
Stithians *Cornw'l*	2	S6
Stobo *Borders*	51	G10
Stock *Essex*	24	P18
Stockbridge *Hants*	15	Q14

Stockenchurch *Bucks* 16 P15
Stockland *Devon* 5 R10
Stockport *Gtr Man* 37 M12
Stocksbridge *S Yorks* 37 M13
Stockton-on-Tees *Clevl'd* 47 J14
Stockton-on-Teme *Heref/Worcs* 29 O12
Stoer *H'land* 68 B6
Stogumber *Som'set* 13 Q10
Stogursey *Som'set* 13 Q10
Stoke by Nayland *Suffolk* 25 P18
Stoke Canon *Devon* 5 R10
Stoke Climsland *Cornw'l* 4 R8
Stoke Ferry *Norfolk* 32 N18
Stoke Fleming *Devon* 5 S9
Stoke Gabriel *Devon* 5 S9
Stoke Hammond *Bucks* 23 P15
Stoke Mandeville *Bucks* 16 P15
Stoke on Trent *Staffs* 29 M12
Stoke Poges *Bucks* 16 P15
Stoke Prior *Heref/Worcs* 20 O11
Stoke Prior *Heref/Worcs* 29 O12
Stoke Rivers *Devon* 12 Q9
Stoke St. Michael *Som'set* 14 Q12
Stoke sub Hamdon *Som'set* 6 R11
Stoke-by-Clare *Suffolk* 24 O18
Stokeinteignhead *Devon* 5 R9
Stokenham *Devon* 5 S9
Stokesley *N Yorks* 42 K14
Stone *Staffs* 29 N12
Stonegrave *N Yorks* 42 K15
Stonehaven *Gramp* 59 E12
Stonehouse *Glos* 21 P12
Stoneleigh *Warwick* 30 O13
Stonesfield *Oxon* 22 P14
Stoney Middleton *Derby* 37 M13
Stoney Stanton *Leics* 30 N14
Stoneykirk *Dumf/Gal* 44 J7
Stoneywood *Gramp* 65 D12
Stony Stratford *Bucks* 23 O15
Stornoway *W Isles* 66 B4
Storrington *W Sussex* 9 R16
Stotfold *Beds* 23 O16
Stourbridge *W Midlands* 29 O12
Stourpaine *Dorset* 7 R12
Stourport-on-Severn *Heref/Worcs* 29 O12
Stourton Caundle *Dorset* 6 R12
Stow *Lincs* 38 M15
Stow *Borders* 52 G11
Stow cum Quy *Cambs* 24 O17
Stowmarket *Suffolk* 25 O18
Stow-on-the-Wold *Glos* 22 P13
Strachan *Gramp* 65 D11
Strachur *S'clyde* 56 F6
Stradbroke *Suffolk* 33 O19
Straiton *S'clyde* 44 H7
Stramshall *Staffs* 29 N13
Strands *Cumb* 40 K10
Stranraer *Dumf/Gal* 44 J6
Stratford St. Mary *Suffolk* 25 P18
Stratford-upon-Avon *Warwick* 22 O13
Strathaven *S'clyde* 50 G8
Strathblane *Central* 50 G8
Strathcarron *H'land* 62 D6
Strathdon *Gramp* 64 D10
Strathkanaird *H'land* 69 C6
Strathkinness *Fife* 58 F11
Strathpeffer *H'land* 63 C7
Strathy *H'land* 70 A9
Strathyre *Central* 57 F8
Stratton *Glos* 21 P13

Stratton *Cornw'l* 4 R7
Stratton *Dorset* 6 R11
Stratton Audley *Oxon* 22 P14
Stratton on the Fosse *Som'set* 14 Q12
Stratton St. Margaret *Wilts* 22 P13
Streatley *Beds* 23 P16
Streatly *Berks* 15 P14
Street *Som'set* 14 Q11
Strete *Devon* 5 S9
Stretham *Cambs* 32 O17
Stretton *Staffs* 29 N12
Stretton *Staffs* 30 N13
Stretton *Leics* 31 N15
Stretton *Ches* 36 M11
Strichen *Gramp* 65 C12
Stromeferry *H'land* 62 D5
Stromemore *H'land* 62 D5
Stronachlachar *Central* 56 F7
Strone *S'clyde* 49 G7
Strontian *H'land* 55 E5
Stroud *Glos* 21 P12
Struan *H'land* 61 D4
Struy *H'land* 63 D7
Stuartfield *Gramp* 65 D12
Stubbington *Hants* 8 R14
Studland *Dorset* 7 R13
Studley *Warwick* 29 O13
Sturbridge *Staffs* 29 N12
Sturminster Marshall *Dorset* 7 R12
Sturminster Newton *Dorset* 6 R12
Sturry *Kent* 11 Q19
Sturton *Lincs* 38 M15
Sutton *Suffolk* 25 P19
Sudbury *Suffolk* 24 O18
Sudbury *Derby* 30 N13
Sulby *I of Man* 72 K8
Summer Bridge *N Yorks* 42 K13
Summercourt *Cornw'l* 3 S7
Sunbury *Surrey* 16 Q16
Sunderland *Tyne/Wear* 47 J14
Sunderland Bridge *Durham* 47 J13
Sundridge *Kent* 17 Q17
Sunningdale *Surrey* 16 Q15
Sunninghill *Berks* 16 Q15
Surfleet *Lincs* 31 N16
Sutcombe *Devon* 12 R8
Sutterton *Lincs* 31 N16
Sutton *Ctr Lon* 17 Q16
Sutton *Cambs* 32 O17
Sutton *Norfolk* 33 N20
Sutton *N Yorks* 41 L13
Sutton *W Sussex* 9 R15
Sutton Benger *Wilts* 21 P12
Sutton Bridge *Lincs* 32 N17
Sutton Coldfield *W Midlands* 30 N13
Sutton Courtenay *Oxon* 22 P14
Sutton in Ashfield *Notts* 38 M14
Sutton Lane Ends *Ches* 37 M12
Sutton on Trent *Notts* 38 M15
Sutton St. James *Lincs* 32 N17
Sutton St. Nicholas *Heref/Worcs* 20 O11
Sutton Scotney *Hants* 15 Q14
Sutton Valence *Kent* 10 Q18
Sutton Veny *Wilts* 14 Q12
Sutton-on-Sea *Lincs* 39 M17
Sutton-on-the-Forest *N Yorks* 42 K14
Sutton-under-Whitestonecliffe *N Yorks* 42 K14
Swadlincote *Derby* 30 N13
Swaffham *Norfolk* 32 N18
Swaffham Prior *Cambs* 24 O17
Swainby *N Yorks* 42 K14

Swainswick *Avon* 14 Q12
Swallowfield *Berks* 16 Q15
Swanage *Dorset* 7 R13
Swanbourne *Bucks* 16 P15
Swanley *Kent* 17 Q17
Swannington *Leics* 30 N14
Swanscombe *Kent* 17 Q17
Swansea *W Glam* 19 P9
Swanton Morley *Norfolk* 33 N19
Swanwick *Derby* 37 M13
Swardeston *Norfolk* 33 N19
Swaton *Lincs* 31 N16
Swavesey *Cambs* 32 O17
Sway *Hants* 8 R14
Swayfield *Lincs* 31 N16
Swerford *Oxon* 22 P14
Swillington *W Yorks* 37 L13
Swimbridge *Devon* 12 Q9
Swindon *Glos* 21 P13
Swindon *Wilts* 21 P13
Swindon *Staffs* 29 N12
Swinefleet *Humber* 38 L15
Swineshead *Heref/Worcs* 31 N16
Swineshead *Beds* 31 O16
Swinford *Leics* 30 O14
Swinstead *Lincs* 31 N16
Swinton *Gtr Man* 37 L12
Swinton *N Yorks* 43 K15
Swinton *Borders* 53 G12
Swynnerton *Staffs* 29 N12
Syderstone *Norfolk* 32 N18
Sydling St. Nicholas *Dorset* 6 R11
Sykehouse *S Yorks* 38 L14
Symington *S'clyde* 50 G8
Symington *S'clyde* 51 G9
Syresham *Northants* 22 O14
Syston *Leics* 30 N14

T

Tacolneston *Norfolk* 33 N19
Tadcaster *N Yorks* 42 L14
Tadley *Hants* 16 Q14
Taffs Well *Mid Glam* 20 P10
Tain *H'land* 64 C8
Takeley *Essex* 24 P17
Tal y Sarn *Gwyn* 34 M9
Talgarreg *Dyfed* 19 O9
Talgarth *Powys* 20 P10
Talladale *H'land* 69 C6
Talley *Dyfed* 19 P9
Talmine *H'land* 68 A8
Talworth *Surrey* 17 Q16
Talybont *Powys* 20 P10
Tal-y-bont *Gwyn* 26 N9
Talybont *Dyfed* 27 O9
Tamerton Foliot *Devon* 4 S8
Tamworth *Staffs* 30 N13
Tannadice *Tayside* 58 E11
Tansley *Derby* 37 M13
Tantobie *Durham* 47 J13
Tanworth in Arden *Warwick* 29 O13
Taplow *Bucks* 16 P15
Tarbert *S'clyde* 49 G6
Tarbert *W Isles* 67 C3
Tarbet *S'clyde* 56 F7
Tarbet *H'land* 62 E5
Tarbolton *S'clyde* 50 G8
Tarfside *Tayside* 58 E10
Tarland *Gramp* 64 D11
Tarleton *Lancs* 36 L11

115

Tarporley *Ches* 36 M11
Tarrant Gunville *Dorset* 7 R12
Tarrant Hinton *Dorset* 7 R12
Tarrington *Heref/Worcs* 21 O11
Tarskavaig *H'land* 61 D5
Tarvin *Ches* 36 M11
Tatsfield *Surrey* 17 Q17
Tattenhall *Ches* 36 M11
Tattershall *Lincs* 39 M16
Taunton *Som'set* 13 Q10
Tavistock *Devon* 4 R8
Tayinloan *S'clyde* 49 G5
Taynuilt *S'clyde* 56 F6
Tayport *Fife* 58 F11
Tayvallich *S'clyde* 49 F5
Tealby *Lincs* 39 M16
Teangue *H'land* 61 D5
Tebay *Cumb* 41 K11
Tedburn St. Mary *Devon* 5 R9
Teignmouth *Devon* 5 R10
Telford *Shrops* 29 N12
Templand *Dumf/Gal* 45 H10
Temple Ewell *Kent* 11 Q19
Temple Normanton *Derby* 38 M14
Temple Sowerby *Cumb* 46 J11
Templecombe *Som'set* 6 R12
Templeton *Dyfed* 18 P7
Ten Mile Bank *Norfolk* 32 N17
Tenbury Wells *Heref/Worcs* 29 O11
Tenby *Dyfed* 18 P7
Tendring *Essex* 25 P19
Tenterden *Kent* 10 Q18
Terling *Essex* 24 P18
Terrington *N Yorks* 42 K15
Terrington St. Clement *Norfolk* 32 N17
Tetbury *Glos* 21 P12
Tetchill *Shrops* 28 N11
Tetford *Lincs* 39 M17
Tetney *Lincs* 39 M16
Tetsworth *Oxon* 22 P14
Tettenhall *W Midlands* 29 N12
Teviothead *Borders* 46 H11
Tewkesbury *Glos* 21 P12
Teynham *Kent* 10 Q18
Thame *Oxon* 22 P15
Thames Haven *Essex* 24 P18
Thankerton *S'clyde* 51 G9
Thatcham *Berks* 15 Q14
Thaxted *Essex* 24 P17
The Craigs *H'land* 69 C7
The Cronk *I of Man* 72 K7
The Hill *Cumb* 40 K10
Theale *Som'set* 14 Q11
Theale *Berks* 16 Q14
Theddlethorpe St. Helen *Lincs* 39 M17
Therfield *Herts* 23 O16
Thetford *Norfolk* 32 O18
Theydon Bois *Essex* 17 P17
Thimbleby *Lincs* 39 M16
Thirsk *N Yorks* 42 K14
Thixendale *N Yorks* 43 K15
Thompson *Norfolk* 32 N18
Thormanby *N Yorks* 42 K14
Thornaby-on-Tees *Clevl'd* 42 J14
Thornage *Norfolk* 33 N19
Thornborough *Bucks* 16 P15
Thornbury *Avon* 21 P11
Thornby *Northants* 30 O14
Thorndon *Suffolk* 33 O19
Thorne *S Yorks* 38 L15
Thorner *W Yorks* 42 L14

Thorney *Cambs* 31 N16
Thornford *Dorset* 6 R11
Thornham *Norfolk* 32 N18
Thornhill *Cumb* 40 K9
Thornhill *Dumf/Gal* 45 H9
Thornhill *Central* 57 F8
Thornley *Durham* 47 J14
Thornthwaite *Cumb* 45 J10
Thornton *Mersey* 36 L10
Thornton *Lancs* 40 L10
Thornton *N Yorks* 41 L12
Thornton *Fife* 58 F10
Thornton le Dale *N Yorks* 43 K15
Thorp Arch *W Yorks* 42 L14
Thorpe *Norfolk* 33 N19
Thorpe *Derby* 37 M13
Thorpe le Soken *Essex* 25 P19
Thorpe on the Hill *Lincs* 38 M15
Thorpe Thewles *Clevl'd* 47 J14
Thorpe Willoughby *N Yorks* 38 L14
Thorpeness *Suffolk* 25 O20
Thorrington *Essex* 25 P19
Thorton Rust *N Yorks* 41 K12
Thorverton *Devon* 5 R9
Thrapston *Northants* 31 O15
Threekingham *Lincs* 31 N16
Threlkeld *Cumb* 46 J10
Thringstone *Leics* 30 N14
Throckley *Tyne/Wear* 47 H13
Thropton *Northum* 47 H13
Thrumster *H'land* 70 B10
Thrupp *Glos* 21 P12
Thruxton *Hants* 15 Q13
Thundersleigh *Essex* 24 P18
Thurcroft *S Yorks* 38 M14
Thurgarten *Notts* 30 M15
Thurlby *Lincs* 31 N16
Thurleigh *Beds* 23 O16
Thurlstone *S Yorks* 37 L13
Thurmaston *Leics* 30 N14
Thurnby *Leics* 30 N14
Thurnham *Lancs* 40 L11
Thurnscoe *S Yorks* 38 L14
Thursby *Cumb* 46 J10
Thursley *Surrey* 16 Q15
Thurso *H'land* 70 A9
Thurston *Suffolk* 24 O18
Thwaite *N Yorks* 41 K12
Thwing *Humber* 43 K16
Tibberton *Glos* 21 P12
Tibenham *Norfolk* 33 O19
Tibshelf *Derby* 38 M14
Tibthorpe *Humber* 43 L15
Ticehurst *E Sussex* 10 Q17
Tickhill *S Yorks* 38 M14
Ticknall *Derby* 30 N14
Tickton *Humber* 43 L16
Tidenham *Glos* 21 P11
Tideswell *Derby* 37 M13
Tigerton *Tayside* 59 E11
Tigharry *W Isles* 60 C1
Tighnabruaich *S'clyde* 49 G6
Tilbury *Essex* 17 Q17
Tillicoultry *Central* 51 F9
Tillingham *Essex* 24 P18
Tilmanstone *Kent* 11 Q19
Tilshead *Wilts* 15 Q13
Tilstock *Shrops* 28 N11
Tilston *Ches* 36 M11
Tilton *Leics* 31 N15
Timberscombe *Som'set* 13 Q10
Timsbury *Avon* 14 Q12
Tingewick *Bucks* 22 P14

Tintagel *Cornw'l* 3 R7
Tintern Parva *Gwent* 20 P11
Tinwald *Dumf/Gal* 45 H9
Tipton *W Midlands* 29 N12
Tiptree *Essex* 24 P18
Tirley *Glos* 21 P12
Tirril *Cumb* 46 J11
Tisbury *Wilts* 14 Q12
Tissington *Derby* 37 M13
Titchfield *Hants* 8 R14
Titchmarsh *Northants* 31 O15
Tittleshall *Norfolk* 32 N18
Tiverton *Devon* 13 R10
Tiverton *Ches* 36 M11
Tobermory *S'clyde* 55 E4
Toberonochy *S'clyde* 55 F5
Toddington *Beds* 23 P15
Todenham *Glos* 22 O13
Todmorden *W Yorks* 37 L12
Tollerton *N Yorks* 42 K14
Tollesbury *Essex* 24 P18
Tolleshunt D'Arcy *Essex* 24 P18
Tolpuddle *Dorset* 6 R12
Tolsarnau *Gwyn* 34 N8
Tomatin *H'land* 63 D8
Tomdoun *H'land* 62 D6
Tomich *H'land* 62 D7
Tomintoul *Gramp* 64 D10
Tomnavoulin *Gramp* 64 D10
Tonbridge *Kent* 17 Q17
Tondu *Mid Glam* 19 P9
Tong *Shrops* 29 N12
Tongland *Dumf/Gal* 45 J8
Tongue *H'land* 70 B8
Tonna *W Glam* 19 P9
Tonypandy *Mid Glam* 20 P10
Tonyrefail *Mid Glam* 20 P10
Topcliffe *N Yorks* 42 K14
Topsham *Devon* 5 R9
Torbay *Devon* 5 S9
Torcross *Devon* 5 S9
Tore *H'land* 63 C8
Tormarton *Avon* 21 P12
Torness *H'land* 63 D8
Torphichen *Lothian* 51 G9
Torphins *Gramp* 65 D11
Torpoint *Cornw'l* 4 S8
Torquay *Devon* 5 S9
Torrance *S'clyde* 50 G8
Torridon *H'land* 62 C5
Torrin *H'land* 61 D4
Torrobell *H'land* 71 B8
Torry *Gramp* 65 D12
Torryburn *Fife* 51 F9
Torthorwald *Dumf/Gal* 45 H9
Torver *Cumb* 40 K10
Toscaig *H'land* 61 D5
Totland *I of Wight* 8 R13
Totley *S Yorks* 37 M13
Totnes *Devon* 5 S9
Tottington *Gtr Man* 37 L12
Totton *Hants* 8 R13
Tow Law *Durham* 47 J13
Towcester *Northants* 22 O15
Tower Hamlets *Gtr Lon* 17 P16
Towie *Gramp* 64 D11
Towiemore *Gramp* 64 C10
Town Yetholm *Borders* 52 G12
Townshend *Cornw'l* 2 S5
Towyn *Clwyd* 35 M9
Trafford *Gtr Man* 37 M12
Tranent *Lothian* 52 G11
Traquair *Borders* 52 G10
Trawden *Lancs* 41 L12

Trawsfynydd *Gwyn*	35	N9
Trecastle *Powys*	19	P9
Tredegar *Gwent*	20	P10
Tredington *Warwick*	22	O13
Trefeglwys *Powys*	27	O9
Trefnant *Clwyd*	35	M10
Trefonen *Shrops*	28	N10
Treforest *Mid Glam*	20	P10
Trefriw *Gwyn*	35	M9
Tregaron *Dyfed*	19	O9
Tregony *Cornw'l*	3	S7
Tregynon *Powys*	27	N10
Treharris *Mid Glam*	20	P10
Treherbert *Mid Glam*	20	P9
Trelawnyd *Clwyd*	35	M10
Trelech *Dyfed*	19	P8
Tremadog *Gwyn*	34	N8
Trenance *Cornw'l*	2	S6
Trent *Dorset*	6	R11
Trentham *Staffs*	29	N12
Treorchy *Mid Glam*	20	P9
Tresaith *Dyfed*	18	O7
Tresillion *Cornw'l*	3	S7
Tressait *Tayside*	57	E9
Tre-Taliesin *Dyfed*	27	O9
Tretower *Powys*	20	P10
Treuddyn *Clwyd*	35	M10
Trevone *Cornw'l*	3	R7
Trevor *Gwyn*	34	N8
Trexine *Dyfed*	18	P6
Trimdon *Durham*	47	J14
Trimdon Colliery *Durham*	47	J14
Trimingham *Norfolk*	33	N19
Trimley *Suffolk*	25	P19
Trimsaran *Dyfed*	19	P8
Tring *Herts*	16	P15
Trinity *Tayside*	59	E11
Trochrie *Tayside*	58	E9
Troon *Cornw'l*	2	S6
Troon *S'clyde*	50	G7
Troutbeck *Cumb*	40	K11
Trowbridge *Wilts*	14	Q12
Trowell *Notts*	30	N14
Trull *Som'set*	13	R10
Trunch *Norfolk*	33	N19
Truro *Cornw'l*	2	S6
Trusthorpe *Lincs*	39	M17
Tudweiliog *Gwyn*	34	N7
Tugnet *Gramp*	64	C10
Tullynessle *Gramp*	64	D11
Tumble *Dyfed*	19	P8
Tummel Bridge *Tayside*	57	E8
Tunbridge Wells *Kent*	10	Q17
Tunstall *Suffolk*	25	O19
Tunstall *Staffs*	37	M12
Tunstall *Lancs*	41	K11
Turnditch *Derby*	30	M13
Turners Hill *W Sussex*	9	Q16
Turriff *Gramp*	65	C12
Turvey *Beds*	23	O15
Tutbury *Staffs*	30	N13
Tuttington *Norfolk*	33	N19
Tuxford *Notts*	38	M15
Tweedsmuir *Borders*	51	G10
Twycross *Leics*	30	N13
Twyford *Hants*	15	Q14
Twyford *Berks*	16	Q15
Twyford *Leics*	30	N15
Twynholm *Dumf/Gal*	45	J8
Tycroes *Dyfed*	19	P8
Tydd St. Giles *Cambs*	32	N17
Tyldesley *Gtr Man*	36	L12
Tyndrum *Central*	56	F7
Tynemouth *Tyne/Wear*	47	H14

Tynewydd *Mid Glam*	20	P9
Tyninghame *Lothian*	52	F11
Tynron *Dumf/Gal*	45	H9
Tysoe *Warwick*	22	O13
Tywardreath *Cornw'l*	3	S7
Tywyn *Gwyn*	26	N8
Tywyn *Gwyn*	35	M9

U

Ubley *Avon*	14	Q11
Uckfield *E Sussex*	10	R17
Uddingston *S'clyde*	50	G8
Udney *Gramp*	65	D12
Uffculme *Devon*	13	R10
Uffington *Oxon*	22	P13
Uffington *Lincs*	31	N16
Ufford *Suffolk*	25	O19
Ugborough *Devon*	4	S9
Ugthorpe *N Yorks*	43	K15
Uig *H'land*	61	C4
Uig *W Isles*	66	B2
Ulbster *H'land*	70	B10
Ulceby *Humber*	39	L16
Ulceby Cross *Lincs*	39	M17
Uldale *Cumb*	46	J10
Uley *Glos*	21	P12
Ulgham *Northum*	47	H13
Ulleskelf *N Yorks*	42	L14
Ullapool *H'land*	69	C6
Ullenhall *Warwick*	29	O13
Ullesthorpe *Leics*	30	O14
Ullock *Cumb*	40	J10
Ulpha *Cumb*	40	K10
Ulrome *Humber*	43	L16
Ulverston *Cumb*	40	K10
Unapool *H'land*	68	B6
Underbarrow *Cumb*	40	K11
Underwood *Notts*	30	M14
Union Mills *I of Man*	72	K7
Unstone *Derby*	38	M14
Upavon *Wilts*	15	Q13
Uphill *Avon*	13	Q11
Upholland *Lancs*	36	L11
Uplawmoor *S'clyde*	50	G8
Uplyme *Devon*	6	R11
Upper Arley *Heref/Worcs*	29	O12
Upper Sapey *Heref/Worcs*	21	O12
Upper Slaughter *Glos*	22	P13
Upper Tean *Staffs*	29	N13
Upper Wyche *Heref/Worcs*	21	O12
Uppingham *Leics*	31	N15
Upstreet *Kent*	11	Q19
Upton *Hants*	15	Q14
Upton *Oxon*	22	P14
Upton *Cambs*	31	O16
Upton *Mersey*	36	M10
Upton *Ches*	36	M11
Upton *W Yorks*	38	L14
Upton *Notts*	38	M15
Upton Grey *Hants*	16	Q14
Upton upon Severn *Heref/Worcs*	21	O12
Upwell *Norfolk*	32	N17
Upwood *Cambs*	31	O16
Urchfont *Wilts*	15	Q13
Urmston *Gtr Man*	37	M12
Urquhart *Gramp*	64	C10
Ushaw Moor *Durham*	47	J13
Usk *Gwent*	20	P11
Utterby *Lincs*	39	M16
Uttoxeter *Staffs*	29	N13

V

Valley *Gwyn*	34	M7
Velindre *Dyfed*	19	O8
Ventnor *I of Wight*	8	R14
Verwood *Dorset*	7	R13
Veryan *Cornw'l*	3	S7
Vickersley *S Yorks*	38	M14
Vickerstown *Cumb*	40	K10

W

Waddesdon *Bucks*	22	P15
Waddingham *Lincs*	38	M15
Waddington *Lincs*	38	M15
Waddington *Lancs*	41	L12
Wadebridge *Cornw'l*	3	R7
Wadhurst *E Sussex*	10	Q17
Wadworth *S Yorks*	38	M14
Waenfawr *Gwyn*	34	M8
Wainfleet All Saints *Lincs*	39	M17
Wakefield *W Yorks*	37	L14
Wakes Colne *Essex*	24	P18
Walberswick *Suffolk*	33	O20
Walberton *W Sussex*	9	R15
Walcot *Lincs*	39	M16
Walcott *Norfolk*	33	N19
Walesby *Notts*	25	O19
Walesby *Lincs*	38	M15
Walford *Heref/Worcs*	39	M16
Walgrave *Northants*	21	P11
Walk Mill *Lancs*	31	O15
Walkerburn *Borders*	37	L12
Walkern *Herts*	52	G10
Walkington *Humber*	23	P16
Wall *Northum*	39	L16
Wallasey *Mersey*	47	H12
Wallingford *Oxon*	36	M10
Wallsend *Tyne/Wear*	22	P14
Walmer *Kent*	47	J13
Walpole Highway *Norfolk*	11	Q19
Walpole St. Andrew *Norfolk*	32	N17
Walpole St. Peter *Norfolk*	32	N17
Walsall *W Midlands*	32	N17
Walsall Wood *W Midlands*	29	N13
Walsham-le-Willows *Suffolk*	29	N13
Waltham *Humber*	33	O18
Waltham Abbey *Essex*	39	L16
Waltham Forest *Gtr Lon*	17	P17
Waltham on the Wolds *Leics*	17	P16
Walton *Som'set*	31	N15
Walton *Surrey*	14	Q11
Walton *Powys*	16	Q16
Walton *Leics*	20	O10
Walton *W Yorks*	30	O14
Walton *Cumb*	37	L14
Walton le Dale *Lancs*	46	J11
Walton on the Hill *Surrey*	36	L11
Walton-on-the-Naze *Essex*	17	Q16
Wanborough *Wilts*	29	N12
Wandsworth *Gtr Lon*	25	P19
Wangford *Suffolk*	15	P13
Wanlockhead *Dumf/Gal*	17	Q16
Wansford *Cambs*	33	O20
Wansford *Humber*	51	H9
Wanstrow *Som'set*	43	L16
Wantage *Oxon*	14	Q12
	22	P14

Wappenham *Northants* 22 O14
Warboys *Cambs* 31 O16
Warcop *Cumb* 41 J12
Wardle *Gtr Man* 37 L12
Ware *Herts* 17 P16
Wareham *Dorset* 7 R12
Warenton *Northum* 53 G13
Wargrave *Berks* 16 Q15
Wark *Northum* 46 H12
Wark *Northum* 53 G12
Warkworth *Northum* 47 H13
Warlingham *Surrey* 17 Q16
Warlington *Suffolk* 32 O17
Warmington *Warwick* 22 O14
Warmington *Northants* 31 N16
Warminster *Wilts* 14 Q12
Warmworth *S Yorks* 38 M14
Warnham *W Sussex* 9 Q16
Warren *Ches* 37 M12
Warrington *Ches* 36 M11
Warslow *Staffs* 37 M13
Warsop *Notts* 38 M14
Warter *Humber* 43 L15
Warton *Lancs* 36 L11
Warton *Lancs* 40 K11
Warwick *Warwick* 30 O13
Warwick *Cumb* 46 J11
Washfold *N Yorks* 41 K13
Washford *Som'set* 13 Q10
Washingborough *Lincs* 39 M16
Washington *Tyne/Wear* 47 J13
Washington *W Sussex* 9 R16
Waskerley *Durham* 47 J13
Watchet *Som'set* 13 Q10
Watchfield *Oxon* 22 P13
Water Orton *Warwick* 30 N13
Waterbeach *Cambs* 24 O17
Waterbeck *Dumf/Gal* 45 H10
Wateringbury *Kent* 10 Q17
Waterloo *Mersey* 36 M10
Waterloo *Tayside* 58 E9
Waterlooville *Hants* 8 R14
Waters Upton *Shrops* 29 N11
Waterside *S'clyde* 44 H8
Watford *Herts* 16 P16
Wath *N Yorks* 42 K13
Wath upon Dearne *S Yorks* 38 M14
Watlington *Oxon* 16 P14
Watlington *Norfolk* 32 N17
Watten *H'land* 70 B10
Watton *Norfolk* 32 N18
Watton *Lancs* 43 L16
Watton-at-Stone *Herts* 23 P16
Waverton *Cumb* 45 J10
Wawne *Humber* 39 L16
Wearhead *Durham* 46 J12
Weaverham *Ches* 36 M11
Weaverthorpe *N Yorks* 43 K15
Wedmore *Som'set* 14 Q11
Wednesbury *W Midlands* 29 N12
Wednesfield *W Midlands* 29 N12
Weedon Bec *Northants* 22 O14
Week St. Mary *Cornw'l* 4 R8
Weem *Tayside* 57 E9
Weeting *Norfolk* 32 O18
Weeton *Lancs* 36 L11
Welbourn *Lincs* 38 M15
Welbury *N Yorks* 42 K14
Welby *Lincs* 31 N15
Weldon *Northants* 31 O15
Weldon *Northum* 47 H13
Welford *Northants* 30 O14
Welford-on-Avon *Warwick* 22 O13
Well *N Yorks* 42 K13

Wellesbourne *Warwick* 22 O13
Wellingborough *Northants* 31 O15
Wellingore *Lincs* 38 M15
Wellington *Som'set* 13 R10
Wellington *Heref/Worcs* 20 O11
Wellington *Shrops* 28 N11
Wellow *Notts* 38 M15
Wells *Som'set* 14 Q11
Wells of Ythan *Gramp* 65 D11
Wells-next-the-Sea *Norfolk* 32 N18
Welney *Norfolk* 32 N17
Welshampton *Shrops* 28 N11
Welshpool *Powys* 27 N10
Welton *Lincs* 39 M16
Welton *Cumb* 46 J10
Welwick *Humber* 39 L17
Welwyn *Herts* 17 P16
Welwyn Garden City *Herts* 17 P16
Wem *Shrops* 28 N11
Wembdon *Som'set* 13 Q10
Wemyss Bay *S'clyde* 50 G7
Wendover *Bucks* 16 P15
Wenhaston *Suffolk* 33 O20
Wennington *Lancs* 41 K11
Wensley *N Yorks* 41 K13
Wentnor *Shrops* 28 N11
Wenvoe *S Glam* 13 Q10
Weobley *Heref/Worcs* 20 O11
Wereham *Norfolk* 32 N17
Wessington *Derby* 37 M14
West Ashby *Lincs* 39 M16
West Aukland *Durham* 47 J13
West Barns *Lothian* 52 G11
West Bay *Dorset* 6 R11
West Bergholt *Essex* 24 P18
West Bridgford *Notts* 30 N14
West Bromwich *W Midlands* 29 N12
West Buckland *Devon* 12 Q9
West Burton *N Yorks* 41 K13
West Butterwick *Humber* 38 L15
West Calder *Lothian* 51 G9
West Chittington *W Sussex* 9 R16
West Coker *Som'set* 7 R11
West Dean *Wilts* 15 Q13
West Dean *W Sussex* 9 R15
West Deeping *Lincs* 31 N16
West Down *Devon* 12 Q8
West End *Hants* 8 R14
West Felton *Shrops* 28 N11
West Geirinish *W Isles* 60 D2
West Haddon *Northants* 30 O14
West Halton *Humber* 38 L15
West Harptree *Avon* 14 Q11
West Heath *Hants* 16 Q15
West Heslerton *N Yorks* 43 K15
West Hoathly *W Sussex* 9 R16
West Hougham *Kent* 11 Q19
West Ilsley *Berks* 15 P14
West Itchenor *W Sussex* 8 R15
West Kilbride *S'clyde* 50 G7
West Kirby *Mersey* 36 M10
West Linton *Borders* 51 G10
West Looe *Cornw'l* 3 S8
West Lulworth *Dorset* 6 R12
West Malvern *Heref/Worcs* 21 O12
West Meon *Hants* 8 Q14
West Mersea *Essex* 25 P18
West Moors *Dorset* 7 R13
West Parley *Dorset* 7 R13
West Pennard *Som'set* 14 Q11
West Rasen *Lincs* 39 M16
West Runton *Norfolk* 33 N19
West Scrafton *N Yorks* 42 K13
West Tanfield *N Yorks* 42 K13

West Walton *Norfolk* 32 N17
West Wellow *Hants* 7 R13
West Winch *Norfolk* 32 N17
West Wittering *W Sussex* 8 R15
West Witton *N Yorks* 41 K13
West Woodburn *Northum* 46 H12
West Wycombe *Bucks* 16 P15
Westbourne *W Sussex* 8 R15
Westbury *Wilts* 14 Q12
Westbury *Shrops* 28 N11
Westbury on Severn *Glos* 21 P12
Westbury-sub-Mendip *Som'set* 14 Q11
Westcott *Surrey* 16 Q16
Wester Balgaldie *Tayside* 58 F10
Westerdale *N Yorks* 43 K15
Westerdale *H'land* 70 B10
Westerham *Kent* 17 Q17
Westfield *E Sussex* 10 R18
Westgate *Durham* 47 J12
Westgate-on-Sea *Kent* 11 Q19
Westham *E Sussex* 10 R17
Westhay *Som'set* 14 Q11
Westhoughton *Gtr Man* 36 L11
Westleton *Suffolk* 33 O20
Westmuir *Tayside* 58 E10
Westnewton *Cumb* 45 J10
Weston *Lincs* 31 N16
Weston *Ches* 36 M12
Weston *Notts* 38 M15
Weston Alconbury *Cambs* 31 O16
Weston Favell *Northants* 23 O15
Weston Rhyn *Shrops* 28 N10
Weston Subedge *Glos* 22 O13
Weston Turville *Bucks* 16 P15
Weston under Lizard *Staffs* 29 N12
Weston under Penyard *Heref/Worcs* 21 P11
Weston upon Trent *Staffs* 29 N12
Westoning *Beds* 23 P15
Weston-in-Gordano *Avon* 13 Q11
Weston-on-the-Green *Oxon* 22 P14
Weston-super-Mare *Avon* 13 Q11
Westonzoyland *Som'set* 13 Q11
Westow *N Yorks* 43 K15
Westruther *Borders* 52 G11
Westward Ho *Devon* 12 Q8
Wetheral *Cumb* 46 J11
Wetherby *W Yorks* 42 L14
Wethersfield *Essex* 24 P17
Wetleyrocks *Staffs* 29 M12
Wetton *Staffs* 37 M13
Wetwang *Humber* 43 K15
Weybourne *Norfolk* 33 N19
Weybridge *Surrey* 16 Q16
Weyhill *Hants* 15 Q13
Weymouth *Dorset* 6 R12
Whaley Bridge *Derby* 37 M13
Whalley *Lancs* 36 L12
Whalton *Northum* 47 H13
Whaplode *Lincs* 32 N16
Whaplode Drove *Lincs* 31 N16
Wharncliffe Side *S Yorks* 37 M13
Wharram-le-Street *N Yorks* 43 K15
Whatton *Notts* 31 N15
Whauphill *Dumf/Gal* 44 J7
Wheathampstead *Herts* 17 P16
Wheatley *Oxon* 22 P14
Wheatley Hill *Durham* 47 J14
Wheaton Aston *Staffs* 29 N12
Wheddon Cross *Som'set* 13 Q9
Wheelock *Ches* 36 M12
Wheldrake *N Yorks* 42 L15
Wherwell *Hants* 15 Q14

Whicham *Cumb*	40 K10	
Whichford *Warwick*	22 O13	
Whickham *Tyne/Wear*	47 J13	
Whiddon Down *Devon*	4 R9	
Whimple *Devon*	5 R10	
Whinnyfold *Gramp*	65 D13	
Whipsnade *Beds*	23 P15	
Whissendine *Leics*	31 N15	
Whissonsett *Norfolk*	33 N18	
Whiston *Staffs*	29 M13	
Whiston *Mersey*	36 M11	
Whitbourne *Heref/Worcs*	21 O12	
Whitburn *Tyne/Wear*	47 J14	
Whitburn *Lothian*	51 G13	
Whitby *Ches*	36 M11	
Whitby *N Yorks*	43 K15	
Whitchurch *Avon*	14 Q11	
Whitchurch *Hants*	15 Q14	
Whitchurch *Oxon*	15 Q14	
Whitchurch *S Glam*	20 P10	
Whitchurch *Heref/Worcs*	21 P11	
Whitchurch *Oxon*	22 P14	
Whitchurch *Bucks*	23 P15	
Whitchurch *Shrops*	29 N11	
Whitchurch *Devon*	4 R8	
White Roding *Essex*	17 P17	
Whitecairns *Gramp*	65 D12	
Whitefield *Gtr Man*	37 L12	
Whitehaven *Cumb*	40 J9	
Whitehill *Hants*	8 Q15	
Whitehills *Gramp*	65 C11	
Whitehouse *S'clyde*	49 G6	
Whitehouse *Gramp*	65 D11	
Whitekirk *Lothian*	52 F11	
Whiteparish *Wilts*	15 Q13	
Whiterashes *Gramp*	65 D12	
Whitfield *Kent*	11 Q19	
Whitford *Clwyd*	35 M10	
Whithorn *Dumf/Gal*	44 J8	
Whiting Bay *S'clyde*	49 H6	
Whitland *Dyfed*	18 P7	
Whitley Bay *Tyne/Wear*	47 H14	
Whitmore *Staffs*	29 N12	
Whitney *Heref/Worcs*	20 O10	
Whitsome *Borders*	53 G12	
Whitstable *Kent*	11 Q19	
Whitstone *Corn'l*	4 R8	
Whittingham *Northum*	53 H13	
Whittington *Shrops*	28 N10	
Whittington *Staffs*	30 N13	
Whittington *Derby*	37 M14	
Whittington *Lancs*	41 K11	
Whittle le Woods *Lancs*	36 L11	
Whittlesey *Cambs*	31 N16	
Whittlesford *Cambs*	24 O17	
Whitwell *Herts*	23 P16	
Whitwell *Derby*	38 M14	
Whitwell *I of Wight*	8 R14	
Whitwick *Leics*	30 N14	
Whitworth *Lancs*	37 L12	
Whixley *N Yorks*	42 K14	
Whorlton *Durham*	41 J13	
Wick *Mid Glam*	13 Q9	
Wick *Avon*	14 Q12	
Wick *H'land*	70 B10	
Wicken *Cambs*	32 O17	
Wickford *Essex*	24 P18	
Wickham *Hants*	8 R14	
Wickham Market *Suffolk*	25 O19	
Wickham Skeith *Suffolk*	33 O19	
Wicklewood *Norfolk*	33 N19	
Wickwar *Avon*	21 P12	
Widdington *Essex*	24 P17	
Widdrington *Northum*	47 H13	
Widecombe in the Moor *Devon*	5 R9	
Widemouth *Corn'l*	4 R7	
Widford *Herts*	17 P17	
Widnes *Ches*	36 M11	
Wigan *Gtr Man*	36 L11	
Wiggenhall St. Mary Magdalen *Norfolk*	32 N17	
Wigglesworth *N Yorks*	41 K12	
Wighton *Norfolk*	32 N18	
Wigmore *Heref/Worcs*	28 O11	
Wigston *Leics*	30 N14	
Wigton *Cumb*	46 J10	
Wigtown *Dumf/Gal*	44 J8	
Wilbarston *Northants*	31 O15	
Wilberfoss *Humber*	42 L15	
Wilburton *Cambs*	32 O17	
Willand *Devon*	13 R10	
Willaston *Ches*	36 M10	
Willaston *Ches*	36 M12	
Willenhall *W Midlands*	29 N12	
Willerby *Humber*	39 L16	
Willersey *Heref/Worcs*	21 O13	
Willingdon *E Sussex*	10 R17	
Willingham *Cambs*	32 O17	
Willingham *Lincs*	38 M15	
Willington *Derby*	30 N13	
Willington *Durham*	47 J13	
Williton *Som'set*	13 Q10	
Willoughby *Warwick*	30 O14	
Willoughby *Lincs*	39 M17	
Wilmcote *Warwick*	21 O13	
Wilmington *Devon*	5 R10	
Wilmslow *Ches*	37 M12	
Wilnecote *Staffs*	30 N13	
Wilpshire *Lancs*	36 L12	
Wilsford *Lincs*	31 N15	
Wilshamstead *Beds*	23 O16	
Wilsill *N Yorks*	42 K13	
Wilton *N Yorks*	43 K15	
Wimblington *Cambs*	32 O17	
Wimborne Minster *Dorset*	7 R13	
Wincanton *Som'set*	14 Q12	
Winchburgh *Lothian*	51 G10	
Winchcombe *Glos*	21 P13	
Winchelsea *E Sussex*	10 R18	
Winchester *Hants*	15 Q14	
Windermere *Cumb*	40 K11	
Windlesham *Surrey*	16 Q15	
Windsor *Berks*	16 Q15	
Windygates *Fife*	58 F10	
Winford *Avon*	14 Q11	
Winfrith Newburgh *Dorset*	6 R12	
Wing *Bucks*	23 P15	
Wingate *Durham*	47 J14	
Wingham *Kent*	11 Q19	
Wingrave *Bucks*	23 P15	
Winkfield *Berks*	16 Q15	
Winkleigh *Devon*	4 R9	
Winnersh *Berks*	16 Q15	
Winnington *Ches*	36 M11	
Winscombe *Avon*	13 Q11	
Winsford *Som'set*	13 Q9	
Winsford *Ches*	36 M11	
Winsham *Som'set*	6 R11	
Winsley *Wilts*	14 Q12	
Winslow *Bucks*	23 P15	
Winster *Derby*	37 M13	
Winster *Cumb*	40 K11	
Winston *Durham*	41 J13	
Winterborne Whitechurch *Dorset*	6 R12	
Winterbourne *Avon*	21 P11	
Winterbourne Abbas *Dorset*	6 R11	
Winterslow *Wilts*	15 Q13	
Winterton *Humber*	38 L15	
Winterton-on-Sea *Norfolk*	33 N20	
Winthorpe *Notts*	38 M15	
Winton *Cumb*	41 K12	
Winwick *Ches*	36 M11	
Wirksworth *Derby*	37 M13	
Wisbech *Cambs*	32 N17	
Wisbech St. Mary *Cambs*	32 N17	
Wisborough Green *W Sussex*	16 Q15	
Wishaw *S'clyde*	51 G9	
Wistanstow *Shrops*	28 O11	
Wistaston *Ches*	36 M12	
Wiston *Dyfed*	18 P7	
Wiston *S'clyde*	51 G9	
Wistow *Cambs*	31 O16	
Wistow *N Yorks*	38 L14	
Witcham *Cambs*	32 O17	
Witchampton *Dorset*	7 R12	
Witchford *Cambs*	32 O17	
Witham *Essex*	24 P18	
Witheridge *Devon*	12 R9	
Withern *Lincs*	39 M17	
Withernsea *Humber*	39 L17	
Withersfield *Suffolk*	24 O17	
Withington *Heref/Worcs*	21 O11	
Withington *Glos*	21 P13	
Withypool *Som'set*	12 Q9	
Witley *Surrey*	16 Q15	
Witney *Oxon*	22 P14	
Wittersham *Kent*	10 Q18	
Witton Park *Durham*	47 J13	
Witton-le-Wear *Durham*	47 J13	
Wiveliscombe *Som'set*	13 Q10	
Wivenhoe *Essex*	25 P18	
Wix *Essex*	25 P19	
Woburn *Beds*	23 P15	
Woburn Sands *Bucks*	23 O15	
Woking *Surrey*	16 Q15	
Wokingham *Berks*	16 Q15	
Woldingham *Surrey*	17 Q16	
Wolferton *Norfolk*	32 N17	
Wolfhill *Tayside*	58 F10	
Wolf's Castle *Dyfed*	18 P7	
Wollaston *Northants*	23 O15	
Wolsingham *Durham*	47 J13	
Wolston *Warwick*	30 O14	
Wolverhampton *W Midlands*	29 N12	
Wolverley *Heref/Worcs*	29 O12	
Wolverton *Bucks*	23 O15	
Wolvey *Warwick*	30 O14	
Wolviston *Clevl'd*	47 J14	
Wombwell *S Yorks*	38 L14	
Wonersh *Surrey*	16 Q15	
Wonston *Hants*	15 Q14	
Wooburn *Bucks*	16 P15	
Woodbridge *Suffolk*	25 O19	
Woodbury *Devon*	5 R10	
Woodchurch *Kent*	10 Q18	
Woodcote *Oxon*	22 P14	
Woodford *Northants*	31 O15	
Woodford *Gtr Man*	37 M12	
Woodford Halse *Northants*	22 O14	
Woodhall Spa *Lincs*	39 M16	
Woodhead *Gramp*	65 D12	
Woodhouse Eaves *Leics*	30 N14	
Woodmansey *Humber*	43 L16	
Woodnesborough *Kent*	11 Q19	
Woodplumpton *Lancs*	36 L11	
Woodside *Tayside*	58 F10	
Woodside *Gramp*	65 D12	
Woodstock *Oxon*	22 P14	

Woodville *Derby*	30	N13
Wookey *Som'set*	14	Q11
Wookey Hole *Som'set*	14	Q11
Wool *Dorset*	6	R12
Woolacombe *Devon*	12	Q8
Woolavington *Som'set*	13	Q11
Wooler *Northum*	53	G12
Woolfardisworthy *Devon*	12	R8
Woolhampton *Berks*	15	Q14
Woolhope *Heref/Worcs*	21	O11
Woolpit *Suffolk*	25	O18
Woolsthorpe *Lincs*	31	N15
Woore *Shrops*	29	N12
Wooton Bassett *Wilts*	21	P13
Wooton Bridge *I of Wight*	8	R14
Wooton Ribers *Wilts*	15	Q13
Wooton under Edge *Glos*	21	P12
Wooton Wawen *Warwick*	22	O13
Wootton *Oxon*	22	P14
Wootton *Beds*	23	O15
Wootton *Humber*	39	L16
Worcester *Heref/Worcs*	21	O12
Worfield *Shrops*	29	N12
Workington *Cumb*	45	J9
Worksop *Notts*	38	M14
Worlaby *Humber*	39	L16
Wormit *Fife*	58	F11
Worplesdon *Surrey*	16	Q15
Worsbrough *S Yorks*	37	L14
Worstead *Norfolk*	33	N19
Worth *Kent*	11	Q19
Worth Matravers *Dorset*	7	R12
Wortham *Suffolk*	33	O19
Worthen *Shrops*	28	N11
Worthenbury *Clwyd*	28	M11
Worthing *W Sussex*	9	R16
Wragby *Lincs*	39	M16
Wrangle *Lincs*	32	M17
Wrawby *Humber*	39	L16

Wray *Lancs*	41	K11
Wrea Green *Lancs*	36	L11
Wrelton *N Yorks*	43	K15
Wrenbury *Ches*	29	M11
Wreningham *Norfolk*	33	N19
Wrentham *Suffolk*	33	O20
Wrestlingworth *Beds*	23	O16
Wretham *Norfolk*	24	O18
Wrexham *Clwyd*	28	M10
Wrington *Avon*	14	Q11
Writtle *Essex*	17	P17
Wrockwardine *Shrops*	29	N11
Wrotham *Kent*	17	Q17
Wroughton *Wilts*	21	P13
Wroxall *I of Wight*	8	R14
Wroxham *Norfolk*	33	N19
Wroxton *Oxon*	22	O14
Wychbold *Heref/Worcs*	29	O12
Wye *Kent*	11	Q18
Wykeham *N Yorks*	43	K15
Wylam *Northum*	47	J13
Wylye *Wilts*	15	Q13
Wymeswold *Leics*	30	N14
Wymington *Beds*	23	O15
Wymondham *Leics*	31	N15
Wymondham *Norfolk*	33	N19
Wyre Piddle *Heref/Worcs*	21	O12

Y

Yalding *Kent*	10	Q17
Yapton *W Sussex*	9	R15
Yarburgh *Lincs*	39	M17
Yarcombe *Devon*	5	R10
Yardley Hastings *Northants*	23	O15
Yarmouth *I of Wight*	8	R13

Yarnfield *Staffs*	29	N12
Yarpole *Heref/Worcs*	28	O11
Yate *Avon*	21	P12
Yateley *Hants*	16	Q15
Yatesbury *Wilts*	15	Q13
Yattendon *Berks*	15	Q14
Yatton *Avon*	14	Q11
Yatton Keynell *Wilts*	14	Q12
Yaxham *Norfolk*	33	N18
Yaxley *Cambs*	31	N16
Yaxley *Suffolk*	33	O19
Yeadon *W Yorks*	42	L13
Yealmpton *Devon*	4	S9
Yelverton *Devon*	4	S8
Yeovil *Som'set*	6	R11
Yetminster *Dorset*	6	R11
Ynyshir *Mid Glam*	20	P10
Ynys-y-bwl *Mid Glam*	20	P10
York *N Yorks*	42	L14
Youlgreave *Derby*	37	M13
Yoxall *Staffs*	30	N13
Yoxford *Suffolk*	33	O20
Ysbyty-Ystwyth *Dyfed*	27	O9
Yspytty-Ifan *Gwyn*	35	M9
Ystalyfera *W Glam*	19	P9
Ystrad Meurig *Dyfed*	27	O9
Ystrad Rhondda *Mid Glam*	20	P10
Ystrad Mynach *Mid Glam*	20	P10
Ystradfellte *Powys*	20	P9
Ystradgynlais *Powys*	19	P9

Z

Zeal Monachorum *Devon*	5	R9
Zeals *Wilts*	14	Q12
Zennor *Cornw'l*	2	S5

NORTHERN IRELAND INDEX

Antrim *Antrim*	77	B7
Armagh *Armagh*	77	B7
Aughnacloy *Tyrone*	77	B6
Ballycastle *Antrim*	77	A7
Ballyclare *Antrim*	77	B7
Ballymena *Antrim*	77	A7
Ballymoney *Antrim*	77	A7
Ballynahinch *Down*	77	B8
Banbridge *Down*	77	B7
Bangor *Down*	77	B8
Belcoo *Ferman*	76	B5
Belfast *Antrim*	77	B7
Bushmills *Antrim*	77	A7
Carrickfergus *Antrim*	77	B8
Castlerock *Derry*	77	A6
Coalisland *Tyrone*	77	B6
Coleraine *Derry*	77	A7
Cookstown *Tyrone*	77	B6
Cushendall *Antrim*	77	A7
Donaghadee *Down*	77	B8
Downpatrick *Down*	77	B8

Draperstown *Derry*	77	B6
Dromore *Tyrone*	76	B5
Dungannon *Tyrone*	77	B6
Dungiven *Derry*	77	A6
Enniskillen *Ferman*	76	B5
Garvagh *Derry*	77	A7
Glenariff *Antrim*	77	A7
Glenarm *Antrim*	77	A7
Greyabbey *Down*	77	B8
Holywood *Down*	77	B8
Irvinestown *Ferman*	76	B5
Kesh *Ferman*	76	B5
Kilkeel *Down*	77	C7
Larne *Antrim*	77	A8
Limavady *Derry*	77	A6
Lisburn *Antrim*	77	B7
Lisnaskea *Ferman*	76	B5
Londonderry *Derry*	76	A6
Lurgan *Armagh*	77	B7
Maghera *Derry*	77	A7
Magherafelt *Derry*	77	B7

Moneymore *Derry*	77	B7
Newcastle *Down*	77	B8
Newry *Down*	77	B7
Newtownabbey *Antrim*	77	B7
Newtownards *Down*	77	B8
Newtownhamilton *Armagh*	77	B7
Newtownstewart *Tyrone*	76	B6
Omagh *Tyrone*	76	B6
Oxford Island *Armagh*	77	B7
Plumbridge *Tyrone*	76	B6
Portadown *Armagh*	77	B7
Portaferry *Down*	77	B8
Portballintrae *Antrim*	77	A7
Portglenone *Antrim*	77	A7
Portrush *Antrim*	77	A7
Portstewart *Derry*	77	A7
Strabane *Tyrone*	76	A6
Strangford *Down*	77	B8
Tandragee *Armagh*	77	B7
Toome *Antrim*	77	B7
Warrenpoint *Down*	77	C7
Whitehead *Antrim*	77	B8

Abbeyfeale *Limerick*	80	E3
Abbeyleix *Laois*	83	D5
Ardee *Louth*	82	C7
Arklow *Wicklow*	83	E7
Askeaton *Limerick*	80	E3
Athenry *Galway*	78	D4
Athlone *Westmeath*	79	D5
Athy *Kildare*	83	D6
Bagenalstown *Carlow*	83	D6
Bailieborough *Cavan*	82	C6
Ballaghaderreen *Roscommon*	78	C4
Ballina *Mayo*	78	B3
Ballinamore *Leitrim*	79	C5
Ballinasloe *Galway*	79	D4
Ballinrobe *Mayo*	78	C3
Ballybofey *Donegal*	76	B5
Ballybunnion *Kerry*	80	E2
Ballyhaunis *Mayo*	78	C4
Ballymahon *Longford*	79	C5
Ballysadare *Sligo*	78	B4
Ballyshannon *Donegal*	76	B5
Baltinglass *Wicklow*	83	D6
Bandon *Cork*	80	F3
Bangor *Mayo*	78	B2
Bantry *Cork*	80	F2
Belmullet *Mayo*	78	B2
Belturbet *Cavan*	79	C5
Birr *Offaly*	79	D5
Borrisokane *Tipperary*	79	D4
Boyle *Roscommon*	79	C4
Bray *Wicklow*	82	D7
Bunbeg *Donegal*	76	A4
Bunclody *Wexford*	83	E6
Buncrana *Donegal*	76	A6
Bundoran *Donegal*	76	B4
Buttevant *Cork*	81	E4
Caher *Tipperary*	81	E5
Cahersiveen *Kerry*	80	F1
Callan *Kilkenny*	83	E5
Cappoquin *Waterford*	81	E5
Carlow *Carlow*	83	D6
Carrick on Shannon *Leitrim*	79	C5
Carrick-on-Suir *Tipperary*	83	E5
Cashel *Tipperary*	81	E5
Castlebar *Mayo*	78	C3
Castleblayney *Monaghan*	82	C6
Castlecomer *Kilkenny*	83	D6
Castleisland *Kerry*	80	E2
Castlepollard *Westmeath*	79	C6
Castlerea *Roscommon*	79	C4
Castletown Bearhaven *Cork*	80	F2
Cavan *Cavan*	79	C5
Ceanannus Mór *Meath*	82	C6
Charlestown *Mayo*	78	C4
Charleville *Cork*	81	E4
Claremorris *Mayo*	78	C3
Clifden *Galway*	78	C2
Clogherhead *Louth*	82	C7
Clonakilty *Cork*	80	F3
Clondalkin *Dublin*	82	D7
Clones *Monaghan*	79	B6
Clonmel *Tipperary*	81	E5
Cobh *Cork*	81	F4
Collooney *Sligo*	78	B4
Cootehill *Cavan*	82	C6
Cork *Cork*	81	F4
Croom *Limerick*	81	E4
Crossmolina *Mayo*	78	B3
Dingle *Kerry*	80	E1
Donegal *Donegal*	76	B5
Drogheda *Louth*	82	C7
Droichead Nua *Kildare*	82	D6
Dublin *Dublin*	82	D7
Dun Laoghaire *Dublin*	82	D7
Dundalk *Louth*	82	C7
Dungarvan *Waterford*	81	F5
Dunglow *Donegal*	76	A4
Dunleer *Louth*	82	C7
Edenderry *Offaly*	82	D6
Ennis *Clare*	80	D3
Enniscorthy *Wexford*	83	E6
Ennistimon *Clare*	78	D3
Ferbane *Offaly*	79	D5
Fermoy *Cork*	81	E4
Fethard *Tipperary*	81	E5
Foynes *Limerick*	80	E3
Frankford *Offaly*	79	D5
Galway *Galway*	78	D3
Glenties *Donegal*	76	A4
Gorey *Wexford*	83	E7
Gort *Galway*	78	D3
Graiguenamanagh *Kilkenny*	83	E6
Granard *Longford*	79	C5
Greenore *Louth*	82	C7
Greystones *Wicklow*	82	D7
Headford *Galway*	78	C3
Inishcrone *Mayo*	78	B3
Kenmare *Kerry*	80	F2
Kilbeggan *Westmeath*	79	D5
Kilcormac *Offaly*	79	D5
Kilcullen *Kildare*	82	D6
Kildare *Kildare*	82	D6
Kilkenny *Kilkenny*	83	E6
Killarney *Kerry*	80	E2
Killorglin *Kerry*	80	E2
Killybegs *Donegal*	76	B4
Kilmallock *Limerick*	81	E4
Kilrush *Clare*	80	E3
Kinnegad *Westmeath*	82	D6
Letterkenny *Donegal*	76	A5
Lifford *Donegal*	76	A5
Limerick *Limerick*	81	E4
Lismore *Waterford*	81	E5
Listowel *Kerry*	80	E3
Longford *Longford*	79	C5
Loughrea *Galway*	78	D4
Macroom *Cork*	80	F3
Malahide *Dublin*	82	D7
Mallow *Cork*	81	E4
Maynooth *Kildare*	82	D7
Midleton *Cork*	81	F4
Millstreet *Cork*	80	E3
Milltown Malbay *Clare*	80	D3
Mitchelstown *Cork*	81	E4
Moate *Westmeath*	79	D5
Mohill *Leitrim*	79	C5
Molville *Donegal*	77	A6
Monaghan *Monaghan*	79	B6
Monasterevin *Kildare*	82	D6
Mostrim Edgeworthstown *Longford*	79	C5
Mountmellick *Laois*	79	D6
Mountrath *Laois*	79	D5
Muine Bheag *Carlow*	83	E6
Mullingar *Westmeath*	79	C6
Naas *Kildare*	82	D6
Navan *Meath*	82	C6
Nenagh *Tipperary*	81	D4
New Ross *Wexford*	83	E6
Newcastle West *Limerick*	80	E3
Newmarket *Cork*	80	E3
Newmarket on Fergus *Clare*	80	D3
Newport *Mayo*	78	C3
Oranmore *Galway*	78	D3
Port Laoise *Laois*	79	D6
Portarlington *Laois*	79	D6
Portumna *Galway*	79	D4
Rath Luirc *Cork*	81	E4
Rathdrum *Wicklow*	83	D7
Rathkeale *Limerick*	80	E3
Rathkenny *Kerry*	80	E3
Rathnew *Wicklow*	83	D7
Rochfortbridge *Westmeath*	79	D6
Roscommon *Roscommon*	79	C4
Roscrea *Tipperary*	81	D5
Rosslare *Wexford*	83	E7
Rosslare Harbour *Wexford*	83	E7
Skerries *Dublin*	82	C7
Skibbereen *Cork*	80	F3
Sligo *Sligo*	79	B4
Stradbally *Laois*	79	D6
Stranorlar *Donegal*	76	B5
Swinford *Mayo*	78	C3
Swords *Dublin*	82	D7
Tallow *Waterford*	81	F4
Tarbert *Kerry*	80	E3
Templemore *Tipperary*	81	D5
Thomastown *Kilkenny*	83	E6
Thurles *Tipperary*	81	E5
Tipperary *Tipperary*	81	E4
Tralee *Kerry*	80	E2
Tramore *Waterford*	83	E6
Trim *Meath*	82	C6
Tuam *Galway*	78	C4
Tullamore *Offaly*	79	D5
Tullow *Carlow*	83	E6
Urlingford *Kilkenny*	83	E5
Virginia *Cavan*	82	C6
Waterford *Waterford*	83	E6
Waterville *Kerry*	80	F1
Westport *Mayo*	78	C3
Wexford *Wexford*	83	E7

Motorway with service area		National Park or Area of Outstanding Natural Beauty	
Primary route (dual)		Sand beach	
Primary route (single)		Sand and shingle beach	
'A' Road (dual)		T.	AA or RAC telephone box
'A' Road (single)		✈	Airport
'B' Road		⊔	Castle
Other road		+	Cathedral or Abbey
Road under construction		🏯 🏞	Country park (England/Scotland)
Motorway junction number	27	★	House/Garden open to the public
Distance between symbols in miles and kilometres	7 11	N.T.	National Trust property open to the public
Car ferries	CAR FERRY	▬	Other place of interest
Toll road or bridge	TOLL	▲	Youth hostel
Hill 1 in 7 or steeper (arrow points downhill)		⛵	Coastal yachting centre
Railway		▶	Golf course
National boundary		⊖	Motor racing circuit
County boundary		Pot ○	Pot holing centre
Navigable river or canal	*Forth*	🏇	Race course
Spot height in feet	·1354	△	Rock climbing centre
Viewpoint	☀	🎿	Skiing centre
Primary route town	EXETER	🏄	Water skiing centre

Scale : 5 miles to 1 inch

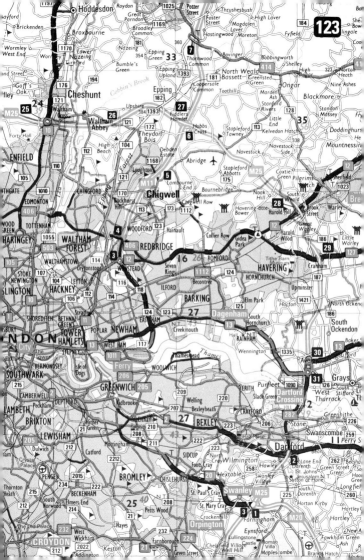

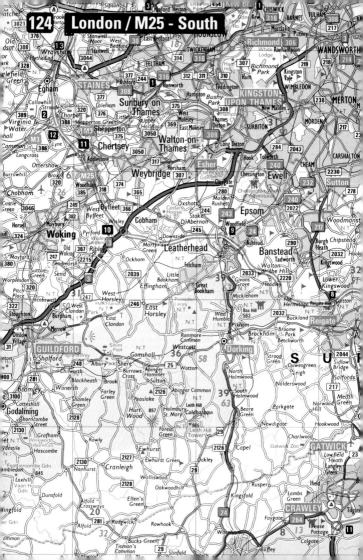

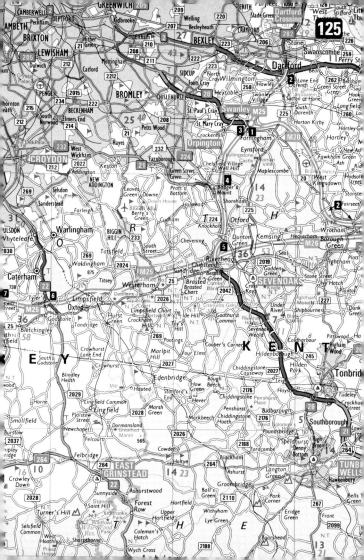

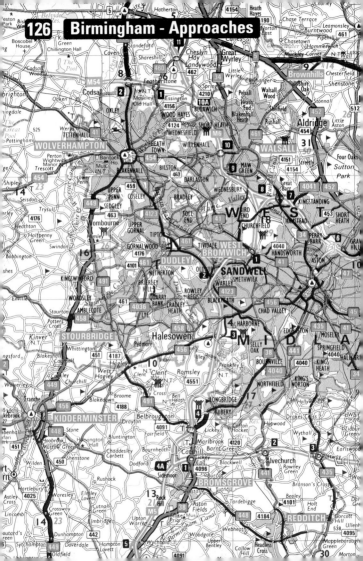

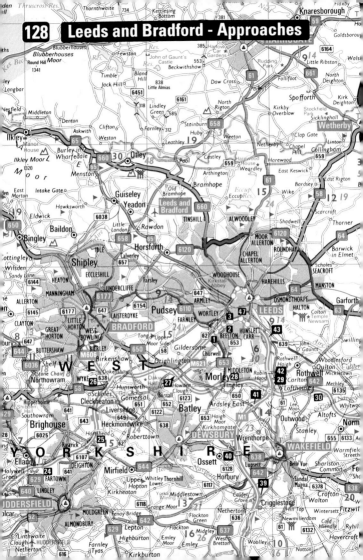

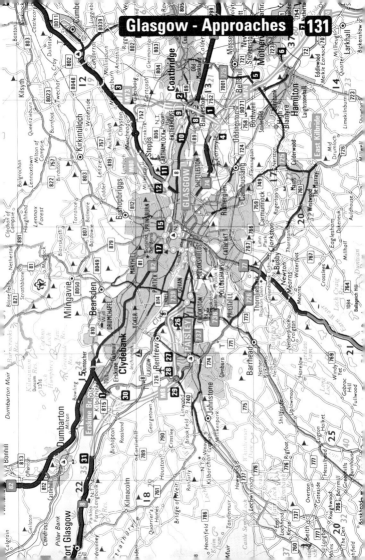

Dealing with an accident

If you are the first on the scene after a road accident, by
following a few simple guidelines the action you take
can help to save lives and prevent an even worse
accident. Here is what to do.

Stop a short distance from the accident, parking your car well
into the nearside of the road. Turn on your hazard warning lights,
as well as fog lights in fog and headlights at night. Leave a gap
between your car and the accident, so that emergency vehicles
can park nearer the accident site.

Make the accident vehicles safe. Put out any fire with a fire extinguisher; switch off the ignition, apply the brakes and put the vehicle in gear. DO NOT move any victim unless he or she is in danger from fire – you could make an injury worse. DO NOT smoke – there may be spilled petrol.

Check that there are no more victims who have been thrown clear of the accident site. Work out the order of priority in treating the victims: deal with breathing difficulties first, bleeding second and unconsciousness third. Keep the victims warm by covering them with rugs or coats.

Set up a red warning triangle at the edge of the road 200 feet (60 metres) behind your car. Send the first available person to phone for the emergency services, stating the site of the accident, the number of people and vehicles involved, and the types of injury. Discourage sightseers.

Stay with any victims while waiting for the emergency services to arrive. Be reassuring when you talk to them, saying that help is on the way. Make a note of names and addresses of victims and witnesses, and record vehicle number plates (to give to the paramedics or police).

Life-saving first aid

The three ways you can save the life of an accident victim concern breathing, bleeding and unconsciousness.

1 If a victim is not breathing, give mouth-to-mouth resuscitation and – if there is no pulse – begin heart massage. You should continue these treatments until breathing and heartbeat return or until professional help arrives.

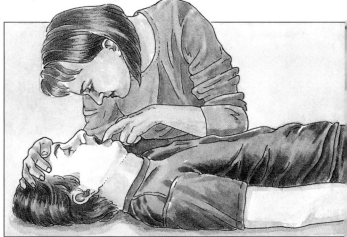

Check for breathing by feeling for movements of the victim's chest or by gently placing your hand over the mouth. Turn the victim on his or her back and tip the head to one side. Remove any foreign body from the mouth. Loosen clothing around the neck.

The information given here is intended to offer emergency first aid guidelines; it does not constitute a comprehensive manual. First aid procedures should be learnt and practised by enrolling in a training course run by an official, recognized organization, such as St. John Ambulance Association, St. Andrew's Ambulance Association or the British Red Cross.

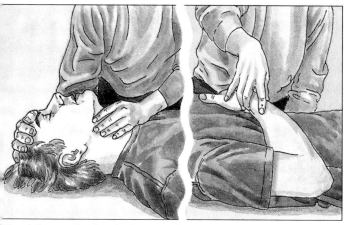

Check for a pulse by placing your fingers on the victim's neck just below the angle of the jaw. Alternatively, feel for a pulse by holding your fingers on the inside of the wrist in line with the victim's thumb. Cold, grey skin and pale lips are also signs that the heart is not beating.

To give mouth-to-mouth resuscitation – the kiss of life – tilt the head and lift the chin gently. Take a deep breath, pinch the victim' nose closed, place your lips around the mouth and breathe out. The victim's chest should rise.

If the chest does not rise, check that the airway is clear. Then continue mouth-to-mouth resuscitation at a rate of about 10 breaths a minute.

For a baby or child, there are special techniques which should be learnt from a course run by an official first aid training organization.

2 If there is any severe bleeding, control it immediately.

The best way to stop bleeding is with pressure; DO NOT attempt t use a tourniquet, which can cause severe damage. For a small

wound, press hard on a clean handkerchief with your fingers at the site of the injury. For a large wound, use a pad of clean cloth to press hard until bleeding stops. If possible, elevate the wounded part. Be prepared to do this until professional help arrives.

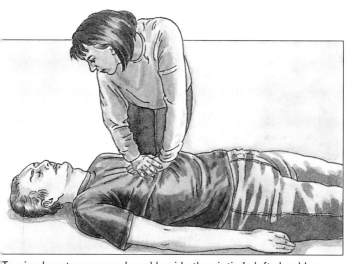

To give heart massage, kneel beside the victim's left shoulder, and place the heel of one hand on the middle of the lower part of the breastbone. Cover this hand with your other one and lean forwards to press the breastbone gently down about 1½ to 2 inches (4 to 5 centimetres).

Release the pressure and then continue pressing at a rate of about 60 times a minute. Somebody whose heart has stopped also stops breathing. You should therefore stop heart massage every 15 seconds to give two breaths of mouth-to-mouth resuscitation. Two first aiders can share these tasks.

3 If the victim is unconscious and can safely be laid on the ground, put him or her in the recovery position (see picture below) ensuring that the head is tilted well back and supported by the victim's hand. This position is chosen so that the tongue does not block the airway and so that blood or vomit can drain out of the victim's mouth and prevent choking.

4 Shock is a common result of a road accident. Its symptoms include pale skin, shallow breathing and a rapid pulse, with anxiety and confusion.

Watch over anybody in shock. The victim may wander off, possibly into moving traffic. Get the victim to lie down, covered with a rug for warmth. DO NOT give hot or stimulating drinks. Check regularly for breathing and a pulse (see Section 1) and reassure the victim.

Car first aid kit

Every car should carry a first aid kit, preferably in a waterproof case underneath the passenger seat. DO NOT carry it in the boot (which can be impossible to open after a rear-end collision). You can help your own passengers if you are involved in an accident, or perhaps save the lives of others if you are first on an accident scene. You should also carry a red warning triangle and a fire extinguisher (compulsory in some other EC countries). The minimum basic contents of a car first aid kit are as follows.

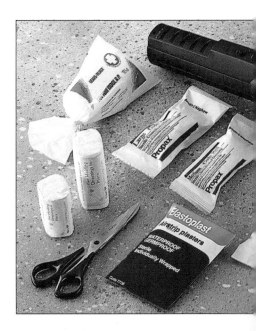